SEMEIA 46

NARRATIVE RESEARCH ON THE HEBREW BIBLE

Guest Editors:
Miri Amihai
George W. Coats
Anne M. Solomon

© 1989
by the Society of Biblical Literature

SEMEIA 46

Copyright © 1989 by the Society of Biblical Literature

All rights reserved. No part of this work may be reproduced or transmitted in any form or by any means, electronic or mechanical, including photocopying and recording, or by means of any information storage or retrieval system, except as may be expressly permitted by the 1976 Copyright Act or in writing from the publisher. Requests for permission should be addressed in writing to the Rights and Permissions Office, Society of Biblical Literature, 825 Houston Mill Road, Atlanta, GA 30329, USA.

ISSN 0095-571X
ISBN 1-58983-187-X

Printed in the United States of America
on acid-free paper

CONTENTS

Contributors to This Issue v

Preface vii

INTRODUCTION

Story upon Story
    Anne M. Solomon 3

ARTICLES

A Theory of Narrative

The Restoration of Biblical Narrative
    Mary Gerhart 13

Can Genesis Be Read as a Book?
    Everett Fox 31

The Genealogical Framework of the Family Stories in Genesis
    Naomi Steinberg 41

The Structure of The Chronicler's History: A Key to
the Organization of the Pentateuch
    Anne M. Solomon 51

The Form-Critical Problem of the Hexateuch
    George W. Coats 65

Narrative Tricks

The Reported Story: Midway between Oral Performance
and Literary Art
    Antony F. Campbell, S.J. 77

Spatial Form in Exod 19:1-8a and in the Larger Sinai Narrative
    Thomas B. Dozeman 87

The Institutional Matrix of Treachery in 2 Samuel 11
  Joel Rosenberg 103

Feminist Criticism of Biblical Narrative

The Harlot as Heroine: Narrative Art and
Social Presupposition in Three Old Testament Texts
  Phyllis Bird 119

His Story Versus Her Story: Male Genealogy and
Female Strategy in the Jacob Cycle
  Nelly Furman 141

The Literary Characterization of Mothers and
Sexual Politics in the Hebrew Bible
  Esther Fuchs 151

RESPONSE

Between Reader and Text: A General Response
  James G. Williams 169

CONTRIBUTORS TO THIS ISSUE

Miri Amihai
  Department of Religious and Classical Studies
  University of Rochester
  Rochester, NY 14627

Phyllis Bird
  Garrett-Evangelical Theological Seminary
  2121 Sheridan Road
  Evanston, IL 60201

Antony F. Campbell, S.J.
  Jesuit Theological College
  175 Royal Parade, Parkville
  Victoria, 3052 Australia

George W. Coats
  Lexington Theological Seminary
  631 South Limestone Street
  Lexington, KY 40508

Thomas B. Dozeman
  Department of Religion
  Calvin College
  Grand Rapids, MI 49506

Everett Fox
  Clark University
  950 Main Street
  Worcester, MA 01610

Esther Fuchs
  Department of Oriental Studies
  University of Arizona
  Tucson, AZ 85721

Nelly Furman
  Department of Romance Studies
  Cornell University
  Ithaca, NY 14853

Mary Gerhart
  Department of Religious Studies
  Hobart and William Smith Colleges
  Geneva, NY 14456

Joel Rosenberg
  Program in Judaic Studies
  Tufts University
  Medford, MA 02155

Anne M. Solomon
  3715 Pinelea Road
  Pikesville, MD 21208

Naomi Steinberg
  Department of Religious Studies
  DePaul University
  Chicago, IL 60614

James G. Williams
  Department of Religion
  Syracuse University
  Syracuse, NY 13244-1170

PREFACE

This issue has been longer coming than the editors and the contributors would have wished. Illness and other such uncontrolled problems stood in the way. Nevertheless, this selection of papers reflects the contribution of the Narrative Research Group of the Society of Biblical Literature during its initial years. Three articles have since appeared elsewhere but, because they form part of the pattern of work of the group, it was decided to include them as originally planned. Parts of "The Institutional Matrix of Treachery in 2 Samuel 11" by Joel Rosenberg duplicate or overlap discussion in *Kings and Kin: Political Allegory in the Hebrew Bible* (Indiana Studies in Biblical Literature; Bloomington: University of Indiana Press, 1986). "His Story Verses Her Story: Male Genealogy and Female Strategy in the Jacob Cycle," by Nelly Furman and "The Literary Characterization of Mothers and Sexual Politics in the Hebrew Bible" by Esther Fuchs have both appeared in *Feminist Perspectives on Biblical Scholarship* (ed. Adela Yarbro Collins; SBL Centennial Publications; Chico: Scholars Press, 1985). The planning of the Research Group and this volume was done by the three editors, Miri Amihai, George Coats, and Anne Solomon, but the painstaking task of preparing the volume for the press fell to Miri Amihai who deserves credit for a remarkable job.

Robert C. Culley
General Editor

Introduction

INTRODUCTION: STORY UPON STORY
Anne M. Solomon

The first time we hear a good biblical story we experience a certain oneness, a wholeness which we recognize, nonetheless, as unifying several currents of reality. As the experience sinks in we become aware of more than one story being told. Some of us may immediately recognize that the narrator has combined several stories together. Others may realize that the narrator has craftily hidden a second story in the very words of the first one. Most will probably recognize our own story tied into the narrator's story. Finally, a few may realize that the story's lines are tied back to a greater silent story—all of reality, which is known only through the words of the present story. Admittedly there are many ways to describe these rich dynamics of hearing a story upon a story. The purpose of this volume is to share some of the ways members of the Society of Biblical Literature's Narrative Research Group on the Hebrew Bible have described these dynamics to one another at annual meetings from 1979–1984.

In the beginning of the research group, no particular theme was announced in the call for papers, nor were there overall titles for our sessions beyond the theme of narrative research since we wished to foster methodological exploration. The eleven papers in this volume thus present many ways of looking at several different stories. Hence the phrase, "story upon story," reflects the broad range of biblical narratives discussed, but also a peculiarly late twentieth century version of the four realizations mentioned above.

A traditional audience may immediately recognize that the narrator's own story has brought together several small stories into one larger unity. It would be like realizing that the narrator speaks for a whole row of storytellers sitting behind her. Others may realize that the very skillful narrator has told one story while actually telling us another. This would be like finding a story hidden in back of the narrator's words. Such realizations have probably always been true for audiences of traditional literature. But with the advent of Higher Criticism and other modes of historical thinking, these realizations became true in a different sense. The final storyteller was thought of as a redactor of traditions which originated in a time and place far removed from the original happenings on the one hand, and from the redactor on the other. Many new possibilities for the hidden story emerged from historical reconstructions of earlier societies. The current twentieth century rediscovery of narrative offers a way to appreciate the artistic wholes out of which and within which a story is constructed. Stylistic criticism more self-consciously directs form and redaction criticism in current narrative research. Some of the contributions in this volume embody the first realization, while others exemplify the second realization.

Another realization, however, may come to the audience of a good story. For a traditional audience this realization is embodied in the saying that the Torah is different each time we hear it because each time we are different. Undoubtedly most of us today would realize that the story we hear is simultaneously two stories: the narrator's and the one in our own ears. This realization in turn has two effects: upon the content of the narrator's story, and upon the ongoing construction of our own stories. Feminist criticism of biblical narrative offers a powerful example of these processes. In three papers in this volume we sense these dynamics, as well as the intertwining of history and herstory.

Finally, some traditional audiences may realize that a story's lines are tied back to an otherwise inaccessible story, which is like realizing that first there is a reality, and then come the words for it. Yet the narrator can only tell us the silent story through the words of the present story. In the modern period we are more likely to realize that because of the sequential nature of perception, a story (which is by definition a literature of sequence) recombines someone's original perceptual sequence into a new story. Thus we begin the collection with a paper on narrative theory which articulates this insight in its relationship to cognition, historicity, and theology. Such narrative theory offers a new way of understanding the begetting and birthing inherent in the root metaphor of *tôlĕdôt*, Hebrew narrative.

In all the activities of the Narrative Research Group, we have attempted to encourage greater awareness of methodology. In our presentations and discussions we benefited from the rich interaction of approaches. Thus we offer this sampler of papers in narrative research to further the creation of stories upon stories. Some explicit suggestions for such creative efforts in biblical criticism are made by Mary Gerhart in her opening essay.

In "The Restoration of Biblical Narrative," Mary Gerhart presents a theory of narrative and then employs it to evaluate recent work considered representative of current biblical criticism. She argues that it is urgent to construct a theory of narrative "faithful to the exigencies of contemporary thought" since, while biblical narrative itself threatens to disappear, its current reinstatement in literary criticism does not meet twentieth century concerns about the genre of narrative. She makes a distinction between precritical questions ("who, what, where, with what help, wherefore, how, at what time?") and her explication of a postcritical theory of narrative on the basis of their presuppositions. Unlike precritical thinking, postcritical theory presupposes more answers to the questions. In answer to the precritical questions, one pointed to only one person per character, one external reality per story, one time per plot, and one inner effect (in the story) per action.

Focusing on the latter three answers, she constructs a postcritical theory which presupposes that the story also points to the reality of the human narrator's consciousness, that narrated time also points to the condition of living in time, and that narrated action also points to the reader's theological activity. Hence her theory is a description of narrative as "generically" cognitive, historical, and theological.

In building this theory, she employs Ricoeur's notions of time-separation (meaning arriving after the original event) and the reader's need to reconstruct the emplotment of the narrative; Gadamer's notion of historicity as the "thrownness" of the reader into inescapable worlds of meanings and as the hallmark of a classic; and Fredric Jameson's notion of dialectical thinking as the historically reflexive study of both an object and the categories we bring to it.

Gerhart's essay has some valuable suggestions for form, redaction, stylistic and canon-criticism. She concludes her theory with the admission of one of its central concerns: the need to question the norm of "realistic narrative reading." She hopes that the question will continue to be asked in biblical criticism and not abandoned for fear of losing the biblical text once obscured by historical and hermeneutical reconstructions, but now restored by literary criticism. In its own way, the answer which a postcritical theory of narrative produces by questioning the "realistic" story shows how a story can beget our twentieth-century story.

The contributions following Gerhart's essay may be viewed from the perspective of the prominence of a given dynamic which originates within a biblical story and proceeds to another story, in addition to that of a particular method or theory of narratology. While these essays do exemplify all the methods of biblical criticism mentioned above, as well as postcritical narratology, another mode of organization is evident: that of the main dynamic interaction from (1) stories to broader story; (2) story to inner stories; and (3) story to reader. The contributions by Fox, Steinberg, Solomon, and Coats ("Achieving Unity in Traditional Narrative") concern understanding how units of biblical text become one big story. Those by Campbell, Dozeman, and Rosenberg ("Narrative Tricks") exemplify how one story is contained within another. Finally, those by Bird, Furman, and Fuchs ("Feminist Criticism of Biblical Narrative"), illustrate the back and forth movement of feminist eyes upon the faces of women and men in the Bible. Therein lie many stories.

In "Can Genesis Be Read as a Book?," Everett Fox argues for the rich structural unity of all of Genesis with the assistance of what he terms a broader form of rhetorical criticism. The four areas in which he demonstrates the book's coherence are (1) character development; (2) style; (3) theme; and (4) plot. He offers a carefully elaborated chiastic plot structure for the whole book which may be summarized in the broader themes of "selection and survival amidst struggle and disaster." Within each of the four major literary units of Genesis are four shared themes: (1) chosen figure; (2) favor to youngest son and response of hatred; (3) family line threatened; and (4) concluding "death notices." He demonstrates how the last chapters of Genesis are fully coherent with respect to all four areas, thus countering Walter Brueggeman's charge of their *post-hoc* nature. Fox perceives Genesis as the thoroughly integrated work of its redactor.

An elaboration of how genealogies function in the structure of Genesis is contained in the article by Naomi Steinberg, "The Genealogical Framework of the Family Stories in Genesis." She employs Tzvetan Todorov's fivefold movement of narrative equilibrium to understand the integration of genealogy into the narratives of Genesis. The initial and final states of equilibrium are provided by the genealogies in the family stories of Genesis 11–50. Intrinsic relationships exist between these genealogies and the narratives (which express states of disequilibrium). The six genealogies of Genesis 11–50 not only closely parallel one another in structure, but the genealogies of the first member of each pair (*Shem* & Terah, *Ishmael* & Isaac, and *Esau* & Jacob) "function as a summary of events describing the stable situation of family history." The genealogies of the second members shift the reader into the narratives which eventually solve the problems of family descent. The narratives are actually the transitions to the genealogies and not the reverse.

From this perspective, Steinberg solves the frequent problem of the proper function of the Shem genealogy. She not only demonstrates how a genealogy is narrative and where to properly begin the family stories in Genesis, but also shows how genealogy provides the unifying stability of Genesis 11–50 and suggests ways of reopening the study of Genesis 1–11.

Another approach to the study of how genealogies provide the structure of biblical narrative is contained in "The Structure of the Chronicler's History: A Key to the Organization of the Pentateuch" by Anne M. Solomon. She argues that the Chronicler has structured major portions of the history (2 Chronicles 10–36 and Ezra-Nehemiah) by means of a fourfold schema which is ultimately derived from Gen 15:13–16 (affliction for four hundred years and a return to the land in the fourth generation), punctuated by references to the generations of high priests and Levites.

The early portions of the Chronicler's history are divided into three parts: 1 Chronicles 1–9 — genealogical introduction; 1 Chronicles 10–29 — David's generation; and 2 Chronicles 1–9 — Solomon's generation. 2 Chronicles 10–36 — four hundred years of affliction, and Ezra-Nehemiah — restoration in four generations, are termed parts four and five of the history respectively.

Solomon then looks back to the Pentateuch and notes a parallel to this fivefold structure in both its overall plan and again within the unit Exodus 15–Deuteronomy 34. Building upon Pfeiffer's observation of parallels between the structure of the Chronicler's history and the Pentateuch, she sees (1) genealogical introduction; (2) Abraham's generation; (3) Isaac's generation; (4) four hundred years of affliction; and (5) four generations to the land. Within this last unit, Exodus 15–Deuteronomy 34, there is a repetition of the fivefold structure: (1) introduction to world of sabbath—Exodus 15-19; (2) covenant established—Exodus 20-24; (3) sanctuary built and dedicated—Exodus 25–Numbers 10; (4) wilderness struggles in four units of journeying—Numbers 11-33; and (5) four units of Torah to prepare for Canaan—Numbers 33–Deuteronomy 34. Generational thinking is thus suggested as a multidimensional redactional mode for structuring biblical stories.

Steinberg's and Solomon's articles take issue with Gerhard von Rad's evaluation of the two "secondary" units in the Hexateuch: the Primeval History and the Sinai traditions. "Another Form-Critical Problem of the Hexateuch" by George Coats also begins with noting rejections of von Rad's view by Artur Weiser and Walter Beyerlin. Coats proceeds to label the question of the Sinai narrative a traditio-historical problem, not a form-critical one. However, he raises another form-critical problem which is not simply a gap between the genre of family saga in the patriarchal theme and the heroic genre of the Moses material, but rather one of the relationship between these two units and the three others before, in the middle, and after them: the Primeval History, the Joseph story, and the Sinai narrative.

Coats sees the relationship between these units in terms of the theme of intimacy. The Joseph story thus answers the problem of broken intimacy which originates in the Jahwist's version of the Primeval History and is exacerbated in the patriarchal stories. The Jahwist ending to the Joseph story, however, shows that the intimacy between the brothers is broken in the supposed message from Jacob to Joseph to spare his brothers after Jacob's death. Ultimately the answer to this broken intimacy is the covenant at Sinai. Thus the Joseph narrative is the storyteller's "tool for reporting the move from Canaan to Egypt." Yet in the last analysis it has intensified the form-critical problem of the Hexateuch.

All four of these articles offer examples of how to move to the redactional level of traditional material. Steinberg's and Coats' articles employ more form-critical bases. Fox's and Solomon's articles have a more rhetorical-critical foundation. Nonetheless, in their discussions of structures and themes one senses the dynamic of movement to the broader story and the attempt to discern the activity of the redactor in achieving that unity. All are aware of the redactor's attempts to overcome the inevitable time separation by forging a final meaningful whole.

Three articles question the notion that a single narrative need be one story, presented in temporal sequence, about an original historical event. Campbell demonstrates how variant stories can be preserved within the framework of seemingly one story, like a storyteller's sketchbook. Dozeman uncovers a story told from revolving perspectives lurking behind broken temporal and spatial lines. Rosenberg shows that even the most historical of narratives, the Court History, is an institutional parable requiring the audience's active involvement. For all three there is a story within the apparent story.

In "The Reported Story: Midway Between Oral Performance and Literary Art," Antony Campbell establishes a new genre which communicates "the gist of a story so that it might be recalled or retold." Proceeding from 1 Sam 19:11–17, Michal's "dummy-in-the-bed" ploy, Campbell recognizes the reported story by omission of key plot elements. Since there are approximately thirty stories in the narrative of David's rise to power, it is understandable why a literary author might wish to report the stories rather than tell each one. Reported stories can also be recognized by "variant ways of telling the same story," for example in 1 Samuel 20. "In an oral performance, a storyteller might choose whichever version was most appropriate to the audience, the mood, or the time available." Twentieth century narratology would suggest that for the literary audience, the one they see is the one they are inclined to perceive.

"Spatial Form in Exod 19:1–8a and in the Larger Sinai Narrative" by Thomas Dozeman builds upon current literary discussions of spatial form-devices in narrative which depart from chronological sequence. Instead, scenes of "characterization, slow pace, lack of resolution, and repetition" provide different but equal perspectives on the same core event, like the sections of an orange. Through a careful analysis of the notoriously difficult interplay of commandments and actions in Exod 19:1–8a, Dozeman demonstrates how redactors continually impel an audience into the immediate present of God's will at Sinai. In the chapters from Exodus 19–34, Dozeman details Moses' six journeys between God encountered on the mountain and Israel met at its base, showing how the legal material has been incorporated into the narrative. The journeys do not move forward in time but rather juxtapose revelations of Torah given "on this day." A story seemingly of time and motion is actually one of immediate revelation.

In "The Institutional Matrix of Treachery in 2 Samuel 11," Joel Rosenberg demonstrates, through a detailed stylistic analysis, that "verisimilitude and factuality" do not account for the story's "literary artfulness." Instead, servants, the battlefield, holy war, protocol, communication, powerful members of court society, all tell the story of the tragedy "in which David is the criminal, and the nation both his accomplice and his victim." The reader is made aware continually of the contradictions of Israel's political life such that we finally share David's astonishment at Uriah's refusal to return home. For Rosenberg, the biblical narrator is not simply the servant of verifiable historical events or the portrayer of moral and psychological struggles, but the teacher of institutional history through a parable.

All three of these authors are indebted to modern literary theory for alerting them to the subtleties of the tiny building blocks of narrative (repetitions, seeming lapses, modes of reference), and also to the overall plan and integrity of a literary unit. They all take these insights to another level. Campbell's definition of the genre "reported story" bridges the gap between literary production and the audience of oral storytelling. Dozeman applies his discussion of "spatial structures" to the processes of redaction criticism. Rosenberg's critiques of modern literary approaches challenge us to acknowledge the wealth of societal knowledge and wisdom transmitted in the art of biblical narration. For all three of these literary sleuths, careful attention to the minutest details of the texts have yielded a story within a story.

In the final articles in this volume ("Feminist Criticism of Biblical Narrative"), all three authors are keenly aware of the societal expectations of women for the female protagonists whose stories they examine. Bird, Furman, and Fuchs all also acknowledge that present society's views of women as mothers, sacred women, wives, and prostitutes are inevitably interwoven in their perceptions of the Israelite and other ancient Near Eastern views of women. All three also build upon the works of feminist thinkers, share feminist concerns, and construct stories through stories.

The differences among them may be seen more clearly by comparing their analyses of the story of Tamar. By arguing for the societal distinction between the sacred woman and the prostitute and for the ambivalent expectations of society toward the latter, Phyllis Bird opens up many levels of irony in the story of Judah's daughter-in-law. Nelly Furman also treats Genesis 38 at some length. Characteristic of her approach is a focus on the differing meanings of attire (in this case the widow's garb, the harlot's veil, and the signet, cord, and staff) for disclosing contrary interpretations of events for women and men. Like the "annunciation type-scenes" which provide the major focus of the article by Esther Fuchs, the story of Tamar illustrates for her the basic view of the patriarchal ideology of motherhood. In this case, Tamar's pluck is motivated by self-seeking concerns for the benefits and security of birthing a male child who continues her husband's line. While presented as a heroine, Tamar's portrayal has a literary flatness due to the constraints on women's roles. Nonetheless, all three authors offer interesting methods for viewing the contours of the narrative dynamics in this and a whole range of biblical stories.

In "The Harlot as Heroine: Narrative Art and Social Presupposition in Three Old Testament Texts," Phyllis Bird examines the stories of Tamar, Rahab, and the two harlots brought before Solomon. She argues that the narrative turns in the stories can only be appreciated and understood by recognizing the "fundamental ambivalence" of the societal role of the harlot in ancient Near Eastern society. Bird rejects the designation of Tamar as a hierodule but insists that she is a harlot, whose role "is a kind of legal outlaw, standing outside the normal social order with its approved roles for women, ostracized and marginalized, but needed and therefore accommodated." She also argues that Rahab should not be understood as a hierodule, and that her marginal role as a harlot is clearly shown from her house in the walls of

Jericho. Our low expectations for any "moral strength, courage, or insight" from a prostitute are reversed in the Deuteronomist's version of her final speech proclaiming the mighty acts of God. Our expectation that no true motherly feelings will be expressed by the two harlots brought before Solomon is reversed in the crisis of the story. Thus in all three examples, the crises of the stories are constructed by reversing our expectations of prostitutes' behavior.

In "His Story Versus Her Story: Male Genealogy and Female Strategy in the Jacob Cycle," Nelly Furman uncovers the conflicting interpretations of reality for women and men by contrasting the meaning of attire in the stories about Rebekah, Tamar, and Joseph and Potiphar's wife. Esau's attire, falsely placed on Jacob's hands and neck, ensure a triumph for Rebekah's son. For Judah, his signet, cord, and staff are a promissory note; for Tamar, they are "proof in a paternity suit." For Joseph his coat is a symbol of trust between men (for his father and for Potiphar). For Potiphar's wife it is "the reminder of her frustrated desire." In all three stories, attire represents conflicting desires between women and men.

Esther Fuchs' article, "The Literary Characterization of Mothers and Sexual Politics in the Biblical Narrative," opens with an analysis of all the "annunciation type-scenes" progressing from Genesis to 2 Kings; they demonstrate an increasing narrative role for female protagonists in procuring their desires — to be mothers of sons. The message of this progression is that "good" women will eventually be rewarded by God in this way. Fuchs then considers a number of other passages which portray biblical motherhood. Hagar, Tamar, Zipporah, Samson's mother, Ruth, the Shunammite, Rizpah, Maacah the mother of Tamar, and Bathsheba are all mothers caught up in the lives of their sons. Thus she illustrates in a thoroughgoing way how the institution of patriarchal motherhood "secures the wife as her husband's exclusive property and insures the continuity of his name and family possessions via patrinomial customs and patrilineal inheritance patterns." In the biblical narratives, mothers have collapsed Adrienne Rich's distinction between the patriarchal social and legal institution, on the one hand, and seemingly their personal and psychological approach to mothering on the other.

This last group also evidences the combination of many methods of biblical criticism and modes of modern narratology. All three articles highlight literary strategies in their examinations of the struggles for power and survival in the biblical world. These three authors, indeed all the authors of this volume and its editors, hope that these articles will further readers' creation of stories upon stories.

ARTICLES

I

A Theory of Narrative

THE RESTORATION OF BIBLICAL NARRATIVE

Mary Gerhart
Hobart and William Smith Colleges

ABSTRACT

Biblical scholarship is enjoying a renaissance, thanks primarily to the use of literary critical analysis. Yet questions of theory and of methodology appear to be caught in a thicket of unexamined assumptions. As a result, it could be argued that exegesis which is good is so more by luck than by design. Focusing on the issue of genre in general, the paper designs a theory of narrative. Three propositions are offered: (1) Narrative is generically cognitive; (2) narrative is generically historical; (3) narrative is generically theological. Brief analyses of specific books which propose to employ literary critical understandings of the Bible as narrative suggest how narrative theory might assist work being done in the field.

Scholars outside the field of Biblical Studies receive mixed impressions about the status of narrative in contemporary biblical scholarship. In his review of Robert Alter's *The Art of Biblical Narrative*, for example, Frank Kermode (6) praises the author's attention to the literary aspects of the biblical text: "Something new and exciting is happening," Kermode declared in his review, entitled "The New Old Testament."

One is puzzled, therefore, to notice Alter's own derogatory attitude toward the newer approaches to literary interpretation—an attitude which seems to contradict Kermode's appraisal. Alter states his disdain bluntly in his introduction:

> This book, then, is directed to anyone concerned with the Bible, whether out of cultural or religious motives, and also to students of narrative. Readers in this last category will find no more than a couple of passing allusions to the new narratology that has flourished in France and America over the last decade because, quite frankly, I find its usefulness limited, and I am particularly suspicious of the value of elaborate taxonomies and skeptical as to whether our understanding of narrative is really advanced by the deployment of bristling neologisms like analepsis, intradiegetic, actantial (x).

So much for damning narratology with no praise whatsoever! Kermode notices (7) that Alter "has taken a point here and there from modernist criticism but ... is distinctly unfashionable in his respect for the author's intention." Nonetheless, even if no outright contradiction exists between what Alter does and how he claims to have done it, the issue of methodology in his book remains confusing at best.

Moreover, on the basis of Kermode's *own* book on biblical narrative, *The Genesis of Secrecy: On the Interpretation of Narrative* (1982), Mary Ann Tolbert, a New Testament scholar, calls for a change in the way most work is done in the field. Tolbert states that "[most] modern New Testament scholarship has concerned itself either with the universe [which] the text supposedly represents ... or with the artist/author." Since these two "orientations," according to Tolbert,

> both necessarily regard gospel narrative as being *at some point* transparent on historical reality, Kermode's absolute denial of this possibility and his emphasis upon the fundamental secrecy of all narrative pose a radical challenge to biblical historians (3).

As a result of this challenge, Tolbert concludes, "It may well be that the biblical guild needs to be forced into rethinking methodological assumptions too facilely or naively accepted." Nevertheless, although she credits Kermode with a "latent challenge" on these terms she does not find his work explicitly directed toward the rethinking that is needed. "For this purpose," she adds, "one might wish a more pointed and rigorous approach" (Tolbert, 2).

As if this were not enough, Hans Frei's pessimistic evaluation (1974) of the results of eighteenth and nineteenth century biblical criticism applies equally well to twentieth century criticism. For the thrust of his argument in *The Eclipse of Biblical Narrative* is that biblical narrative itself is in danger of obfuscation by the form-critical and hermeneutical methods used to interpret it.

We will return to Frei's challenge later, but for the moment let us summarize the combined message as follows: *Biblical scholarship is enjoying a renaissance of sorts, thanks primarily to the use of literary critical analysis. Yet questions of theory and of methodology appear to be caught in a thicket of unexamined assumptions. As a result, it could be argued that exegesis which is good is so more by luck than by design.*[1] If my assessment is correct, the most urgent need is to construct ways of sorting out and evaluating current methodological assumptions and principles, and the best way to accomplish this goal is to formulate a theory of narrative that is faithful to the exigencies of contemporary thought.

How does a postcritical theory of narrative differ from a precritical one? First of all, we expect postcritical theory to be different from, for example, medieval biblical criticism which Thomas Wilson analyzed in his handbook on rhetoric (*Arte of Rhetorique*, 1553).[2] Wilson's account answers questions considered to be appropriate for a narrative: who, what, where, with what help, wherefore, how, at what time? We notice that these precritical questions focus on the character (considered as a replica of a person). These questions presume also that only one time is significant in the explication of narrative, viz., the action. Further, the action is conceived of in terms of a naive realist epistemology: It appears as the "already, out there now real," and does not take cognizance of the operations of consciousness of the one who conceived of the action, i.e., the explicator. Finally, the action is conceived of in terms of the effect it has in itself, i.e., apart from the work it accomplishes by means of the reader's activity.

I propose to make explicit a postcritical theory of narrative by considering narrative to have three aspects: (1) narrative is generically cognitive; that is, narrative is both a mode of cognition and a genre; (2) narrative is generically historical, which is to say that narrative discloses the phenomenon of historicity; and (3) narrative is generically foundational, by which we mean that *biblical* narrative has an implicit theological orientation. I will then show the appropriateness of the theory by applying it to representative types of biblical scholarship. Finally, I shall consider how a postcritical theory of narrative addresses the issue of the relationship of theory to method in an attempt to come to a different assessment of method than that which is implied by Frei's historical and Alter's literary critical studies.

I. Narrative Is Generically Cognitive

It has been the ambition of genre criticism, which originated with Hermann Gunkel, to identify the *sub*genre of specific texts—such as gospel, midrash, story of the Living Oracle, parable, etc. Most of these subgenres are sufficiently established so that the evocation of a generic identity concomitantly sets in motion certain expectations for the reader. With respect to biblical narrative in general, however, it is more difficult to specify just which expectations.

Notwithstanding this difficulty, some expectations are always made evident whenever we try to read a text aloud and find ourselves adopting certain tones or ways of expression rather than others. We are also made aware of such expectations whenever we are led to ask what mode of cognition is represented by narrative in general. What is the cognitive status of narrative in relation to those other major modes of cognition designated by discipline as philosophical, scientific, historical? What is its status among the modes of thought viewed as binary oppositions cutting across several disciplines: oppositions such as linear/hermeneutical; synchronic/diachronic; reductionist/distortionist; apodictic/polemical; theoretical/commonsensical; analogical/metaphorical; mimetic/impressionistic; etc.? We find that narrative participates in more than one mode of cognition, viewed either as a discipline or as a binary opposition, and it overarches many of the traditionally designated literary genres. In short, narrative surpasses both the class "major modes of cognition" and the class "major literary genres" in ways that none of the other members of either class does.

Narrative belongs to, and therefore is, both a mode of cognition and a genre at once. In order to make explicit, first of all, the cognitive character of narrative, let us construct a phenomenology of narrative under the auspices of what Paul Ricoeur calls the "competence" each of us has for following a story (esp. 52–94). In Ricoeur's hermeneutical theory, narrative persuades neither by means of formal logic or by the results of thought brought directly to judgment but rather by multiple means, such as juxtaposition of qualities, reinforcement by images, jarring of assumptions by means of metaphor, suspense, coincidence, failure of logic, sympathy, identification, repulsion, and appropriate and inappropriate instances of abstraction. The conception of narrative as a distinctive mode of thought clarifies the indispensability of a literary analysis of narrative and the recognition that the narrative mode of thought may not be substituted for without remainder by other modes of thought.

The notion of the competence every reader must have for following a story is intrinsic to a postcritical theory of narrative. This notion objectifies the minimal conditions for the act of intelligent reading and brings to light what will be our first premise, namely, that a narrative "whole" is located between the text and the reader's reconstruction of its parts. Next, it discloses what will be our second premise, that there are, minimally, two time-elements in a narrative: the time of events told about and the time of telling. That is, narrative sentences refer to at least two time-separated events, and explicitly aim to describe the earliest event to which they refer. It is this time-separation which accounts for the essential difference between literary-historical narrative on the one hand and philosophical-scientific explanation on the other. This factor also has the potential for overcoming the naive realist expectation that an event has a fixed meaning which can be recorded by a perfect witness who can give a full description of it as soon as it has occurred.[3] A narrative sentence, then, describes an event A by making reference to a future event B which could not be known at the time when A occurred.

This factor of the time-separation of the events to which the text refers from the event(s) of narration is familiar to us, of course, especially from redaction criticism, which has, as its first objective, to distinguish narrated events from the event(s) of narration. In redaction criticism, the time of narration is as important as the time of the events referred to in a text. The success of redaction criticism can be seen, for example, in the deciphering of four strands of narration in the Pentateuch.

Ricoeur's analysis is especially helpful for instances in which the time of narration is presumably singular and in which events A and B can be understood to be related in terms provided only by hypothetical circumstances belonging to the time of narration. I say "*hypothetical* circumstances" to emphasize that, strictly speaking, both the narrated events and the original narration are inaccessible to the reader except through "texts" and must be reconstructed in interpretation. Robert Alter makes this kind of hypothesis (although not explicitly) when he observed, for example, that in traditional criticism, the story of Tamar (Genesis 38) has been treated as an anomalous fragment inserted into the Joseph story between Genesis 37 and 39. By paying close attention to the language of narration, however, Alter perceives certain coincidences between the verbs which describe Jacob's recognition of Joseph's coat brought to their father by his other sons and Judah's recognition of his own seal, cord, and staff brought to him by his servants from Tamar. These coincidences lead to the awareness of larger similarities of emplotment in the two stories and eventually disclose a link between the stories of Joseph and Tamar. This link is the uprooting of the law of primogeniture which Alter finds to be at the heart of both stories. In Alter's example, the events referred to in the two stories have no intrinsic connection with each other. It is only through the event of narration that they can be said to be related and ultimately even to be part of the same story (Alter:4–12).

We can say, then, that the precritical notion that a narration is merely the reenactment of what characters originally thought, felt, or did, must be replaced with the postcritical realization that actors' actions are described in the light of events that they did not and could not know (as, for example, the reason for Judah's being singled out in the first episode in the story of Joseph). According to Ricoeur, it is frequently the case that a sufficient condition for the meaning of an event occurs later than the time of the original event.

We are now prepared to return to the first premise which was designed to overcome the precritical notion that a text is an "already-out-there-now-real" phenomenon by making explicit the hermeneutical insight that a narrative "whole" is located between the text as a unit and the reader's reconstruction of it. This premise corresponds to our recognition in the second premise that the distance between two time-separated events (the presumed original happenings and the events of telling) sets up a tension which the reader attempts to resolve by relating the events in some way so as to grasp the best sense of the whole story. What now is our new notion of text? A narrative text describes a sequence of actions and experiences which are attributed to a number of characters, whether based on historical personages or wholly imaginary. These agents of action are presented in situations that they change or to whose changes they react. In turn, these changes reveal hidden aspects of the situation, and the actions give rise to a new predicament calling for thought, or action, or both. The response to this predicament brings the narrative to its conclusion.

What now is our new notion of reader? To follow a narrative means to understand the successive actions, thoughts, and experiences as having a particular directedness. That person is a reader who is pulled forward by the succession of acts and responds to the directedness with expectations concerning the outcome and the ending of the whole process. In this sense, the "conclusion" of the story as read is the attracting pole of the process. But unlike scientific or philosophical modes of thought, wherein a conclusion can be deduced or predicted, the conclusion of a narrative must be "acceptable." For every story holds surprises, coincidences, encounters, revelations, and recognitions, and its conclusion surpasses the disciplined lines of logic. Looking backward from the conclusion to the episodes which led to it, the reader must rather be able to say that this end required those events and this chain of actions. The affirmation rising out of this retrospective look of the acceptability of it all is made possible by the mode of thought which guided every movement of the reader's expectations when s/he followed the narrative. To follow a narrative, then, is not to master, but to find events cognitively acceptable *after all*.[4]

We know from nineteenth century hermeneutical critics that we are drawn to read narratives because they are about human action. What is represented in narratives is, in the largest sense, human actions. However far these particular human actions may be from the reader's present feelings or interests, the emplotment of the actions imposes itself on the reader's basic interest in the human realm. But this ultimate interest in human beings and actions is not enough. In Ricoeur's theory, a narrative lures the potential reader into reading because in narrative, human actions have been radically disintegrated. Narrative constructs a felt need to reintegrate these actions into the continuity of a narrative. The reader's own life-project, the world which the reader is constructing, comes into view when the reader begins to explain the relations of the parts to the whole, and vice versa. The entire process of understanding a narrative begins with the reader's reconstructing its emplotment.

The act of reconstructing the emplotment brings us back to the issue of genre. Readers are aware, if only minimally so, that the text contains certain clues which lead to understanding it in one way rather than another. In *Fiction and the Shape of Belief* (1–69), Sheldon Sacks demonstrates, for example, why Henry Fielding's *Tom Jones* needs to be read as "represented action" rather than as satire or apologue. In *Rhetoric of Fiction* (243–70), Wayne Booth explores Jane Austin's *Emma* as a comedy of manners. In fact, whenever we understand a text, we understand it *as* a particular genre. By means of its generic disposition, narrative produces effects in the world in ways similar to other work in the world. We recognize this "praxis-dimension" of different kinds of narrative, for example, in the abbreviated typology of the effects of myth, parable, action, apologue and satire, in John Dominic Crossan's *The Dark Interval*:

> Story establishes world in *myth*, defends such established world in *apologue*, discusses and describes world in *action*, attacks world in *satire*, and subverts world in *parable* (1975:9).

However limited such typologies are in their ability to provide an overarching sense of the work that narrative in general does, they do remind us that narrative "works" in multiple ways. Narrative is designed to generate new meaning, to manifest meaning in nascent form, and to lure us into recognition of ways of being in the world other than our own.

II. Narrative Is Generically Historical

The history of genres is a concept familiar to twentieth century scholars. Genre-history, i.e., the tracing of specific kinds of narrative in terms of their rise, reappearance, combination, and decline, is only peripheral, however, to the phenomenon of historicity as disclosed through the study of narrative.

Hans-Georg Gadamer's notion of historicity is helpful in setting the stage for a discussion of narrative as generically historical. For Gadamer, historicity consists initially in the reader's awareness that s/he comes to the text with prejudgments and foremeanings. Absolute neutrality with respect to any text is an impossibility since everyone is "thrown into" worlds of meanings at birth and consequently thinks in terms of those meanings.

Contrast Gadamer's understanding with that of the naive realist, for whom the historical is the extrinsic linking of events to the time matrix of "history" and to the space matrix of "geography." To know something historically for the naive realist is to reconstruct, insofar as possible, the relationships — social, political, economic, religious — which can be "found" to have been present. For the naive realist history is strictly two-dimensional. For Gadamer, on the other hand, human beings are inescapably historical and manifest their historicity in a number of ways. Indeed, the way reflection constantly understands and exercises itself constitutes historicity.

Narratives which have become classics are among the most important manifestations of historicity. According to Gadamer, a classic makes explicit the mode of "being historical" in the sense that it illustrates the historical process of preservation. In other words, a classic is an "historical domain which precedes all historical reflection and continues through it" (Gadamer:225).

The foremeaning that belongs to a classic is precisely the sense we sometimes have, in reading texts or in viewing art, or being rescued from the immediacy of the present for the sake of the enduring, of the significance that hasn't been lost — that sense which leads us to understand a classic in relation to all past and future significance. A classic means not only what it says, but all that has and will be said as well.

It is somewhat ironic that classics *become* classics only after we have noticed that a stylistic ideal has been fulfilled in a certain time and place and we have become aware of the decline and distance in subsequent works. Classics are climaxes, then, that articulate the history of narrative in terms of the past, the present, and the future. Gadamer emphasizes that the climactic points of a genre—here, the different forms of narrative—usually come within a brief period of time. Although genre is history-bound, it is at the same time its own uprooting. For as a narrative form endures, its classics generate an element of self-criticism: "the classical is what is preserved precisely because it signifies and interprets itself" (Gadamer:257). The uncritical Romanticism of Gadamer's theory of interpretation, noted by Habermas and others, however, begins to appear at this point: A classic, Gadamer says, is not merely a statement about the past, a witness to what still needs interpretation, not only a communication with the present, but a communication which overcomes its own historical distance.

The notion of dialectical thinking, as explained by Fredric Jameson (107–109), refines our sense of history of genres as mere chronology. He argues that genres must be understood in two necessarily unreconcilable ways: first, phenomenologically, or semantically, in terms of what a text means and what "spirit" or "world view" it aims to describe; second, structurally, or syntactically, in terms of effective mechanics and processes that may constitute a text. Jameson suggests that one can regard these two ways of understanding genre as cohabiting in what then becomes the dual nature of genre. This approach yields conventional understandings of history in the forms of histories of thought and histories of genre. Or, one can rethink the two ways of understanding genre dialectically.

Jameson characterizes dialectical thinking as "historical reflexivity, that is, as the study of an object which also involves the study of the concepts and categories (themselves historical) that we necessarily bring to the object." Jameson gives a good example of dialectical thinking in his study of Northrop Frye's concept of romance. For Frye, a romance is a "Utopian fantasy" which aims at the transfiguration of the world of everyday life into a space-time continuum from which all imperfections will be removed. Jameson notices the phenomenological impossibility of regarding one's "world" (of which one is empirically a part) as a simple object of perception, despite the tendency for the "world" in romance narrative to be personified. In Frye, according to Jameson, world assumes the roles of traditional romantic characters; scenes usurp the "attributes of Agency and Act."[5]

Jameson credits Frye with providing an immense description of the basic elements of romance and an ingenious arrangement of these "semes" in terms of binary oppositions, but views his own study of romance as a dialectical mediation between character-positions and the "narratively 'meaningful'" world. He also proposes an historical reexamination of binary opposition, "a form [itself] without content which nonetheless ultimately confers signification on the various types of content (geographical, seasonal, social . . .) which it organizes."

Jameson's analysis completes our exposition of narrative as generically historical. His analysis suggests that what he has done with the form *binary opposition* and the genre *romance* would have to be done similarly by the postcritical interpreter with central terms, such as "consciousness," "the mind of the author," "the first audience," etc., used in studying various kinds of biblical narrative.

III. Narrative Is Generically Theological

Consideration of narrative as theological follows necessarily from our recognition (1) that narrative generates meaning; (2) that those meanings inform the worlds which shape us, and we, them; (3) that the forms of explanation employed to interpret narratives are themselves historically intrinsic to our understanding. When we question a narrative and allow it to question us, new questions arise, questions of *which* meanings to affirm and of *how* to relate those meanings into meaningful "wholes," or what Jameson calls "master stories." In other words, to ask such questions as *Which* texts? *Which* interpretations? and By what *criteria*? is to engage in activities which become foundational to our understandings of self and world.

In saying that narrative is generically theological, I am claiming that a biblical scholar *cannot not* engage in implicit theological reflection. Most minimally, by choosing to read biblical as distinct from or in addition to other texts, the reader makes an investment in what they express. But what do biblical texts express? One theologian specifies the object of religious texts in the following manner:

> For the Jewish, Christian and Islamic traditions, [the] experience of the whole is an experience of a who: a loving and jealous, living, acting, covenanting God, a God who discloses who God is, who we are, what history and nature, reality itself ultimately are. . . . [S]criptures are themselves only a relatively adequate expression of the earliest . . . community's experience. . . . They remain open to new experiences—new questions, new and sometimes more adequate responses for later generations who experience the same event[s] in ever different situations. Yet throughout the . . . tradition these scriptures will serve as finally normative: as that set of aspirations, controls and correctives upon all later expressions, all later classical texts, persons, images, symbols, doctrines, events that claim appropriateness to the classic witnesses to that event (Tracy:248–49).

The foregoing statement is an expression of *explicit* theological reflection on the scriptures. We notice, however, that even in this maximal (i.e., explicit act of taking a position before the text, of allowing the text to become a "whole" in front of the reader), no threat exists either of translating narrative into some other mode of cognition, such as doctrine, or of substituting some credal statement for any of the multiple genres which constitute the original text and its original interpretations.[6] The implication is that narrative (as well as other biblical genres) serves as the relatively adequate originating expression and norm for God's self-manifestation. Every other mode, however appropriate and expeditious, is subject to the same need for interpretation and evaluation.

But is it not true that by certain choices of texts, interpretations, criteria, we preclude other choices? Is it possible to be a Proteus of the scriptures, appropriating them all in turn, thereby maintaining for ourselves a pluralism of texts and interpretations? Furthermore, does not every expression of a "whole" tend "in spite of itself to give the impression of a facile totalization, a seamless web of phenomena"? Such is the charge made by Louis Althusser, a major Marxist, revisionist critic. In examining Althusser's charge and his counterthesis that "[a text] is a process without a *telos* or a *subject*," Fredric Jameson admits that the Althusserian critique is irrefutable on its own terms:

> it demonstrates the way in which the construction of a . . . totality necessarily involves the isolation and privileging of one of the elements *within* that totality (a kind of thought habit, a predilection for specific forms, a certain type of belief, a "characteristic" political structure or form of domination) such that the element in question becomes a master code or "inner essence" capable of explicating the other elements or features of the "whole" in question (28-29).

Althusser's claim represents a limit of thought for Jameson, one which is appropriate to accept, he thinks, because it corresponds to our experience of reading texts. There is a difference, therefore, between "pluralism" which refers to "the coexistence of methods and interpretations in the intellectual and academic marketplace" and that which is used as a "proposition about the infinity of possible meanings and methods and their ultimate equivalence with and substitutability for one another." Jameson concludes:

> I suspect, indeed, that there are only a finite number of interpretative possibilities in any given textual situation. . . : to forestall that systematic articulation and totalization of interpretive results . . . can only lead to embarrassing questions about the relationship between them. . . .

Interestingly, Jameson finds Americans especially unhearing with respect to what he calls "an upper methodological limit" (31-32).[7]

By considering the ways in which narrative is theological, we have discovered both the extent and the limits of our theory of narrative. This theory began with a phenomenological description of what it means to be able to follow a story and of the work that narrative accomplishes as a genre. The theory then moved to a consideration of what is disclosed by means of the time-bound and time-surpassing character of narration. Finally, the theory extends as far as the sense in which, together with other genres, it functions foundationally and thereby brings about a closure (however partial and temporary, some real closure) to our reflections on narration. This "relatively adequate" closure, we have claimed, is also explicitly or implicitly theological.

There are those, of course, who, like Althusser, decry any kind of closure to thought, but on different grounds. Some find narrative a "reactionary" form in the sense that it imposes an *illusory* order upon an essentially chaotic reality. Others, like Johannes Metz, use certain kinds of narrative, for example, narratives of the memory of suffering, to challenge bourgeois expectations of order. All of these denials of closure, however, implicitly affirm the limits of the genre of narrative as such. They also affirm the possibility that following a story may have reversible as well as predictable outcomes. These alternate views of narrative are important, and while, in the long run, one would not expect them seriously to undermine the theory of narrative outlined above, still that possibility serves as a potential corrective to it.

There are, finally, further questions about narrative, major questions, such as that of the relationship of narrative to experience, of history to fiction, or of specific genres to a "canon." Some of these further questions will be touched upon as we now turn to apply our theory to representative approaches to the understanding of biblical narrative.

IV. Application of Theory to Representative Texts in Biblical Criticism

The theory of narrative proposed in the three previous sections should be useful for the purpose of evaluating criticism; however, because of the number of variables involved in the application of the theory, its predictive value is limited. Nevertheless, the presumption is that if one understands the theory, one will have gained different ways of conceiving of what one does. Our major objective in the following brief analysis is to test the usefulness of the theory, i.e., its capacity for illuminating how a representative critical text might have been improved by attention to the issues raised here.

As one of the most engaging representatives of the literary-critical method of "close" reading, Robert Alter's *The Art of Biblical Narrative* (1981) affords us an opportunity to assess literary-critical approaches to scripture in general. We have already noticed Alter's rejection and disparagement of the newer literary-critical approaches, which he refers to in general as "narratology." But the method he advocates is not above criticism.

Alter compares his approach to biblical texts with that of "the midrashic exegetes," suggesting that "in many cases a literary student of the Bible has more to learn from the traditional commentaries than from modern scholarship. . . . [T]he makers of the Midrash were often as exquisitely attuned to small verbal signals of continuity and to significant lexical nuances as any 'close reader' of our own age" (11). But only to be attuned to small verbal signals leaves several methodological issues unresolved. Alter acknowledges that the midrashic genius for making connections is lacking in two ways: (1) It lacks a sense of a "coherent unfolding story in which the meaning of earlier data is progressively, even systematically, revealed or enriched by the addition of subsequent data"; (2) The "literary integrity" of biblical narrative tends to get lost in the "didactic insistence" characteristic of midrashic exegesis (11). Yet Alter's own approach remains bound unreflectively to the connections he makes within texts. Moreover, his claim that he limits himself to conventional exegetical and literary-critical devices within the text is contradicted by his use of concepts which come from other than the midrashic tradition. He employs the Freudian notion of "overdetermination," for example, to explicate the narration of Michal's contemptuous rebuke of David for dancing.

Besides failing to acknowledge the prejudgments and presuppositions which he brings to the texts, Alter seldom questions those of the texts themselves. It is ironic, therefore, that he faults contemporary literary-critical approaches for their neglect of "a deeper understanding of the values, the moral vision embodied in a particular kind of narrative" (Alter: x). For this neglect, which assumes the autonomy of the text with respect to anything extrinsic to the text while at the same time presumes to be able to *report* on "moral visions embodied in texts," characterizes his own approach as well. What is lacking, perhaps equally in both Alter's work and the work of those whom he criticizes, is an awareness of the implications of their own performance, that is, of the effects of their own moral visions on their interpretations and of the extent and limits of the approach they are taking.[8] What is lacking, in other words, is attention to the historical and foundational aspects of interpretation, without which their literary interpretations appear to be ensnared in moral naiveté and false objectivism.

A second shortcoming of Alter's work is his unreflective attribution of the patterns of meaning, which he finds in the text to the "author's intention."[9] Such attribution is a consequence of his desire to regard redactionist writers as creative rather than as passive transmitters or mere copyists of earlier texts. Even if his analysis does support the thesis that the redactionists were creative, a quite different claim is involved in asserting that what is found in the text is evidence of their intention—a claim which, as it stands, violates the principle of the time-separation of events. Alter would need to distinguish between the two claims as well as between the different evidence for each. His book is therefore a good example of the old criticism, not the beginning of the new.

Space does not permit a detailed analysis of other kinds of narrative studies of the bible, but general observations can be made about several other recent endeavors. In the following brief comments, I make no attempt to do justice to what the texts accomplish.

Johannes Metz's *Faith in History and Society: Toward a Practical Fundamental Theology* (1980) is one of the first German theologies to pay attention to narrative as a critical concept.[10] Metz is attuned to the exigencies of historical consciousness. He states, for example, that fundamental theology, is "concerned with experience, insights and theories with a theological character that cannot always be ascertained in advance because it has to be rediscovered again and again in a historical, experimental synthesis" (28).[11] Narrative and memory, for Metz, "are not added as an ornament" to theology but rather they "form part of the basic structure" of theology (51). However noteworthy Metz's attempt to introduce the concept of narrative into theology, his work contains few of the insights that come from an analysis of narrative as genre.

Two difficulties stem from Metz's lack of clarity about narrative as a genre: First, his reading of particular stories to make a conceptual point often forces specific elements of the narrative into inadequate interpretations. Arguing that narrative-practical theology must *replace* transcendental-idealistic theology, for example, he cites a well-known German folktale, the race between the hare and the hedgehog. The hedgehog, who challenged the hare to a number of laps in adjacent furrows of a field, got his wife to stand at one end of the furrow so that it appeared as though the hedgehog had already arrived, no matter toward which end of the furrow the hare raced. Metz interprets the hare, who dies of exhaustion, as having "opted to enter the field of history . . . [as well as] to expose the idealistic guarantee of the threatened identity of Christianity." Metz interprets the hedgehog as perpetrating a "trick which aims to safeguard the identity and triumph of Christianity without the experience of the race (that is, without the experience of being threatened and possibly of being defeated)." Surely this is a forced interpretation, however. Moreover, the two hedgehogs are not duplicates of each other: One is male and the other, female.[12]

Another slight of thought occurs in his claim regarding the non-discursive and non-argumentative character of narrative. "As distinct from pure discourse or argument, narrative makes it possible to discuss the whole history and the universal meaning of history in such a way that the idea of this universal meaning is not transferred to a logical compulsion of totality or a kind of transcendental necessity" (Metz:164–65).

It is not clear, however, just how narrative, as he explicates it, is able to achieve what he claims for it. Nor is it self-evident how narrative theology is an adequate replacement for transcendental theology. Perhaps Metz's is a none-too-subtle inflation of the notion of narrative.

From the perspective of the foregoing theory of narrative, Raymond Brown's *The Birth of the Messiah* (1979) could also have been strengthened. First, a genric analysis might have resolved the internal contradiction that arises in his treatment of "infancy narrative." For, on the one hand, he objects to the classification as being "inaccurate and inadequate," cautioning that "as for narrative, one may well wonder whether this term is applicable to a series of short scenes with accompanying Scripture citation" (Brown:25). Later he rejects as well the classification as "midrash" of the texts he is dealing with (37). He asserts that genric criticism has been a stage of criticism passed for a "more fruitful stage of research." Yet he identifies the texts in question as infancy *narrative* and, aside from the exceptions noticed above, does not consider other possibilities. One might conclude that Brown's concept of genre is only classificatory, rather than generative and praxis-oriented.

Second, Brown's work is organized around questions which we have above identified as precritical; he says that he will expand Stendahl's formula, which offers a "basic approach": "... *Quis et Quomodo, Ubi et Unde* (Who, How, Where, Whence)" (Brown:53). These questions are precritical in the sense that they exhibit no self-reflective methodological awareness on the part of the interpreter. Third, like Alter, Brown thinks that the "quest for the evangelist's intent" constitutes the "task of the whole commentary." Given the contemporary discussion of the issue of authorial intentionality, one might expect to find some discussion of the extent and limits of this approach to the text.[13] Because such discussion is lacking in Brown's study, the non-specialist again finds internal contradictions between the sometimes carefully qualified statements on what it is possible to know about the narratives and the assertions of certitude regarding, for example, Luke's intentions and knowledge (Brown:466).

John Dominic Crossan's *Cliffs of Fall: Paradox and Polyvalence in the Parables of Jesus* (1980) runs into two major difficulties. The first pertains to the limits of what can be accomplished by redaction criticism. His study has as its first priority to determine which is the original text, i.e., what are the sayings of *Jesus*. Crossan, like Alter, justifies this goal in terms of redaction criticism. To the degree that this method is successful, it may yield information about the life of Jesus or the early Christian and Jewish communities. But even if one were to ascertain, for example, which parables are probably the texts of Jesus, can one presume thereby (as Crossan seems to do) that these texts become normative for interpreting all other Christian scripture? In other words, Crossan would have to argue the sense in which the parables are normative; to assert that the parables are the original sayings of Jesus is not enough.

The second difficulty is with the meaning of the "canon" operative here as normed by the parables. As we have seen in Part III, individuals as well as communities will choose to read certain texts first—some texts more than others, and some as the key to all the rest. In addition, religious communities use canons to identify and to limit what were the originating texts of their complex traditions. The canonical texts, however, are in fact interpreted in relation to one another and to those "discovered" since the canon was formulated. The danger is to assert the normativeness of certain texts to the exclusion of others. Crossan's tendency toward exclusivity in his early work could be emended by the notion of a "working canon," a theological concept which, while it acknowledges the matter-of-fact normativeness of certain texts, does not result in the principled rejection of others.[14]

V. *Conclusion*

What happens in the debates between the literal, historical position and the various challenges to that position or variations on it, Frei says, is that the "realistic narrative reading of biblical stories ... went into eclipse." What happens, in other words, is that new methods such as form criticism and hermeneutical theory tend, in Frei's view, to move interpretation away from the text. In the case of historical criticism, it is to look "for what the narrative refers to or what reconstructed historical context outside itself explains itself" (Frei:135). In the case of hermeneutical theory, it is to substitute knowledge of a structure of consciousness for the meanings of the text.

But Frei does not merely critique various methods. He also proposes an alternative, and that alternative is, surprisingly, what appears to be a precritical reading of the texts: "the words and sentences meant what they said, and because they did so they accurately described real events and real truths that were rightly put only in those terms and no others." In precritical reading, figural interpretations are permitted so long as they do not "offend against a literal reading of those parts which seemed most obviously to demand it" (Frei:1). To the degree that Frei's suspicion of hermeneutical theory and, for different reasons, historical criticism is representative of biblical studies, this suspicion, whether or not explicit, may account for much of the confusion perceived by scholars from other fields. For, in his book (and perhaps also in the field), the norm of "realistic narrative reading" is neither sufficiently questioned, modified, nor relativized by the historical character of the debates he reports.

The questioning of this norm is the very heart of contemporary narrative theory.

NOTES

[1] See Alter's account of the somewhat accidental character of the success of his first excursion into the field of biblical studies: "I put my notes for the colloquium (on the literary study of the Bible) away in a drawer, and some four years later, on an impulse, I asked the editors of *Commentary* whether they would be interested in an article on the need for a literary approach to the Bible" (xi).

[2] As cited in Buss (19). The example is, more precisely, from *post*medieval form-criticism.

[3] In Arthur Danto's view, an ideal chronicle, i.e., one which is recorded moment by moment and which ends peremptorily without any conclusion, constitutes a scientific, rather than a narrative statement (1965: chap. 8; see also 1962).

[4] See below, Part III, for an interpretation of the theological aspect of genre to be the act of making explicit these relationships within a "master story."

[5] Although I find Jameson in general positivist in his Marxist assumptions, an analysis based on his work need not be impaired thereby.

[6] See also Kelsey (158–59, 205–7).

[7] Jameson has an intriguing view of the medieval system of the four levels of interpretation (anagogical, moral, allegorical, literal) and how it discloses the "incommensurability between the private and the public" (29–31).

[8] Of the three readings Alter (125) suggests for 2 Sam 6:23, it is not clear why the third reading is "less likely than the other two readings."

[9] See also Note 13 below.

[10] Metz is a liberation theologian who has as his primary goal the restoration of what he calls the "dangerous memory" of Jesus—a memory which would call into question any bourgeois consciousness lacking an understanding of freedom and critical praxis.

[11] To develop his thesis that a remembrance of suffering and the dead is intrinsic to a praxis-oriented theology, he argues that the Enlightenment criticism of traditions does not preclude the necessity of recognizing memory as the "inner element" of the critical consciousness that tries to get a sense of its own direction (Metz:39).

[12] Peter Hodgson (31-33) notices that "Actually the two are not 'exactly the same.' One is the husband, the other the wife—a subtle difference that escaped the hare, the difference, perhaps, of beginning and end?"

[13] Such a critique has been available in literary-critical studies since William Wimsatt's classic article on the "intentional fallacy," appears more recently with the debates over E. D. Hirsch's principle of the normativeness of such intentionality, and currently has been revised. See Juhl.

[14] See Tracy, 254-59, 264, 272-73, 290 n. 29, 296-98 n. 81, 309, 313-14, 333 n. 3.

WORKS CONSULTED

Alter, Robert
    1981 *The Art of Biblical Narrative.* New York: Basic Books.

Booth, Wayne
    1961 *The Rhetoric of Fiction.* Chicago: University of Chicago.

Brown, Raymond
    1979 *The Birth of the Messiah.* New York: Doubleday.

Buss, Martin
    1977 "The Study of Forms." Pp. 1-56 in *Old Testament Form Criticism.* Ed. John H. Hayes. San Antonio: Trinity University.

Crossan, John Dominic
    1975 *The Dark Interval: Towards a Theology of Story.* Niles, IL: Argus Communications.
    1980 *Cliffs of Fall: Paradox and Polyvalence in the Parables of Jesus.* New York: Seabury.

Danto, Arthur
    1962 "Narrative Sentences." *History and Theory.* 2:146-79.
    1965 *Analytical Philosophy of History.* Cambridge: Cambridge University.

Frei, Hans W.
    1974 *The Eclipse of Biblical Narrative: A Study in Eighteenth and Nineteenth Century Hermeneutics.* New Haven and London: Yale University.

Gadamer, Hans-Georg
    1975 *Truth and Method.* New York: Seabury.

Hodgson, Peter
    1981 Review of Johannes B. Metz, *Faith in History and Society: Toward a Practical Fundamental Theology. RelSRev* 7:31-33.

Jameson, Fredric
    1981 *The Political Unconscious.* Ithaca: Cornell University.

Juhl, P. D.
    1980 *Interpretation: An Essay in the Philosophy of Literary Criticism.* Princeton: Princeton University.

Kelsey, David
  1975 *The Uses of Scripture in Recent Theology.* Philadelphia: Fortress.
Kermode, Frank
  1981 "The New Old Testament." *New York Times Book Review.* July 19:6–7.
Levenson, Jon D.
  1983 Review of Robert Alter, *The Art of Biblical Narrative. BA* 46:124–25.
Metz, Johannes B.
  1980 *Faith in History and Society: Toward a Practical Fundamental Theology.* Trans. David Smith. New York: Crossroad.
Ricoeur, Paul
  1984 *Time and Narrative.* Vol. I. Chicago: University of Chicago.
Sacks, Sheldon
  1964 *Fiction and the Shape of Belief.* Berkeley: University of California.
Tolbert, Mary Ann
  1982 Review of Frank Kermode, *The Genesis of Secrecy: On the Interpretation of Narrative. RelSRev* 8:1–6.
Tracy, David
  1981 *The Analogical Imagination.* New York: Crossroad.

CAN GENESIS BE READ AS A BOOK?

Everett Fox
Clark University

ABSTRACT

In line with recent literary scholarship and its concerns with the unity of biblical books, this paper examines Genesis for structural coherence. Accepting a fourfold division for the book, I will attempt to demonstrate progression in its handling of character development (including that of God) and the style of the text, suggesting thereby a final shaping consciousness. Theme-words that bind the four sections together will be noted, and a general structuring of the book on the basis of important motifs will be presented. The resulting chart will show both balanced and chiastic elements. I will then compress the list of motifs into a central "message" of Genesis; this may tell us something about the audience for which the canonical book of Genesis was intended.

The title of this paper fully reflects the era in which it has been written. It seldom occurred to believing Jews and Christians of centuries past to ask questions concerning the coherence of biblical books. The book of Genesis, for one, was an established fact as a unity and was reverently read as such. It has remained for biblical scholarship of the last two hundred years to perform the dissection whose procedures and results are well known to all in the field. These have become such a matter of course that one still finds, in recent commentaries on Genesis, a basic acceptance of Gunkel's judgment, rendered over eighty years ago (159):

> We may perhaps regret that the last great genius who might have created out of the separate stories a great whole, a real "Israelite national epic," never came. Israel produced no Homer.... the individual portions have been left side by side and in the main unblended.

This clear reference to source-criticism is buttressed not only by standard commentaries and introductions to Genesis (e.g., Driver; Eissfeldt; Speiser) but by introductory articles as well (e.g., in *The Interpreter's Dictionary of Bible* and the *Encyclopedia Judaica*). Even leaving aside the question of sources, one observes that some critics treat the text as almost an accident of editing, whose importance lies mostly in its overall role in the Pentateuch. Sandmel, for instance, writes (370):

> Genesis exists as a separate book because it contains sufficient material for a scroll, rather than because it was planned as a unit. The division was strictly a matter of convenience. One should read on into the beginning of Exodus without pause.

Judgments such as these, combined with the added weight of the so-called comparative approach to biblical texts (which tends often to treat smaller, individual sections in isolation), could lead to the conclusion that nothing much may be gained from an attempt to limn the unity of Genesis. In addition, the fact remains that the various sources of Genesis *do* lie side by side, virtually begging for the scholarship of the past few generations to appear and put each piece in its proper place.

Nevertheless, the question of the coherence of Genesis as a book cannot be ignored. An oral, written, redactional, and scribal tradition as complex as Israel's cannot be presumed to have been ignorant of artistic values, one of which is surely coherence. What might be termed the "P mentality," a cast of mind that focused on order and on the inherent meaningfulness of things, is made a mockery of if it is assumed that its practitioners possessed no sensitivity to literary structure. Furthermore, recent work on biblical narrative has led to a growing conviction among scholars that a consideration of macrostructures in the biblical text needs more elucidation and elaboration.[1]

It has been my experience as a translator of Genesis that when one takes a broad view of the text, issues of structure and coherence become compelling.[2] This is particularly true where the literature bears a strong oral stamp, as is the case with the Pentateuch. The Hebrew consonants of the book of Genesis are, in the main, an incontrovertible fact, and that fact leads to the perception of obvious inner links in the text, forged first by sounds and subsequently by ideas. Such an approach might be dubbed Rhetorical Criticism on a Grand Scale—that is, the hearing and perception of large literary constructs and their evaluation within the context of an entire book or complex of books (also similar to Canonical Criticism).[3]

A preliminary overview of Genesis as a book uncovers a clear basic structure. Most critics agree that the book falls into four main sections: the Primeval History (chapters 1–11), the Abraham Cycle (11:27 or 12:1–25:11), the (Isaac-)Jacob Cycle (25:12–36:43), and the Joseph Narrative (37–50). Once these divisions have been established, however, what the sections have in common outside of chronological and familial ties is not entirely clear. The Primeval History is almost always treated in isolation;[4] the Abraham Cycle differs from the rest of the Patriarchal sagas in both its form (short scenes rather than a continuous chronological account) and the character of the protagonist (except for an occasional white lie told on foreign territory,

Abraham is a paragon of biblical virtue); the Jacob material is biographical with strong aetiological content; and the Joseph narrative, as has often been noted, is a long short story with an unusual wealth of psychological detail for Genesis, and a changed locale (Egypt).

In light of those major differences, the unity of Genesis cannot be explained by calling it a book of origins (although it is), or a history of early Israel, or a collection of legends about the Patriarchs accompanied by a universal prologue. Yet many critics have been reluctant to go any further.

I would argue that, to be read as a book, Genesis must possess some compelling structural coherence, in some or even all of the following areas: character development; style; use and development of theme words and thematic threads; and ability to plot out a reasonable, balanced scheme for the book.

The human characters of the book of Genesis present a varied picture for analysis. Some of them, notably, Jacob, Judah, and Joseph, undergo marked and vivid transformation, and fully half the book details the changes they experience. Other protagonists, such as Cain, Noah, and even Abraham, appear not to change at all, conveying the text's message more by the consistency of their behavior than by their ability to grow. What is significant about the overall picture is the sense of development of character that unfolds as the book progresses: the further one reads in the text, the more complex and human the heroes become. It is, however, somewhat deceptive to single out any one of these characters for scrutiny, since the main figure of the book is undoubtedly YHWH himself.

Can one speak of character development in the redactor's portrayal of the God of Genesis, or of his relations with human beings? At the very least one may make three brief observations. First, as the book progresses, there is notably less and less human contact with the deity. The God who walks about in the Garden of Eden, freely conversing with his creatures, gives way to one who appears, occasionally in human guise, occasionally in dreams, and finally, in the Joseph story, to one who never directly talks to the hero at all.[5] It is possible that this progression reflects a postexilic view of Israel's religious development. Second, YHWH is himself presented as undergoing character transformation, especially in the early sections of the book, where both the realities of human nature (after the Deluge) and Abraham's eloquence (at Sodom and Gomorrah) prevail upon him to defer the destruction of the wicked, however temporarily. The latter is a favorite prophetic theme, familiar from the book of Jonah, but also found frequently in the Wandering narratives of the Pentateuch. By the second half of the book of Genesis, God appears more decisively in control of events, manipulating them with the skill of a master puppeteer (whose puppets are allowed at least a modicum of free will). Finally, the book in all its sections draws a powerful portrait of a deity who acts in human history, whether directly, as in the stories about the Deluge and the Tower of Babel, or discreetly, with Joseph. By the end of Genesis, there can be no doubt that God will take what is planned for evil and "plan it over" (*ḥšb*) for good (50:20), and will "take account" (*pqd*) of the people in their situation of exile (50:24). Here once more, the progression is striking; the Joseph story is the clearest and most full-blown illustration of this central characteristic of the biblical God.

Another line of development, likewise suggestive of an intentional final unity, may be observed in the area of style. What has apparently happened in the case of Genesis is that the redactor, skillfully utilizing the vast range of traditional material at his disposal, has fashioned a whole in which the style of each section is more expansive and smoother than the last. The text moves from a combination of short fragments (especially chapters 4–6) and longer narratives (Garden, Deluge) in the Primeval History, to the fuller vignettes of the Abraham cycle, through to a more coherent biography (Jacob) and finally to the self-integrated tale of Joseph.[6] In addition, each section of the book is actually longer than the previous one in sheer bulk of text. The book thus moves from a rapid-fire mix of stories to a more sustained narrative and, in so doing, effects strong movement of thematic material, with magnification of its concerns and ultimate resolution in the Joseph story. Simply put, the narrative process in the book of Genesis gradually slows down and concentrates, culminating in the high drama of chapters 37–50.[7]

It is in the third area, thematic development, that the book of Genesis attains its greatest demonstrable coherence. Theme-words serve as the point of departure. Exegetes have long observed, for example, that the recurrence of the word *tôlĕdôt* functions as the backbone of the entire book (see Buber:25–26). The repetition of this word serves to conceptually join Israel's history to that of the world — or, more precisely, to make Israel's history the culmination of the world's (Andriolo). Structurally, it also vitiates the oft-made claim that the Primeval History is basically apart from the rest of the book, since about one half of the occurrences of *tôlĕdôt* come in chapters 1–11. A second significant theme-word is the root *brk*. Here, like the previous theme-word, a broad concept is expressed: God both extends and narrows down his bestowal of blessing to the family of Abraham, from whom blessing is to proceed to "all the clans of the soil" (12:3). From its first mention in chapter 1, the root recurs in the renewal of Creation after the Deluge (9:1); the Abraham stories start with its fourfold sounding in 12:1–3, the Jacob cycle is built around the recounting of its transfer from Isaac (see chap. 27), and the Joseph narrative ends with it (48:9, 15, 16; 49:25–26).

Numerous other theme-words are used within smaller textual units, but our concern here is to outline major thematic threads that can be observed to provide literary continuity. Before treating the far-reaching themes, however, another issue of the coherence of Genesis must be broached: Has the redactor been able to link the various sections of the book together thematically? In other words, does each succeeding section build on what has gone before? Many examples could be adduced to support a positive answer; we will cite only a few. Abraham mirrors Noah as a recipient of YHWH's covenant, in his witnessing divine judgment on evildoers, and in the adjectives applied to his character—"righteous" (*ṣaddîq*) and "whole" (*tāmîm*). Jacob and Abraham have in common, at the very least, barren wives, contact with YHWH in dreams, association with sacred sites, centrality of blessing, material success, and the experience of wandering. Joseph and Jacob share sibling strife, favored-son status despite inferior birth position, success as adults achieved away from the parental home, incidents involving their father's deception, and eventual confrontation and reconciliation with brothers. One could draw up similar sets of linkages among all three major patriarchal figures (Isaac is a separate and weaker case, who nonetheless mirrors his father). What is striking about these patterns is not only their repetitiveness but also their variability from one figure to the next—for example, the contrast between Abraham's reaction to the impending annihilation of the wicked and Noah's passivity in a similar situation. Such variation may be evidence not only of a final editorial hand but of an earlier narrative consciousness of central concerns. In any event, it is evident that the canonical text of Genesis is the result of a well-worked-out scheme of development, thanks to its use of narrative juxtaposition.

This type of analysis does not preclude viewing each section of the book as a separate unit with separate concerns. The Primeval History, for instance, may be seen as a series of texts polemicizing against Israel's Mesopotamian origins;[8] the Abraham Cycle provides a view of prophetic consciousness through the protagonist's vision and behavior (Buber:37–43);[9] the Jacob cycle addresses anthropological problems of kinship marriage, and thus effects the biologically and culturally proper foundation of the people of Israel (Donaldson; Wander; Oden); and finally, the Joseph story deals with issues of divine providence and the curious relationship between biblical man, who proposes, and the biblical God, who disposes (similarly in the Jacob material). The fact that the entire book can thus be broken down into large and smaller units, and that each section nevertheless maintains its own integrity, is an indication of the level of artistry with which one is dealing in the book of Genesis.

When we turn to a listing of major themes in Genesis and attempt a structural overview on that basis, it becomes apparent that, whatever the history behind the different strands of the book, everything has, in the end, been integrated into an architectonic whole that is by turns consistent and chiastic. The following outline (revised from Fox, 1983) is a skeletal ordering of some of the book's thematic material.[10]

Primeval History	A	Chosen Figure (Noah)
	B	God favors Youngest Son (Abel); Hatred (Cain-Abel)
	C	Family Continuity Threatened (Abel murdered)
	D	Ends with Deaths (Haran, Terah)
		E Humanity Threatened (Deluge; repeated use of *kol* in 7:21–23)
		F Ends Away from Land of Canaan ("in Haran")
Abraham Cycle	A	Chosen Figure (Abraham)
	B	God Favors Youngest Son (Isaac); Hatred (Sarai-Hagar)
	C	Family Continuity Threatened (Sarai Barren; Isaac almost killed)
	D	Ends with Deaths (Sarah, Abraham, Ishmael)
		G Barren Wife (Sarah)
		H "Wife-Sister" Incident (chaps. 12 and 20)
		I Rivalry Between Wives (Sarah-Hagar)
		J Hero Renamed (Abraham)
		K Ends with Genealogy of Non-Covenant Line (Ishmael)
Jacob Cycle	A	Chosen Figure (Jacob)
	B	God Favors Youngest Son (Jacob); Hatred (Esau-Jacob)
	C	Family Continuity Threatened (Jacob almost killed)
	D	Ends with Deaths (Deborah, Rachel, Isaac)
		G Barren Wife (Rachel)
		H "Wife-Sister" Incident (chap. 26)
		I Rivalry Between Wives (Leah-Rachel)
		J Hero Renamed by God (Jacob)
		K Ends with Genealogy of Non-Covenant Line (Esau)
Joseph Story	A	Chosen Figure (Joseph)
	B	God Favors Younger Son (Joseph); Hatred (Brothers-Joseph)
	C	Family Continuity Threatened (Joseph almost killed; Judah's sons die; family almost dies in famine)
	D	Ends with Deaths (Jacob, Joseph)
		E Humanity Threatened (Famine; repeated use of *kol* in 41:54–57)
		F Ends Away from Land of Canaan ("in Egypt")

Although this chart is quite simple in its choice of themes, we may make several observations. Genesis operates in a manner similar to the treatment of myths in some other cultures, where, as G. S. Kirk (60–61) puts it, "a limited (but large) number of myths [is] recounted over and over again, with variations that can usually be found significant within an expanding cultural scheme." The reason for such repetition is that it shows "as in linguistic reduplication that there is a significant message, partly to insure that the message ultimately comes through complete" (Kirk, 61).

What might the "significant message" of Genesis be? The thematic material listed in the above chart lends itself to compression, and could be reduced to a fourfold scheme: (1) selection, (2) favor shown to younger sons, (3) struggle between those living in close intimacy, and (4) serious threats to the lives of the characters. But are there four themes here or two, comprising two groups of positive and negative? I would argue for a final reduction to one basic, composite structure: selection and survival amidst struggle and disaster.[11] One can say, then, that the initial audience of Genesis as a book apparently lives at a time of national and cultural crisis, a time of disarray and despair; events pit brother against brother, and survival seems precarious. Nevertheless, intimates the text, God has chosen the people of Israel, even though outward circumstances do not seem to warrant this conclusion. If we add to this the other important thematic content of Genesis (the constant promises of land and innumerable descendants), we are left with a text that sends a strong message of hope and confidence in the redeeming power of YHWH, as well as a vivid illustration of human difficulties that are encountered along the road to his service.

Such a reading would seem to suggest an exilic or postexilic dating for Genesis.[12] On the other hand, one must be careful not to limit a text as rich as Genesis to a particular historical audience. The book survived precisely because its messages were felt to have deep application even after direct historical analogies were no longer applicable. One could, for example, examine a single motif—such as that of the Younger Son Triumphant—and show how it is possible to extrapolate several major, cogent interpretations from it that bear on different historical periods, sociological circumstances, and ideological presumptions.[13]

In the end, it appears that the book of Genesis, far from being a mere collection of traditions about Israel's beginnings, is a text of considerable layering that has been painstakingly knit together with artistic tools of a high caliber. The question that remains is: Is such a view adversarial to what has preceded it in Biblical Studies? There was a time, rather recently, when this would have to have been the case. But it may be perceived that in current literary studies of biblical texts, there is greater willingness to accept the findings of historical scholarship and to utilize them; on the other side, there is slowly a recognition that source-critics, form-critics, and rhetorical critics have much to learn from one another. Consideration of what George W.

Coats (41) has called the "functional unity" of texts such as Genesis, a process that I have sketched out above on one particular model, will continue to complement earlier historical and literary methods, and will hopefully be combined with those methods in the future to provide a full view of the biblical corpus.[14]

NOTES

[1] See, for instance, Anderson; a recent and strong stand is taken by Kikawada and Quinn.

[2] See Fox (1983) and earlier, Buber and Rosenzweig, whose German translation of the Hebrew Bible also served as my translation model.

[3] As represented by Childs.

[4] The *Cambridge Bible Commentary*, for one, allots a separate volume to chapters 1–11.

[5] Despite the close similarities between the portrayals of Joseph and Jacob, the contrast in their contact with God is striking. At the same time, it should not be forgotten that at every turn, Joseph credits God as the source of his wisdom (e.g., Gen 40:8; 41:16; 45:5, 7, 9).

[6] For a view of how the traditionally troublesome chapter 38 has been integrated into the Joseph material, see Goldin and Fox (1983).

[7] Compare a parallel case in the area of thematic progression, albeit on a smaller scale, the cycle of stories about Samson in Judges 13–16. There, the key concepts and teachings of the narrative are brought to a head and resolved in the final two episodes (chap. 16); indeed, there is virtually no motif in that chapter that has not been anticipated earlier in the story. See Fox (1978:66).

[8] For more on the unity of Genesis 1–11, see, for instance, Anderson.

[9] For a current assessment of the unity of the Abraham Cycle, see Rosenberg.

[10] Other structurings are, of course, possible; for a suggestive one based on the genealogical material in Genesis, see the paper by Steinberg elsewhere in this volume. In addition, one should mention the theme of Promise, so prominent in Westermann, which I have omitted from my chart.

[11] Something like this complex of ideas has been posited by Miller in a study that takes a structuralist point of view in approaching the body of narrative from Genesis 37–Exodus 20. I would move the "message" of the texts back into the Primeval History, as my chart indicates.

[12] Miller, on the other hand, views the decline of Judah and Israel in the wake of the rising Assyrian empire as the psychological precondition for the themes of Genesis.

[13] The possibilities are manifold, ranging from views anthropological (see Stager) to those psychological (Bettelheim) and ideological (Sternberg). My own view, that the Younger Son motif may also include an Israelite critique of ancient Near Eastern ideas of nature and power, will be more fully developed in a future study.

[14] Space does not permit here treatment of the important structural relationship between Genesis and the rest of the Pentateuch. Suffice it to say that Genesis seems to do double duty, as both a self-contained work and as an integrated introduction to the whole of the Pentateuch (a similar role is played within Genesis by the Primeval History).

WORKS CONSULTED

Anderson, Bernhard W.
    1978   "From Analysis to Synthesis: The Interpretation of Gen. 1–11." *JBL* 97:23–39.

Andriolo, Karin R.
　1973　"A Structural Analysis of Genealogy and Worldview in the Old Testament." *American Anthropologist* 75:1657–1669.

Bettelheim, Bruno
　1977　*The Uses of Enchantment.* New York: Random House.

Buber, Martin
　1968　*On the Bible.* New York: Schocken.

Buber, Martin and Franz Rosenzweig
　1936　*Die Schrift und ihre Verdeutschung.* Berlin: Schocken.

Childs, Brevard S.
　1979　*Introduction to the Old Testament as Scripture.* Philadelphia: Fortress.

Coats, George W.
　1976　*From Canaan to Egypt: Structural and Theological Context for the Joseph Story.* CBQMS 4. Washington: Catholic Biblical Association.

Donaldson, Mara
　1981　"Kinship Theory and the Patriarchal Narratives: The Case of the Barren Wife." *JAAR* 49:72–87.

Driver, S. R.
　1926　*The Book of Genesis.* 12th ed. London: Methuen.

Eissfeldt, Otto
　1965　*The Old Testament: An Introduction.* New York: Harper and Row.

Fox, Everett
　1978　"The Samson Cycle in an Oral Setting." *Alcheringa: Ethnopoetics* 4:51–68.
　1983　*In the Beginning.* New York: Schocken.

Goldin, Judah
　1977　"The Youngest Son or Where Does Genesis 38 Belong." *JBL* 96:27–44.

Gunkel, Hermann
　1964　*The Legends of Genesis.* New York: Schocken.

Kikawada, Isaac and Henry Quinn
　1985　*Before Abraham Was.* Nashville: Abingdon.

Kirk, G. S.
　1970　*Myth.* Cambridge/Berkeley: Cambridge University/University of California.

Miller, Alan
　1977　"Claude Levi-Strauss and Gen. 37–Ex. 20." Pp. 21–52 in *Shiv'im*, ed. Ronald Brauner. Philadelphia: Reconstructionist Rabbinical College.

Oden, Robert A., Jr.
　1983　"Jacob as Father, Husband and Nephew: Kinship Studies in the Patriarchal Narratives." *JBL* 102:189–205.

Rosenberg, Joel
　1986　*King and Kin: Political Allegory in the Old Testament.* Bloomington: Indiana University.

Sandmel, Samuel
    1978   *The Hebrew Scriptures.* New York: Oxford University.

Speiser, Ephraim A.
    1964   *Genesis.* AB 1. New York: Doubleday.

Stager, Lawrence E.
    1985   "The Family in Ancient Israel." *BASOR* 260:1–35.

Sternberg, Meir
    1985   *The Poetics of Biblical Narrative.* Bloomington: Indiana University.

Wander, Nathaniel
    1981   "Structure, Contradiction, and 'Resolution' in Mythology." *JANES* 13:75–99.

Westermann, Claus
    1980   *The Promises to the Fathers.* Trans. David E. Green. Philadelphia: Fortress.

THE GENEALOGICAL FRAMEWORK OF THE FAMILY STORIES IN GENESIS

Naomi Steinberg
DePaul University

ABSTRACT

This paper utilizes the work of French literary critic Tzvetan Todorov for analyzing the structure of narrative plot in the family stories of Genesis. Todorov's five-stage plan of movement from one state of narrative equilibrium to another is applied to explain the interrelationship of genealogy and narrative in Genesis 12–50. Genealogy reflects family succession which moves action forward and is the redactional device used by P to organize family history into narrative cycles. Thus, narrative serves as a transitional device between genealogies. When the genealogy of Shem is included within the boundaries of Israel's specific ancestry, a parallel structural pattern in the histories of Abraham, Isaac, and Jacob emerges. All three of these narrative cycles focus on resolving the genealogical disequilibrium mentioned in the genealogies which preceded their stories.

I. Introduction

Genesis is a book whose plot is genealogy. Through the interrelationship of narratives within a genealogical framework, a chronology is established which recounts the general ancestry of universal history leading to Israel's specific beginnings. Few would disagree on this point. The transition from human history to Israelite history is, however, more controversial. Von Rad argues that the link between these two eras comes at Gen 12:1–3. He bases his thesis on a division of primeval history into narrative cycles organized around the Fall, Cain, the Song of Lamech, the Marriage of the Angels, the Flood, and the Tower of Babel. According to von Rad, primeval history represents the integration of older independent stories into cycles of narratives characterized by the pattern of sin, punishment, and divine provision. But the Tower of Babel story lacks the provision which von Rad discerns in the other narrative cycles of primeval history. As von Rad sees it, the provision for the story of the Tower of Babel is found in the call of Abraham; here, in Gen 12:1–3, the particularism of Israel's history begins (24). However, scholarly consensus has traditionally located the beginning of the so-called patriarchal history at Gen 11:27, where the genealogy of Terah begins. Vawter's recent commentary is representative: with the genealogy of Terah the focus of the story narrows down to the one family which marks the transition from universal to Israelite history (167–74).

Whether one follows von Rad or accepts the traditional location of the beginning of Israel's specific history at Gen 11:27, the problem of evaluating the genealogy of Shem, Gen 11:10–26, in its present position in the text remains. Neither von Rad nor more traditional analysis which separates primeval from Israelite history can adequately account for this genealogical unit in the structure of the book of Genesis. Von Rad refers to it as an "external genealogical link," (155) while Vawter focuses on the connections between Genesis 5 and the genealogy of Shem. He believes that the former serves as the structural model for the latter (159–63). Neither scholar provides a convincing argument for the integrity of the priestly redactional technique which incorporates Gen 11:10–16 in the structural design of the book of Genesis.[1] Therefore, this article will evaluate the function of the Shem genealogy in its present context, and, at the same time, address the question of genealogy as a redactional framework (P) which seems to overlay an earlier series of family stories in Genesis 12–50 in which genealogy is, to be sure, present as well (Cf. Tengström; Weimar).

II. Narrative as a Transition Device in Genesis

In his analysis of the structure of narrative plot, Todorov writes:

> An "ideal" narrative begins with a stable situation which is disturbed by some power or force. There results a state of disequilibrium; by the action of a force directed in the opposite direction, the equilibrium is reestablished; the second equilibrium is similar to the first, but the two are never identical.
>
> Consequently, there are two types of episodes in a narrative: those which describe a state (of equilibrium or disequilibrium) and those which describe the passage from one state to the other. The first type will be relatively static and, one might say, iterative; the same kind of action can be repeated indefinitely. The second, on the other hand, will be dynamic and in principle occurs only once (111).

According to Todorov's scheme, there are five stages in the movement from one state of equilibrium to another. When this five-stage plan is applied to the family stories in Genesis, an interrelationship of narratives within a genealogical framework is revealed. The first stage, a stable situation, corresponds to genealogy. Genealogy in Genesis 12–50 reflects the ideal stable movement of a family concerned with family continuity. The second stage in Todorov's analysis is the introduction of a force which upsets prior narrative stability. In the book of Genesis, the problems each of the patriarchs has in designating an heir constitutes the second stage, which results in the third stage, an unstable situation, i.e., narratives focused on the topic of a suitable heir to continue the Israelite lineage of his father. In this fourth stage, Todorov argues, a force is introduced which works against the problem of disequilibrium. In the book of Genesis, this results in a solution to the problem of maintaining genealogical continuity. The fifth and final stage is another state of equilibrium, or stability. This resolution is provided in Genesis through a genealogy which indicates progression from one generation to the next. But no sooner do we get this resolution than the cycle begins again.

It becomes clear from Todorov's analysis of the structure of narrative plot that, in Genesis 12–50, narrative represents a state of disequilibrium designed to return family life back to the state of equilibrium found in genealogy. In the book of Genesis, genealogy expresses the ideal stable succession for any family wishing to continue its lineage into the future. Moving from one generation to another is one way for literature to indicate the passage from one stage of family equilibrium to another. Thus, rather than seeing genealogies only as later redactional additions by P with no intrinsic relationship to the narratives which they now shape, I am arguing that, in a family setting such as the stories in Genesis suggest, the family relationships expressed through the genealogies are the point of continuity (Oden: 192–93; Westermann, 1985:128). Seen from the perspective provided by Todorov, the genealogies in the family stories can be expected to display a patterned, systematizing structure which relates these genealogies to each other, and then to the narratives which advance and supplement the genealogical plot of the book of Genesis.[2]

The application of Todorov's scheme yields a pattern in which the genealogical material in the family stories of the book of Genesis has been organized into three cycles of literature which are structurally parallel. The narratives comprising these three cycles move genealogical concerns forward until the point where one cycle of literature ends and a new genealogy begins. The following pattern emerges.

Gen 11:10–16, the genealogy of Shem, is the genealogical superscription which begins the first family cycle; it introduces the genealogy of Terah in 11:27–32 which is actually the heading for the story of Terah's sons and their wives.

The second genealogical cycle commences at Gen 25:12–18; the genealogy of Ishmael is the genealogical superscription to the genealogy of Isaac in 25:19–26 which introduces the stories of Isaac's sons and their wives.

The final cycle begins in 36:1–37:1 with the genealogical superscription concerning the descendants of Esau. This genealogy is the introduction to the genealogy of Jacob in 37:2, an abbreviated form of the stereotypical *tôlĕdôt* formula, "These are the generations of. . . ." In the case of the Jacob genealogy, the pattern changes and moves directly from "These are the generations of Jacob" (37:2) to a statement about Joseph's age at the time that the stories of Jacob's sons begin.[3] The genealogy of Jacob is the introduction to the stories of Jacob's family.

Thus, the initial genealogy of each of the three family cycles is a superscription in stereotypical language beginning, "These are the generations of . . ." and detailing the descendants of Shem, Ishmael, and Esau. These superscriptions prepare the reader for the genealogies of Terah, Isaac, and Jacob, each of which is actually the introduction to the narratives concerning their offspring and how these, in turn, beget their own offspring to continue the lineage. The latter group of genealogies is also characterized by the use of stereotypical language. Here again, the formula "These are the generations of . . ." is used to mark the beginning of the genealogical unit.

In the cases of Shem, Ishmael, and Esau, no further information is provided in narrative form to detail their fates; this feature provides additional support for the division of these six genealogies into two groups of three structurally similar units. Their histories are provided in their genealogies; their genealogies are their stories. By having no narratives to which they are later connected, the genealogies of Shem, Ishmael, and Esau take on narrative qualities and function as a summary of events describing the stable situation of family history moving from one generation to the next. A man begets a son who begets his own son, and so the family line is perpetuated into the future. The genealogies of Shem, Ishmael, and Esau are the dramatization of family equilibrium, according to Todorov's scheme.

However, the genealogies of Terah, Isaac, and Jacob differ from those of Shem, Ishmael, and Esau. Each of these characters has already been referred to in the genealogical superscription preceding his own genealogy. And each of their genealogies is actually a vehicle for shifting to the narratives that will constitute the genealogical progression of the descendants of each of these three individuals.

Based on our use of Todorov for analyzing Genesis 12–50, the introduction of narratives after the genealogies of Terah, Isaac, and Jacob indicates that these three genealogies are marked by situations of family disequilibrium. While the problems raised by each of these genealogical cycles differ, all three have some point of disequilibrium concerning the identity of an heir in the generation following the son or sons fathered by Terah, Isaac, and Jacob (Silberman: 18).

The precedent of equilibrium established in Gen 11:10–26 is that a man begets a family, but that only one of his sons is reckoned as his true heir. In the genealogies of Terah, Isaac, and Jacob, disequilibrium in the family makes it questionable whether this pattern in the progression of descendants can be carried forward. In the genealogical unit concerning Terah, Gen 11:30 notes the fact—seemingly out of place by the standards of Gen 11:10–26 and unexpected at first glance—that Abram's wife Sarai is barren.[4] This information provides the focus for the problem that will characterize the entire group of narratives relating to the Terah genealogy, how Abram will obtain an heir from his barren wife so that his father's genealogy can progress to a state of equilibrium and so that another generational cycle may begin (Helyer: 82). In contrast to Abram's problem, in the genealogical unit found in Gen 25:19–26 regarding Isaac, the problem of a man whose wife has borne him two sons, twins, is introduced. In this family cycle, the point of family disequilibrium centers around deciding which of the man's two sons will serve as the chosen genealogical link that will move the family line forward to the next generation and once again establish genealogical continuity. The structure of the Jacob genealogy is different from the preceding two because the problem of family disequilibrium focuses around a man with two wives, who are sisters, who have provided him with numerous sons. The introduction of two women with equal family standing provides a unique source of disequilibrium in the generation of Jacob.[5]

The distinctions made above between the three genealogical superscriptions and the three genealogical units interrelated with narratives casts a shadow on the three individuals mentioned as the leading figures in the former genealogies. Shem, Ishmael, and Esau are not distinguished as individuals chosen to be figures in the transmission of the primary Israelite family line. Rather, theirs is a secondary line of descent. They are placed outside the limelight given to the characters who are named in the genealogical narratives associated with the chosen Israelite lineage (Childs: 146).

This analysis of the structural pattern of the genealogies in Gen 11:10–50:26 indicates that there are three cycles of family stories which are characterized by a parallel design in which genealogies and narratives are closely related. We have seen that the generations-formula is a systematizing device which gives structure to narrative traditions. Todorov's scheme for narrative plot allows us to argue that narratives advance and resolve the family problems raised in the genealogies of Terah, Isaac, and Jacob. Once a stable family situation is established in the genealogy of the individuals involved, family history moves from disequilibrium to equilibrium. Yet, no sooner has equilibrium been reestablished than another situation of family disequilibrium arises.

An examination of the genealogies of Ishmael and Isaac provides a more specific illustration of the relationship between equilibrium and disequilibrium in the genealogical plot of the book of Genesis. A brief analysis of Gen 25:12–18 and 25:19–26 will now be presented in order to see clearly how Todorov's categories help us to understand the relationship between genealogy and narrative in the resolution of the problem of generational continuity.

III. Example of Model—Gen 25:12–26

A. Gen 25:12–18

The narratives which moved the genealogical cycle of Abraham's generation from beginning to end and took on meaning in the context of the genealogy of Gen 11:27-32 progress to a point that is structurally similar to the genealogical superscription recording the generations of Shem. In Gen 25:12-18, the genealogical superscription to the next narrative cycle details the descendants of Ishmael, the son of Abraham who will not carry on the chosen Israelite lineage of his father. The genealogy of Ishmael in Gen 25:12-18, like the genealogy of Shem, serves as the introduction to the genealogy of the one whose descendants will be responsible for the transmission of the special Israelite lineage. Like the genealogy of Shem, the genealogy of Ishmael contains no narrative components. In this context, genealogy functions as though it were narrative and provides the readers with a summary of events in the history of Ishmael's lineage. The stable progression of the family line from one generation to the next is recorded. Family stability, the ideal narrative state in the book of Genesis, characterizes the history of Ishmael's descendants. The family flows from one generation to the next with no hint of any disequilibrium in the process. In every respect, the generations of Ishmael recorded in Gen 25:12-18 are the structural equivalent of the generations of Shem in Gen 11:10-26.

B. Gen 25:19-26

The genealogical superscription of the son not chosen to carry on the Israelite lineage of his father moves to the genealogical unit concerning the chosen heir. In Gen 25:19-26, the genealogy of the generation of Isaac's descendants begins. In structure, it follows the pattern given in the genealogy of Terah.[6] The design of the material is such that the genealogy of Isaac serves as an introduction to the descendants of Isaac, whose lives will take the genealogy of their father forward to the next narrative cycle. In the case of Isaac, the narratives which interrelate with his genealogy and which resolve its generational disequilibrium, concern the fates of his sons Esau and Jacob born to him by Rebekah. The genealogy of Isaac, like that of Terah earlier, introduces the stories of his children who are mentioned in the unit Gen 25:19-26.

The genealogy of Isaac introduces a situation of disequilibrium which is potentially threatening to the continuance of his genealogy. The stable family situation in the generations of Ishmael, one of Abraham's two sons, contrasts with the disturbing force which creates disequilibrium in the generations of Isaac, the other of Abraham's sons. Although we learn in Gen 25:12 that Rebekah was barren — and because of Sarah's situation earlier are led to consider that her condition will serve as the source of disequilibrium in Isaac's family — Yahweh quickly corrects the problem in this family's affairs, and Rebekah becomes the mother of twins. But this seemingly harmonious situation actually raises the problem of generational continuity from a new perspective, inasmuch as no rule of primogeniture has been explicitly established at this stage in the narrative. If a man has two sons, born moments apart by the same woman, how is he to decide which one will be his true heir if custom ordains that a man's lineage may only pass through one offspring?

This ambiguity is deepened through the motif of rivalry between Esau and Jacob in Gen 25:19–26. In v 23, Yahweh informs Rebekah of this rivalry: the two will be divided against each other, and one will be stronger than the other. The construction of the poetic piece leads the reader to believe that the stronger one is the older one, the one Yahweh tells Rebekah will be a servant to the younger, weaker twin. This rivalry is evident from the moment the two sons are born; although Esau is ready to be born first, Jacob grabs onto his heel in the womb and seemingly supplants Esau as the firstborn son.

This struggle, already anchored within the genealogy, introduces narratives which will provide the vehicle to advance family relationships from disequilibrium back to a state of equilibrium. Once the rivalry between Jacob and Esau is resolved, and Jacob is recognized as his father's special heir, narrative once again gives way to genealogical equilibrium in Genesis 36, where a new family cycle begins.

IV. Conclusions

The application of Todorov's design for analyzing narrative plot leads us to conclude that the family stories of the book of Genesis must be read in the context of the genealogies of Israel's ancestors. The genealogies are of great importance; they are not merely a skeleton for the narratives. It is toward this goal of genealogy that the stories move.

The plot of the book of Genesis, therefore, is genealogy. Genealogy serves four functions in the material we have considered. First, genealogy describes the ideal temporal sequence of family succession. Second, genealogy provides the structure for Genesis; it systematizes family history into three cycles of literature which are structurally parallel. Third, genealogy allows for narrative to explore the problem of generational continuity; only within the context of genealogical structure do the narratives take on meaning. Finally, genealogy allows for the transition between universal history and Israelite history. I have argued that by including the genealogy of Shem within the boundaries of the so-called patriarchal history, a structural and thematic unity in the life histories of Abraham, Isaac, and Jacob emerges which corresponds to the passage from one state of narrative equilibrium to another as described by Todorov. Thus, this analysis provides an answer to the question raised as the outset of this paper: how to evaluate the genealogy of Shem in the larger design of Genesis? We have already seen that the separation of Gen 11:10–26 from vv 27–32 is an arbitrary division which cannot be supported by a structural analysis of these traditions. The special history of Israel must begin at least as early as Gen 11:10.

Our failure to recognize the structural position of the Shem genealogy may be the result of intentional textual ambiguity on this division. The separation between primeval and the so-called patriarchal history is one we superimpose upon the text. The text itself speaks of the time before the great deluge and then of the postdiluvian generations. In following this division, it might even be necessary to begin the second epoch of history at Gen 10:1. Regardless of what one thinks of the suggestion of beginning Israel's special history at Gen 10:1, it would seem that the Shem genealogy functions both as the start of the history of the ancestors and the conclusion of primeval history. But, the search for such a division between epochs may actually be unncessary:

> Does the structure therefore not point to a closer bond between primeval sagas and the sagas about the patriarchs for P than is to be seen in the transition from patriarchs to the exodus or from the wilderness to the conquest? (Coats: 105).

NOTES

[1] Cassuto (250) breaks with scholarly consensus by viewing Gen 11:10–32 as a unit. Although Coats develops a different structural design for Genesis than the one argued for here, he too considers the Shem genealogy to have a structural function in its present position which connects it with what follows (18; 30).

[2] There are many connections between my arguments and those made by Silberman. Relying on Russian Structuralism, Silberman also speaks of narrative cycles and argues that the plot of Genesis is that of the "True Heir." I am in total agreement with his argument that an over-emphasis on tearing narrative units apart from each other instead of looking at how they work together to tell a story has prevented the modern reader from hearing what the text has to say. But I take issue with the divisions he makes between the three narrative cycles and with the significance he attaches to some of the episodes as they relate to the plot. More importantly, Silberman does not develop his analysis around the structural significance of genealogy in the overall design of the three narrative cycles. Although he mentions specific genealogies in his study, he nowhere states that they provide the framework for the narratives of the matriarchs and patriarchs.

[3] With the generation of Jacob's twelve sons, there is a switch from linear/vertical to segmented/horizontal genealogy. I believe that this shift in genealogical pattern results from accepting both Leah and Rachel as the legitimate mothers of Jacob's children. While one could argue that the narrative ultimately focuses on Judah as the chosen heir (Silberman: 24), I would suggest that all twelve of Jacob's sons are presently accepted as his heirs. For the time being, the prior primary interest in finding a single heir is lost. Of course, this switch prepares the reader for acknowledging all of Jacob's progeny as the manifestation of the twelve tribes of Israel. This generation bridges the gap between the ancestors and the exodus epoch. Thus, I consider this shift in genealogical reckoning to be highly significant for understanding the narratives.

[4] Westermann (1980:133) argues that Gen 11:30 "the motif of the childless mother" is actually the beginning of the Abraham narratives.

[5] It is worth noting that the tensions in the family generational schema are all tied to the women of that generation. So too, the resolution of disequilibrium results only after the true heir finds the "chosen" wife/wives or the appropriate wife gives birth. The women are every bit as important as the men to the continuance of the generational story.

⁶ Cross (304–5) notes that 25:19b is unparalleled in other genealogies. He argues that it is a scribal gloss. What has resulted is that the genealogy recounting the events of the descendants of Isaac actually begins with the notice of Isaac's birth. Cf. Gen 11:27.

WORKS CONSULTED

Andriolo, Karin R.
    1973   "A Structural Analysis of Genealogy and Worldview in the Old Testament." *American Anthropologist* 75:1657–1669.

Cassuto, Umberto
    1964   *A Commentary on the Book of Genesis*. Vol. 2. Jerusalem: Magnes.

Childs, Brevard S.
    1979   *Introduction to the Old Testament as Scripture*. Philadelphia: Fortress.

Coats, George W.
    1983   *Genesis*. FOTL I. Grand Rapids: Eerdmans.

Cross, Frank M.
    1973   *Canaanite Myth and Hebrew Epic: Essays in the History of the Religion of Israel*. Cambridge: Harvard University.

Fishbane, Michael
    1979   "Composition and Structure in the Jacob Cycle (Gen 25:19– 35:22)." Pp. 40–62 in *Text and Texture*. New York: Schocken.

Fisher, Loren R.
    1973   "The Patriarchal Cycles." Pp. 59–65 in *Orient and Occident. Essays Presented to Cyrus H. Gordon on the Occasion of his Sixty-Fifth Birthday*. Ed. Harry A. Hoffner. AOAT 22. Neukirchen-Vluyn: Neukirchener.

Helyer, Larry R.
    1983   "The Separation of Abram and Lot: Its Significance in the Patriarchal Narratives." *JSOT* 26:77–88.

Johnson, Marshall D.
    1969   *The Purpose of Biblical Genealogies*. Cambridge: Cambridge University.

Noth, Martin
    1972   *A History of Pentateuchal Traditions*. Trans. Bernhard W. Anderson. Englewood Cliffs: Prentice-Hall.

Oden, Robert A.
    1983   "Jacob as Father, Husband, and Nephew: Kinship Studies and the Patriarchal Narratives." *JBL* 102:189–205.

Prewitt, Terry J.
    1981   "Kinship Structure and the Genesis Genealogies?" *JNES* 20:87–98.

Rad, Gerhard von
    1972   *Genesis*. Rev. ed. Trans. John H. Marks. OTL. Philadelphia: Westminster.

Seters, John van
  1975   *Abraham in History and Tradition*. New York and London: Yale University.
Silberman, Lou H.
  1983   "Listening to the Text." *JBL* 102:3-26.
Speiser, Ephraim A.
  1964   *Genesis*. AB 1. Garden City: Doubleday.
Tengström, S.
  1981   *Die Toledotformel und die literarische Struktur der priestlichen Erweiterungsschicht im Pentateuch*. ConBOT 17. Lund: Gleerup.
Thompson, Thomas L.
  1974   *The Historicity of the Patriarchal Narratives. The Quest for the Historical Abraham*. BZAW 133. Berlin: de Gruyter.
Todorov, Tzvetan
  1977   *The Poetics of Prose*. Ithaca: Cornell University.
Vawter, Bruce
  1977   *On Genesis: A New Reading*. Garden City: Doubleday.
Weimar, P.
  1974   "Die Toledot-Formel in der priesterschriftlichen Geschichtsdarstellung." *BZ* 18:65-93.
  1984   "Struktur und Komposition der priesterschriftlichen Geschichtsdarstellung." *Biblische Notizen* 23:81-134.
Westermann, Claus
  1967   *Handbook to the Old Testament*. Minneapolis: Augsburg.
  1980   *The Promises to the Fathers*. Trans. David E. Green. Philadelphia: Fortress.
  1985   *Genesis 12-36*. Trans. John J. Scullion. Minneapolis: Augsburg.
Wilson Robert R.
  1975   "The Old Testament Genealogies in Recent Research." *JBL* 94:169-89.
  1977   *Genealogy and History in the Biblical World*. New York and London: Yale University.

THE STRUCTURE OF THE CHRONICLER'S HISTORY: A KEY TO THE ORGANIZATION OF THE PENTATEUCH

Anne M. Solomon

ABSTRACT

This paper presents a fivefold structural pattern which is common to both 1-2 Chronicles, Ezra-Nehemiah, and the Pentateuch, where the pattern occurs twice. The five units in the Chronicler's work are: (1) 1 Chronicles 1-9 — Genealogical Introduction; (2) 2 Chronicles 10-29 — David; (3) 2 Chronicles 1-9 — Solomon; (4) 2 Chronicles 10-36 — Four Generations of Struggle; (5) Ezra-Nehemiah — Four Generations to Restoration in the Land. It will be shown how these distinct units parallel the Genesis 1-Deuteronomy 34 corpus: (1) Introduction; (2) Abraham; (3) Isaac; (4) Four Generations of Strife from Jacob to Moses; (5) Four Generations from Exodus to Inheritors of the Land. The clustering of the themes of proper sacrifice in the sanctuary, proper role for the Levites and the unity of all Israel is shared by Exodus 15-Deuteronomy 34 and the Chronicler's work. Methodologically I proceed from the question, How did teachers of the 5th century B.C.E. structure the historical experience of Israel in the land? Obviously there could be more than one answer to this question, yet I wish to explore the idea that a common grid for organizing traditions exists in the Chroniclers' work and the Pentateuch. In the aftermath of the criticism of von Rad's "historical credo" hypothesis, it appeared unwise to proceed from a particular example of historical recital upon an occasion, since I was convinced that the occasion shaped the traditions to a closely focused level of particularity. Rather this paper attempts to demonstrate a method which operates on a broader level of literary and redactional organization, and which engages with premodern notions of "generations."

The postexilic restoration must have provided several occasions for recounting the story of Israel's origin, rise, fall, and renewal. I am interested in the question of how the fifth and fourth century authors of 1-2 Chronicles and Ezra-Nehemiah structured Israel's historical experience. In particular, on what basis did the final author of the Chronicler's work organize the story? For I believe that the pattern which emerges there is also one which operates in the Pentateuch, a pattern tied to a kind of generational thinking evident in Gen 15:13–16 — God's promise to Abram that his seed would return to the land of Canaan.

I would like to proceed by first, focusing on a key passage in the Pentateuch, the promise to Abram in Gen 15:13–16; second, examining various meanings of *tôlĕdôt*, "generations," and *dôr*, "life-cycle," in order to lay the groundwork for a kind of thinking about generations; third, outlining the structure of the Chronicler's history; and then fourth, suggesting how this pattern organizes the Pentateuch. Thereby I hope to present a further contribution to the dialogue between form, rhetorical, and redaction-critical methodologies and to offer an illustration of studying the structure of a text.

I. Gen 15:13–16 and Generations

The key passage which first caught my eye is Gen 15:13–16, a promise which the Holy One made to Abram:

> Know for sure that your seed will be a stranger in a land which is not for them, and they shall serve them: and they shall afflict them four hundred years. . . . But in the fourth generation they shall return here.

There are at least three important things to be noted about this famous passage: (1) a span of four hundred years of affliction for Abram's seed; (2) a return to the land in the fourth generation; and (3) the implication that a generation equals one hundred years, if one interprets the two verses by means of each other (as have Wellhausen and many others). With the long life-spans of the generations in the Pentateuch, at first sight it does not appear improbable that for the biblical author four hundred years is a span composed of four times a generational unit of an average one hundred years. Yet commentators from Rashi to the present have noticed the many difficulties in computing 400 years on the internal evidence of the texts themselves. Either the combined numbers of total life-spans for the four generations like Levi, Kohath, Amram, and Aaron are too great, or the number of years from Jacob's entry into Egypt to the Exodus, computed by subtracting overlapping years in children's and parents' life-spans, is too small. Ultimately the Midrash abandons the four-generation schema altogether by tracing the period from Isaac onward and by using *gematria* to make the 400 years plausible (Rashi: 61). Indeed, I would like to argue that even though one may wish to understand the 400 years as a span composed of four times an average one-hundred-year unit, the key to the full patterning is revealed by separating v 13 (the 400 years of affliction) from v 16 (the return in the fourth generation) for a moment, and by realizing that the basic notions are a period of affliction and a period of return, each expressed in a multiple of four for a basic unit.

Of course the statement in Exod 12:40–41 that the duration of the sojourning in Egypt was 430 years raises further difficulties. Since 430 sounds more precise than 400, there have been even more valiant attempts to compute the 430 years in Egypt. Cassuto has explained the number 430 in two ways: (1) as a combination of 360 and 70, which was supposed to indicate a very long period of time "in accordance with the customary practice in the Ancient East" (148); and (2) as a sum of the life-spans of four generations minus a sixty-year unit. Let us examine this second method more closely.

Cassuto begins by raising the classic problem of the overly large sum derived from adding the approximately 135-year life-spans of Levi, Kohath, and Amram plus 80 years of Moses' life. If one subtracts for the overlap of years in fathers' and sons' lives, the sum is too small. He also mentions the midrashic tradition that "the period of four hundred years, of four hundred and thirty years, is to be reckoned from the time of Isaac's birth or of the 'Covenant between the Pieces'" (86), a midrashic tradition which is also reflected in the LXX and SP's addition of "in the land of Canaan" to the words "in the land of Egypt." He then returns to adding; but this time he adds Levi's, Kohath's, Amram's, and *Aaron's* life-spans, in a fashion not unlike the Sumerian King List, and then subtracts a Near Eastern unit of time (a *šuš* of sixty years) to allow for the time Levi spent in Canaan before going to Egypt. Thus he arrives once more at the number 430. The 400 number of Gen 15:13 he considers to be a compromise, another way of saying four generations.

It is hard to know whether Cassuto's ingenious suggestions for obtaining the 430 were in the mind of the biblical author, but he provides us another example of preferring a solution based upon four generations, and then considering the 400 years of Gen 15:13 as a variation on this theme. The historical probability of these years is another whole problem, of course, and Martin Noth among others has decided that these figures have "all historical probability" against them (100). While not wishing to enter this aspect of the problem any further, I do wish to note the general uncomfortableness many commentators feel with these numbers, and to raise the question of how the Chronicler understood them.

Surely the Chronicler must have realized that there was something unusual about the numbers 400 and 430. A far more likely figure would have been between 150 and 200 years, which could be derived either by adding the segments of life-spans from four generations to include overlapping years, or by assigning a schematic forty years to each generation from Levi to Moses and Aaron, and then multiplying by four. In any case, no matter on what basis the author of Genesis and Exodus wrote 400 or 430 years, it is my contention that the Chronicler realized that the numbers 400 and 430 strangely corresponded to a period of affliction in Israel's more recent history, the time from the division of the Northern and Southern Kingdoms to the end of the

Babylonian Exile. I would contend further that when he told this story in 2 Chronicles 10–36, he used Gen 15:13 as the basis for its patterning. He divided the history into four parts with four covenant renewal ceremonies, roughly one hundred years apart from each other. Further, I would argue that he recognized Gen 15:16's "return to the land in the fourth generation" as a means of organizing Ezra-Nehemiah on a four-generation schema. Let us look briefly at the genealogies in the Pentateuch that would substantiate this latter mode of generational thinking.

II. Generational Thinking

A careful study of the genealogies in Exodus and Numbers (as well as in 1 Chronicles) reveals an interesting dimension to the interpretation of Gen 15:13–16. There are *two* batches of *four* generations in the expanded genealogies of the tribes of Judah and Joseph: four generations for those who went down and suffered in Egypt, and four generations from those who left Egypt to those who settled in the land. A sample line for Judah is: Jacob, father of Judah, father of Perez, father of Hezron; and then his son Ram, father of Amminadab, father of Nahshon, father of Salma. The line of Joseph similarly takes eight generations to get from the time in Egypt to the time of the settlement: Jacob, father of Joseph, father of Menasshe, father of Makhir; and then his son Gilad, father of Hefer, father of Zelofehad, father of the assertive daughters Mahla, Noa, Hogla, Milcah, and Tirzah (see Numbers 7; 26; Josh 17:5–6). But, you may object, it took only two generations to get from Egypt to the land! That may have been true for the Levites (Exod 6:13–30; Numbers 26 and Josh 24:33). But from the stories in Exodus and Numbers and the subsequent narratives in Joshua, I think that the generation which had to die in the wilderness included the fifth, sixth, and seventh males in the lines of Judah and Joseph, while only the fifth, that is Aaron, in the line of Levi. That is, when the scripture uses the word "generation," it may be referring to three physical generations or to one life-cycle. Since the Hebrews and Israelites could have children at the ages of 13 for males and 12 for females, it is possible to have two or even three generations born to one male within a forty-year period. Thus this very flexibility in the definition of "generation" from the side of nature could lead to its use by the authors of the Pentateuch, 1–2 Chronicles, and Ezra-Nehemiah in a variety of schematic ways.

The terms *tôlĕdôt* and *dôr*, which I would translate "generations" and "life-cycle" respectively, seem to be used interchangeably for the two basic biological facts of life in the first millennium B.C.E., the interval needed to generate a child, which averaged around 12–15 years, and the longest normal length of a male person's life, 40 years. However, there are many other uses of these words than for the time to generate offspring or one's life-span. When using the terms in either a more schematic or more metaphorical fashion, the length of the basic unit of time could vary from as few as ten years in Bar 6:3, to 100 years in Gen 15:13, to a "day" of the creation of the world in Genesis 1–2. Let us look at these three examples, but begin with the bridge between the natural cycle and the schematic ones, the forty years of the high priest's tenure.

It is clear that there are several ways of organizing Israelite history on the basis of generations. In 1 Kgs 6:1 it states that "in the four hundred and eightieth year after the children of Yisrael were come out of the land of Egypt" (Koren JB), Solomon began to build the temple in Jerusalem. This unit of 480 years is understood by many commentators, e.g., de Vaux (193, 375), Rowley, and Kaufmann (308), as a reference to twelve forty-year generations of high priests, from Aaron to Azarya (1 Chr 5:29–34; 6:35–37), as well as a reference to a subsequent 480-year unit based on twelve more generations of high priests, from Azarya to Jeshua, that is, from the First Temple to the Second Temple. Thus "generation" here refers to the service-life of the high priest, which can be expressed schematically as forty years. The pattern of twelve generations, that is 480 years, divides history into two parts: from the Sanctuary to the First Temple in twelve generations, and from the First to the Second Temple, also in twelve generations. As many commentators have also pointed out, however (Brown: 407), this symmetry is obtained by omitting the names of three other high priests: Yehoyada (2 Chr 22:11), Uriah (2 Kgs 16:11), and Azaryahu (2 Chr 26:20). (Later we shall see that the author of 2 Chronicles is constructing another pattern with the mention of Yehoyada and Azaryahu.) In any case, the 480 years is an example of a pattern of religious history based on a generational unit of forty times twelve.

In line with this sort of thinking, the 430 years of Exod 12:40–41 could be understood and reinterpreted for a postexilic community as referring to the oppression from 922–587 B.C.E.[1] Perhaps the Chronicler initially read 430 as a way of saying that the Exile ended in the life of the eleventh high priest from the time of Solomon's Temple. However, he preferred to pattern the story of the oppression on the 400 years of Gen 15:13–16 with four one-hundred-year units, as we shall see. The fact that he mentioned the names of only four high priests in the narrative would further this latter generational schema.

The generational unit could be much shorter or considerably longer than forty years, depending on what the "generation" symbolized and on the length of the time needed for significant change. For as we know from the first chapters of Genesis, generational thinking is a metaphor for the creation of the heavens and the earth, a process which took who knows how long? Perhaps the shortest interval for a "generation" is the ten years implied in Bar 6:3, which states that the exile in Babylon may last as long as "seven generations," which many interpret as a recasting of Jeremiah's famous seventy-year interval for the Exile, that is, seven times a unit of ten years.

In summarizing these two sections, then, I would like to enrich the definition of "generation" by adding to the concepts of "life-span" (*dôr*) and generations produced in "generating-time" (*tôlĕdôt*) these three ideas: (1) the possible relationship between them of from one to three generations equaling one life-span; (2) the high priest's forty-year tenure which has its own rhythm and integrity; and (3) the metaphorical use of "generation" for units which are either larger or smaller than the natural cycles. In interpreting Gen 15:13–16 and Exod 12:40–41, then, the Chronicler may well have realized from a careful study of the genealogies that there were two different four-generational groups being referred to in Gen 15:13–16 — one for the affliction, and one for the return to the land. Further, from the habit of thinking in forty-year units for the high priesthood, the 430 years of Exod 12:40 may have urged him to parallel not just the period from the Sanctuary to the First Temple with that of the First to the Second Temple as the author of 1 Kings 6 had done, but to parallel the affliction in Egypt with the strife from 922–539 B.C.E., and the return to Canaan with the postexilic Restoration. Finally, from the very flexibility in the use of "generations," he chose different modes of interpreting the two parts of Gen 15:13–16, using four covenant renewals about a hundred years apart for the first, and the problems faced by four generations of returnees for the second part. Now let us examine how this generational thinking helped him structure 2 Chronicles 10–36 and Ezra-Nehemiah, in particular.

III. The Structure of the Chronicler's History

No one who has studied the books of 1–2 Chronicles and Ezra-Nehemiah can doubt their authors' concerns with genealogies, particularly those of the Levites, the liturgical and teaching functions of the Levites, proper worship in Jerusalem, and all Israel united in the capital of Jerusalem. The glorious reigns of David and Solomon are clearly narrated with these special interests of the Chronicler in mind, and the preface to their story, 1 Chronicles 1–9, is a genealogical retelling of Genesis–1 Samuel with special emphasis on Levites' genealogies and those who settled in Jerusalem as representative of the whole people. Nearly all would agree that the basic structure of these chapters of the Chronicler's history, then, is:

I. Genealogical Introduction	1 Chronicles 1–9
II. David	1 Chronicles 10–29
III. Solomon	2 Chronicles 1–9

Later in this article I would like to discuss the ways in which these divisions parallel the Pentateuch. Other commentators have drawn attention to this as well, e.g., Pfeiffer (574). But I would rather press on to the harder questions of structure in the rest of the Chronicler's history, to show how the clustering of these concerns in 2 Chronicles 10–36 and Ezra-Nehemiah produce a rhythmic structure in these chapters which reveals one fourfold generational pattern in 2 Chronicles 10–36 and another one in Ezra-Nehemiah. We will finally see how the infamous redacting of Ezra-Nehemiah adjusted the schema based on worship in 2 Chronicles 10–36 to a more literal four-generational schema based on the problems of the generations of returnees. In doing so, the Chronicler used the chief priests' and Levites' genealogies as his anchors.

The Chronicler also refers to chief priests in 2 Chronicles 10–36, but in an even more fascinating manner, to reinforce a fourfold pattern based on covenant renewal. As I have suggested above, one way the Chronicler could have redacted the stories of the kings of Judah from Rehoboam to Zedekiah would have been to arrange them by the tenure of the high priests, thus producing eleven units with the Exile coming in the tenure of the eleventh high priest on the basis of an interpretation of the 430 years in Exod 12:40. Instead he chose the four hundred years of Gen 15:13, and thus divided this history into four parts: (1) from Rehoboam to Asa (10–16); (2) Jehoshaphat to Joash (17–24); (3) Amaziah to Hezekiah (25–32); and (4) Manasseh to Josiah (33–35), with the conclusion in chap. 36 told from the temple's point of view. In each of these four units there is a proper worship ceremony in Jerusalem as a climax to the cleansing of foreign deities from the land, a carefully defined role for the Levites, and a covenant renewal with all of the people and God (2 Chr 15:12; 23:16; 29:10 and 34:31). Note that there are no parallels in the Deuteronomistic history for the covenant renewals under Asa and Hezekiah (2 Chr 15:12 and 29:10); and further, there are no parallels for the Levites' roles in the reforms of Jehoyada and Josiah (2 Chr 23:16 and 34:31). Each of these four units has been carefully crafted on the basis of the key words *tôrâ, biqqēš/dāraš* ("seeking") and *bĕrît*.[2] Thematically the covenant ceremony represents the climax of each of the four units. These four covenant renewals are roughly a hundred years apart (ca. 900, 830, 715, and 620 B.C.E.). The fact that there is mention of only four high priests in 2 Chronicles 10–36 (Amaryahu in 2 Chr 26:20; 31:10; and Hilkiyah in 2 Chr 34:9) may also be intended to reinforce a fourfold schema, for otherwise their presence and order in the text are quite problematic.[3] The catastrophe of the end of Judah is told precisely in terms of the priests polluting the temple, and then the Babylonians looting and burning it. This sets the stage for the restorations of Ezra-Nehemiah, particularly the great covenant ceremonies in Jerusalem.

In the original structure of Ezra-Nehemiah there was a fourfold continuation of the cycle based on proper worship in Jerusalem with all that entailed: two ceremonies in Ezra 1–6 (Ezra 3:1–6 dedicating the altar; 6:16–22 dedicating the temple), one in the Ezra cycle (Nehemiah 8–10 covenant renewal and cleansing), and one in the Nehemiah cycle (Neh 12:27–43 dedicating the walls of Jerusalem). But I think the words of Gen 15:16 "in the fourth generation they shall return here" influenced the Chronicler to show that the major events of the restoration happened in the fourth generation of returnees, and not simply to parallel the work of Ezra and Nehemiah as so many commentators have thought.

A careful and sympathetic study of the Chronicler's work cannot help but make one aware of the problems this traditional storyteller faced. He had autobiographical sources in Aramaic and Hebrew from Ezra and Nehemiah, which could be elaborated upon to make two coherent units, each climaxing in a magnificent ceremony in Jerusalem. But the striking thing about the present order of the text of Ezra-Nehemiah is how intrusive Nehemiah 8–10 is upon the narrative of Nehemiah 7 and 11. I think this was done in order to preserve a better generational order in the book. The Chronicler wished to begin with Ezra, because he had references in Ezra's own genealogy showing that Ezra was of the second generation from the exile (Ezra 7:1–5 lists Ezra as a son of Seraiah who was a contemporary of the chief priest Jeshua). He wanted to end with Nehemiah's bridging the fourth and fifth generations. Most importantly, he wished to place the major ceremonies affecting the fourth generation side by side (Nehemiah 8–10 and 12). Let us trace this generational arrangement more carefully through Ezra-Nehemiah, for ultimately what emerges is not so much the answer to the question of to which generation Ezra or Nehemiah themselves belonged, as the order of the generations whose problems they tackled. Then I will corroborate this order by the references to the Levitical genealogies in the Chronicler's work, a more harrowing adventure.

In this structure, I have employed the names of the high priests to indicate the generations. The usual way of dating things by references to kings or high priests is quite problematic in the Chronicler's work. Once Ezra and Nehemiah leave Babylon and Susa, respectively, they no longer refer to Persian kings' years for dating; and the marriage reforms they both pursue affect the very families of the high priests, who thus may or may not be participants in a given episode. However, there can be little doubt that the chief priest Eliashiv, son of Yoyakim, son of Jeshua, that is, the third generation of the Restoration, is involved in Nehemiah's story (Neh 3:15). The absence of any high priests' names from the Ezra story, including even the Torah ceremonies and covenant document in Nehemiah 8–10, is rather problematic. The reference in Ezra 10:6 to Ezra staying overnight and mourning in a chamber belonging to one of Eliashiv's sons, Johanan, would allow us to conclude that both Ezra's and Nehemiah's first reforms occurred in Eliashiv's chief priesthood. This fact in itself could have led the Chronicler to redact his history to show their contemporaneity more clearly. The structure and the bases for its divisions are:

1.	Ezra 1–6	Problems of first generation — Return, Restoring Worship, and Rebuilding the Temple People listed in Ezra 2; High priest Jeshua in Ezra 2:2; 3:2; 5:2; Neh 12:1–9.
2.	Ezra 7–10	Problems of second generation — Marriage to non-Jews People listed in Ezra 10:18ff. (sons of Jeshua, the high priest); Neh 12:1–21.
3.	Neh 1–7	Problems of third generation — Rebuilding Walls and Resettling Jerusalem People listed in Nehemiah 3; High priest Eliashiv in Neh 3:1.
4a.	Neh 8–10	Problems of third and fourth generation — Relearning Torah and Covenant Renewal People listed in Neh 8:4 and 10; priests and leaders of third and fourth generation correlate with Nehemiah 3 and 11.
4b.	Neh 11–13:3	Problems of third and fourth generation — Resettling Jerusalem, Dedicating Walls, and Reinstituting Levitical Offerings People listed in Nehemiah 11; 13:31ff.; note the genealogy of Maaseiah in Neh 11:5 for fourth generation.
5.	Neh 13:4–31	Problems of fourth and fifth generation — Restoring Levites' Tithes, Combating Sabbath Violation and Mixed Marriages People listed in Neh 3:13, 28; note Yoyada's son is fifth generation in Neh 13:28.

The final generation mentioned in the book is contained in the chronological inserts of chief priests in Neh 12:22 and of David's descendants in 1 Chr 3:17–24, which bring the genealogy down to the sixth generation, perhaps the time of the author. The inserts in Nehemiah 12 are also important for their Levitical references, by which the Chronicler summarizes the references to all the generations' problems handled from Ezra 7–Nehemiah 12. That is, from the frequency of the occurrences of many of the names in Neh 12:24–25 throughout all the generations in Ezra 7–Nehemiah 12, it is probably best to understand this list of Levites as a summary of the most frequent names, a kind of midrashic summary, not just those Levites who worked in Yoyakim's time.

But can the generational schema above, based on priests' and leaders' names, be substantiated by Levitical references apart from the list in Neh 12:24–25? Yes, by carefully tracing the genealogies of a few infrequently mentioned Levites in the Chronicler's history, a correlation can be established. Mattanya is clearly of the first generation (1 Chr 9:14; Neh 12:8), and is mentioned as the great grandfather in two other genealogies, that is Uzzi in Neh 11:22 among those who resettle in Jerusalem, and Zechariah in Neh 12:35 at the wall dedication ceremony, which allows us to date these two chapters in the fourth generation. Yozavad, son of Jeshua, is clearly of the third generation and is listed in Nehemiah's resettlement policy (Neh 11:15). Finally, the Levites in the lists of Nehemiah 8–10 contain a span of second through fourth generation names.

In summary, then, it is clear that the Chronicler employed a fourfold structure of themes (Levites and priests involved with proper worship and covenant renewal for all Israel in Jerusalem) in editing 2 Chronicles 10–36, thereby paralleling the four generations of affliction from Jacob to Moses. He also employed a four-generational schema for redacting the story of the return to the land in Ezra-Nehemiah, climaxing with a covenant renewal in the fourth generation of returnees, thereby paralleling the four generations who leave Egypt in order to return to the land. As a result 2 Chronicles 10–36 parallels Genesis 25–Exodus 15, and Ezra-Nehemiah parallels Exodus 15–Deuteronomy 34. As mentioned above, other commentators have noted the similarities between the first books of the Bible and the work of the Chronicler. Pfeiffer thought that the Chronicler's plan followed the P document (Adam, Noah, Abraham, Moses, and Joshua paralleling Adam, David, Solomon, Rehoboam, and Ezra/Nehemiah).[4] From the argument above concerning Genesis 15, I believe it is far more likely that the Chronicler had the Torah before him, and not simply the P document. Further, the parallels between David and Abraham, and Solomon and Isaac are more direct than Pfeiffer's suggestions.[5] However, the idea of the Chroniclers' patterning his story on the basis of traditional material is very probable. Now I would like to explore the Solomon/Isaac parallel. It appears at first sight to be problematic, for the story of Isaac, as much as it represents the first reference to the Jerusalem Temple (in Genesis 22's setting on Mt. Moriah) is not a story-cycle of its own in Genesis, and it is only a partial precedent for Solomon. The story of the building of the sanctuary in Exodus 25–40 provides a closer parallel to Solomon's story in 2 Chronicles 1–9. But here lies the clue, I believe, to the further unravelling of the structure of the Pentateuch, and the generational thinking underlying it, as well as the paradigm for the cleansing, worship in the Temple, and covenant renewal for all Israel of the Chronicler.

IV. A Generational Outline of the Pentateuch

To this point, we have isolated five major units in the Chronicler's work: (1) Introduction; (2) David; (3) Solomon; (4) Four covenant renewals in the midst of struggles from Rehoboam to Josiah; and (5) Four generations from the Return to full Restoration. Paralleling these in the Pentateuch are: (1) Introduction; (2) Abraham; (3) Isaac; (4) Four generations of strife from Jacob to Moses; and (5) Four generations from the Exodus to the inheritors of the land. Within the last unit of the Pentateuch (Exodus 15–Deuteronomy 34), the entire fivefold structure is repeated again. Now the people enter the world of formal covenanting, as God tests their ability to truly listen to His voice. This moral transposition of the story of the generations is grounded over and over in the ritual unique to Israel: the Sabbath. (The Chronicler does not repeat the whole story-cycle within Ezra-Nehemiah. However, he does allow the paradigm of moral renewal in one of the subunits, Exodus 25–40 — the building of the sanctuary, the cleansing of idols, and the covenant renewal performed with the special help of the Levites for all Israel, to structure 2 Chronicles 10–36, and to provide the climax of Ezra-Nehemiah.) Now let us turn to the elaboration of the repetition of the fivefold pattern in Exodus 15–Deuteronomy 34, the turning toward the land. An outline of the structure is as follows:

1. Exod 15–19   Introduction to World of Sabbath: Seven Stages to Mountain, Marah — Sinai (Num 33:8–15); Sabbath: Exod 16
2. Exod 20–24   Covenant Established
                   Sabbath: Exod 20:23
3. Exod 25–Num 10 Sanctuary Built and Dedicated
                   Sabbath: Exod 31; 34; 35; Lev 19; 23; 24; 25; 26
4. Num 11–33   Struggles in the Wilderness: Four Units of Seven Stages (Num 33:16–47)
                      Num 33:16–23 Kibroth-Hataavah to Mt. Shepher
                      Num 33:24–30 Haradah to Moserath [Mt. Hor]
                      Num 33:31–37 Bene-jaakan to Mt. Hor
                      Num 33:41–47 Zalmonah to Abarim Mts.
                   Sabbath violation: Num 15
5. Num 33–Deut 34 Preparation for Life in the Land from the Plains of Moab: Four Units of Torah
                      Num 33–36 Destroying Idols and Dividing Land (33:50–51 Levites)
                      Deut 1–4:43 Moses Begins to Explain Torah (1:5)
                      Deut 4:40–26:19 "This is the Torah" (4:44)
                      Deut 27–34:12 Torah Ceremonies and Promulgation by Moses and Levites (32:46–47 Torah for Life in the Land).

The major structuring devices noted here are: (1) the sevenfold rhythm in the summary of the itinerary in Numbers 33, in which every seventh stage is a mountain. Notably the introduction to Sinai has these seven stages (Exodus 15–19), but so do the four subunits of the wilderness traditions in unit 4 (Numbers 11–33) from Sinai to the plains of Moab. (2) The Sabbath is mentioned at the beginning and/or the end of the law codes within units 2 (Exodus 20–24) and 3 (Exodus 25–Numbers 10): Exodus 20–23; 25–31; 32–34; 35–40; and Leviticus 19–26. (3) The Torah for the Life in the Land is the major structuring device for the four subunits of unit 5 (Numbers 33–Deuteronomy 34), the preparations made in the plains of Moab. Let us examine each of these more closely.

In both cases where the "seven stages to the Mountain" schema from Numbers 33 is told in fuller narration (Exodus 15–19 and Numbers 11–33), stories are set at the beginnings and the ends of the lists. Within the Marah to Sinai list, stories are set at Marah (Exod 15:23–26), Elim (Exod 15:27–16:1), Sin (Exod 16:1–17:10), then on to Rephidim (Exod 17:10) and Sinai (Exod 19:1–Num 10:11–12). Within the Kibroth Hataavah to Mt. Hor sequence (three full subunits), stories are told for Kibroth-Hataavah (Num 11:1–35) and Hazeroth (Numbers 12), then on to Kadesh (Num 13–20:22) and Mt. Hor (Num 20:23–21:4). A parallel to the Zalmonah to Abarim itinerary can be found in narrative from Num 21:4–Num 22:1 where they reach the plains of Moab. There is a remarkable clustering of the themes common to the Chronicler's work and Exodus 25–40 mentioned above in the actual narrative of Exodus 15–19 and at the beginning and end of the Numbers 11–32 narratives. These themes are (1) proper celebration of the Sabbath (Exodus 16; Num 15:32ff. and Numbers 28); (2) roles for the Levites (Exodus 18; Numbers 16–18; and Numbers 26); (3) proper eating and sacrifices in the sanctuary (Exodus 16; Numbers 11; 15; 19; 28–29); and (4) all Israel (Exod 16:1; 17:1; Numbers 14[7x]; 32:15). Thus the Pentateuch also exhibits a similarity to the Chronicler's narrative in the existence side by side of a pattern based on regular schematic beats (four units of seven stages to the mountain//four one-hundred-year units of covenant renewal, and four units of giving Torah//four generations to Restoration), and a rhythmic pattern indicating major movement in the narratives based on the clustering of the same themes of proper sacrifice in the sanctuary, a proper role for the Levites, and the unity of all Israel. To speak metaphorically, the Levitical music of the Torah and the Chronicler's work is very similar.

The Pentateuch and the Chronicler's History both display a special interest in the Sabbath. For the law collections of Exodus 20–40 and Leviticus 19–26, mention of the Sabbath is either at the beginning or the end or *both* of every collection. The Chronicler treats the Sabbath in regard to both covenant renewal and the walls of Jerusalem. In Nehemiah 10, in the list of emphases among the covenant stipulations, alongside the renunciation of marriage and the providing of tithes for the Levites is the renunciation of trade on the Sabbath. From Nehemiah's story, we learn that one of the beneficial side effects of rebuilding the walls and appointing responsible Levitical gatekeepers is the ability to control the access of the merchants on the Sabbath (Neh 13:15–22). However, the Sabbath does not appear to be the structural device for the Chronicler that it is in the Pentateuch.

The third structural device in the Pentateuch is an emphasis on the prohibition against idols in the presentation of the Torah by which the Israelites are to live in the land (Numbers 33–Deuteronomy 34). There is special emphasis within each subunit on the commandment to have no other deity but the Holy One, and not to worship any images. This theme is in the first command of Num 33:51-52; in the sermon of Deuteronomy 4 which concludes the beginning of Moses' explanation of Torah; in the preface to the Deuteronomic law code (Deuteronomy 5-11); and highlighted as the cardinal offense in the warnings of Moses' song in Deut 32:15-18 and the conclusion to Moses' blessing in Deut 33:26-29. Also the word "torah" is found in Deut 1:5, 4:44, at the beginnings of each of these sections, and in the summary of Deut 32:46-47:

> Take to heart all the warning which I now have given you and which you must impress on your children, that you may carry out carefully every word of this torah. For this is no trivial matter for you; rather, it means your very life, since it is by this means that you are to enjoy a long life in the land which you will cross the Jordan to occupy.

The final reference is in the blessing of Moses over the Levites in Deut 33:9b-10a: "Thus the Levites keep your words, and your covenant they uphold. They promulgate your decisions to Jacob and your torah to Israel." Undoubtedly the Chronicler drew inspiration for his writing from this description of Levitical functions as well.

These are the conclusions concerning the structure of the Pentateuch, then, which may be drawn from the study of the structure of the Chronicler's History. There is a fivefold structure of (1) Introduction; (2) Covenant; (3) Sanctuary; (4) Affliction in four stages; and (5) Returning to the land in four stages. This cycle is repeated twice in the Pentateuch, once from Genesis 1-Deuteronomy 34, and again within Exodus 16-Deuteronomy 34. The patterning which arises from generational thinking is at the backbone of Genesis 1-Deuteronomy 34 and in the Chronicler's History, while within the four physical generations or two moral generations of Exodus 15-Deuteronomy 34, the fourfold rhythm of returning to the sanctuary and the Torah is the spiritual transposition of the generational cycle. This cycle is apparent to us because of the structure of the Chronicler's History. To complete the circle, however, I shall conclude with the contention that he derived these ideas from the Pentateuch, from Exodus 25-40 and Gen 15:13-16 in particular.

NOTES

[1] The number 430 is also the sum of the days for which Ezekiel is commanded to lie on his side, corresponding to the years of the iniquities of Israel (390) and Judah (40) (Ezek 4:5-6). Moshe Greenberg comments: "Counting back from Ezekiel's time 390 years brings one to the beginning of the tenth century B.C.E., roughly when the temple was built—perhaps the start of an era for Ezekiel" (105). Perhaps Ezekiel derived the total of 430 from the Exodus story as well, and by patterning the troubles of a later period of history on it, he may be exhibiting the same kind of thinking as the Chronicler.

[2] The precise details of these literary patterns are in manuscript and await further presentation.

[3] Myers (46) points out the problems with the mention of the chief priests in the Chronicler's work: (1) the list in 1 Chr 6:4–15 is not complete, omitting Jehoiada and Urijah, "for what reason we can only speculate"; (2) the Amariah and Azariah mentioned in 2 Chr 19:26 and 31 seem to be chronologically misplaced, for reasons "beyond us at present"; and (3) he implies a problem with the first two Azariah's, seeming to recognize that the phrase "the one who served as priest in the house that Solomon built" should modify the first Azariah, apparent from the parallel in 1 Kgs 4:2 which he cites. I would suggest the following solutions to some of these problems. (1) Once the author had ascribed service in the temple in Solomonic times to the wrong Azariah, he lost the proper sense of the sequence of Amariah (II) and Azariah (II), nor could he fit in Jehoiada at the proper place. (2) He had to mention Amariah first in the narrative of 2 Chronicles 19, since Azariah II was placed in Solomonic times. If we simply reverse the two names and insert Jehoiada between them, the correct sequence would be restored.

[4] Pfeiffer notes various correspondences with P, but his paralleling of Noah with David, and then Abraham with Solomon, is not persuasive.

[5] The reasons for paralleling Genesis 1–11 with 1 Chronicles 1–9, and the fivefold pattern apparent in both cases are in manuscript and await further presentation. Thanks to my students at St. Bonaventure in the summer of 1985 for urging the articulation of this parallel in full form.

WORKS CONSULTED

Brown, Raymond E., Joseph A. Fitzmyer, and Roland E. Murphy, eds.
    1968   *Jerome Biblical Commentary*. Englewood Cliffs: Prentice-Hall.

Cassuto, Umberto
    1967   *A Commentary on the Book of Exodus*. Jerusalem: Magnes.

Greenberg, Moshe
    1983   *Ezekiel: 1–20*. AB 22. Garden City: Doubleday.

Kaufmann, Y.
    1972   *The Religion of Israel*. Trans. Moshe Greenberg. New York: Schocken.

Myers, Jacob M.
    1983   *II Chronicles*. AB 13. Garden City: Doubleday.

Noth, Martin
    1962   *Exodus*. Trans. J. S. Bowden. OTL. Philadelphia: Westminster.

Pfeiffer, R. H.
    1962   "Chronicles, I and II." Pp. 572–80 in *Interpreter's Dictionary of the Bible*. Vol. 1. Ed. G. A. Buttrick. Nashville: Abingdon.

Rashi
    1973   *Pentateuch and Rashi's Commentary: Genesis*. Ed. M. Rosenbaum and A. M. Silberman. Jerusalem: Silberman.

Rowley, H. H.
    1938   "Israel's Sojourn in Egypt." *BJRL* 22:1–12.

Vaux, Roland de
    1965   *Ancient Israel*. New York: McGraw-Hill.

ANOTHER FORM-CRITICAL PROBLEM OF THE HEXATEUCH

George W. Coats
Lexington Theological Seminary

ABSTRACT

Gerhard von Rad identified a "form-critical" problem of the Hexateuch, a problem that has provoked many responses from the previous generation of biblical scholars. The purpose of this paper is to argue, quite apart from the success or failure of von Rad's thesis, that there is another form-critical problem of the Hexateuch: the structural relationship between the article of faith in the credo or the theme of traditions in the Hexateuch that recounts the events of the patriarchs in Canaan and the article of faith or theme of tradition that recounts the exodus from Egypt. The Joseph story fits into that gap. But the gap still poses problems in the history of traditions in the Pentateuch and the Hexateuch. The Yahwist exploits that gap by using it to undercut the degree of reconciliation in the family at the center of the Joseph story. The question for the Yahwist is then focused on issues of reconciliation. If not in the patriarchal tradition, then where does the story ever describe reconciliation for Israel with God, with family, and with nature?

The form-critical problem of the Hexateuch emerges with clarity, according to Gerhard von Rad, when one compares the structure of the Hexateuch as it now stands in the MT with the structure of the "little historical credo," a stereotyped recital of key events from the past represented by several texts scattered throughout the Old Testament (1969a). The articles of confession in the credo vary only in detail from credo to credo, at least until the latest examples expand the scheme. These articles of confession correspond not only in content but also in sequence to the principal elements in the whole narrative pattern of the Hexateuch. The obvious exceptions are the primeval history and the traditions about the events surrounding God's gift of the law at Sinai. Von Rad concludes by suggesting that the primeval history serves as a theological foil for the remaining narratives in the Hexateuch (1966a:63–67, 1966b). The more pressing issue in the form of the Hexateuch is the position of the Sinai narratives. Everywhere except in the very latest stages of the tradition's history, references to events at Sinai are missing from the credo. And indeed, the Sinai narratives appear to be secondary in the literary composition of the Hexateuch. Therefore, the Sinai traditions, according to von Rad (1966a:53–54), must have been originally quite distinct and independent of the credo traditions.

Martin Noth (59–62) builds on von Rad's analysis of the Pentateuch-Hexateuch form derived from the credo by suggesting that the form reveals four fundamental themes of traditions as principal elements in the structure of both the credo and the Pentateuch.[1] These four themes—patriarchs, exodus, wilderness, and conquest—were originally distinct and, indeed, independent collections of traditions. The theological, canonical scheme that holds these four themes together would be secondary to the themes themselves. But in Noth's discussion, as in von Rad's work, the Sinai traditions would represent an obviously independent and quite separate collection of narratives.

The von Rad-Noth analysis of the form-critical problem in the construction of these narratives, the problem represented by the distinctive manner of relationship to the whole for the Sinai traditions, has influenced a generation of research on the Pentateuch-Hexateuch. But the hypothesis advanced for solving the problem by von Rad and Noth has not won a consensus from other contributors in the field of research. Artur Weiser argues, for example, that

> the subject matter of the Sinai traditions is not a historical event in the same sense as the historical events of the exodus and the entry; it is on the contrary an encounter with God which leads up to the acceptance by the people of the will of God proclaimed in the commandments: and in its cultic setting it represents a particular action in the course of the festival. Consequently it is not mentioned in the same breath with God's acts of salvation in those texts which are concerned only with the latter. The reason why certain texts do not mention the Sinai tradition beside the saving acts of Yahweh . . . is due to the fact that they *restrict* themselves to the recital of the saving acts. . . . (169)[2]

Therefore, the critic has no right to expect the Sinai tradition to appear as an article of confession at all levels of the credo tradition. The form-critical problem as identified by von Rad is thus a phantom.

Walter Beyerlin develops a different point of criticism. The relationship between the exodus tradition and the tradition about Sinai can be understood on the basis of old Hittite treaties from the fourteenth and thirteenth centuries B.C.E. These statements of relationship contain a historical prologue describing the beneficent acts of the author of the covenant. If this form underlies the structure of the Pentateuch, it increases the possibility that historical tradition functions necessarily as the basis for law in the body of the covenant. "We may conclude, therefore, that the traditions of the deliverance from Egypt and the events on Sinai were connected at a very early date under the influence of an old covenant form going back to the pre-Mosaic period" (Beyerlin:169).

My own research on the form-critical problems of the Pentateuch and the Hexateuch supports Noth's analysis of the Pentateuch in terms of four narrative "themes" of tradition.[3] Moreover, the four "themes" correspond to the articles of confession in the units labeled as credo by von Rad. Specifically, the organization of the Hexateuch reveals four clearly defined units that mark the exposition of the major elements of structure: Gen 12:1-3 exposes the theological content and the leading principal for the theme about the patriarchs (Wolff).[4] Exod 1:1-14 sets the stage for the narratives about the exodus event (Coats, 1972a). Exod 13:17-22 accomplishes the same goal for the wilderness traditions (Coats, 1972b). And Joshua 1-5 contains the patterns for an exposition for the conquest stories (Coats, 1985). These texts mark their narrative units off from the preceding narratives as distinct, although not necessarily independent, units. It is of decisive importance, however, that no similar text exposes the principals or topics for a Sinai "theme" of tradition. Moreover, the structure of the wilderness "theme" defined by an itinerary of stations on the wilderness journey (Coats, 1972c; Davies, 1974, 1983) embraces the Sinai narratives as a part of the wilderness theme. Sinai is one station in the wilderness journey, no different for the structure of the wilderness theme than the station at Kadesh with the traditions associated with that site. I would suggest, then, that the Sinai traditions do not constitute a formal and distinct element of narrative in the structure of the Pentateuch-Hexateuch. They are not parallel and coordinated with the tradition themes in the credo. But the failure does not result from a markedly different kind of tradition. The Sinai tradition is in fact a tradition about an event. God gave the law to Moses on the mountain, and Moses gave the law to the people. Rather, it is a part of the wilderness theme, a station among several stations that comprise the structure of the wilderness theme. And, accordingly, it cannot be treated form-critically as a distinct theme in the structure of the Pentateuch-Hexateuch, any more than the stories about the springs at Meribah and Marah or the quail and manna stories can be. The principal form-critical problem of the Pentateuch-Hexateuch is thus not the position of the Sinai traditions in the whole. The Sinai traditions may be in fact problematic, distinct from the other traditions in the whole. But the problem is a tradition-historical one, not a form-critical one.

There is nevertheless a form-critical problem in the Pentateuch-Hexateuch which emerges clearly when one considers the relationship between the patriarchal theme and the exodus theme: the former depicts the fathers in Canaan while the latter sets the Israelites, the sons of Jacob, in Egypt. It is thus a problem in the structure of the Pentateuch, unrelated to the issues of the conquest theme and the book of Joshua. In the present form of the Pentateuch, the Joseph story fills the gap between the fathers in Canaan and the Israelites in Egypt (Coats, 1976:89-93), but in a position that is tradition-historically secondary to the structure of the patriarchal sagas. The gap also appears in the credo (von Rad, 1966a:54–63).[5] Thus, for example, Deut 26:5 refers to the patriarchal element only in terms of the wandering father. None of the distinctive elements in the patriarchal theme, such as promise for progeny, land, or blessing, the complex patterns of strife and broken intimacy, the movement toward reconciliation, appear here. The allusion to the patriarchs in Deut 26:5 simply sets the stage for the article of confession about the exodus. The brief reference to the tradition in 1 Sam 12:8 fits into the same category. Jacob is not the recipient of a divine promise or engaged in strife with a brother. He is simply the one who went to Egypt. Deut 6:21–23 fails to mention the fathers (cf. also Psalms 106; 135; 136; Exod 15:4–16). Neh 9:7–8 recites the tradition about the divine promise to Abraham with a note that the promise to give him and his descendants the land was fulfilled. But then, without transition, v 9 remembers that God heard the affliction of the fathers in Egypt. Josh 24:2–4 follows the pattern of the present form of the Pentateuch, including the genealogical order of the patriarchs: Abraham, Isaac, and Jacob. And the account covers the gap with an explicit reference to Jacob as the one who migrated to Egypt. Psalm 105 fits the same category, with the gap closed by an explicit reference to Joseph. But as texts that simply repeat the order of the Pentateuch-Hexateuch, they offer no insight into the nature of the gap.

The form-critical problem of the Pentateuch-Hexateuch at issue here is the nature of the gap in the structure of the whole between the article of faith that remembers the fathers in Canaan and the article of faith that remembers the exodus from Egypt. How does one account for the movement from Canaan to Egypt, both in the history of the traditions and in the various examples of the tradition that give evidence of the structure of the confession? It may well be that the gap derives from the radical differences in origin for the two bodies of tradition involved: the patriarchal traditions *vis à vis* the Moses traditions. Indeed, genre studies of the narratives would support this observation. The patriarchal traditions appear now in the form of family sagas, while the Moses traditions have been cast as a heroic sage (Coats, 1983). My intentions here, however, are not to explore the sociological dimensions of that observation: Do the two saga groups derive from two quite distinct institutions in the fabric of Israel's life? Rather, my intention is to explore the peculiarities in the Yahwist's narrative that result from the gap.

The primeval saga in Genesis 2–11 functions for the Yahwist as an introduction for the patriarchal theme and, only through that complex, as an introduction for the remaining elements of tradition in the Pentateuch. Indeed, the primeval saga sets the stage for the Abraham saga by posing a fundamental, theological question. For the Yahwist, creation of the human includes an act of God that calls the human to intimacy with God, with nature, and with fellow creatures. The human creature, unable to find a complement for life among the animals of the Garden, becomes by the grace of

God two human creatures, intimate in the finest order of the Garden. But the human pair broke that intimacy. And in response, God drove them from the Garden, the place of their intimacy. In fact, the break was so severe that God was sorry that he had started the whole thing in the first place. And in response, this time, he destroyed the world with a flood. Starting a new creation with Noah, however, God secured intimacy for the human pair, at least with nature, by means of a covenantal promise. But the creatures broke the intimacy again. Gen 8:21 captures this element of tragedy by duplicating the description of the creature from 6:5. In 6:5, a part of the justification for the flood notes that "the Lord saw that the wickedness of man was great in the earth, and that every imagination of the thoughts of his heart was only evil continually." In 8:21, the text reports that after the flood, God smelled the odor of the human's sacrifice and responded: "I will not again curse the ground because of man, for the imagination of man's heart is evil from his youth." The decisive element that marks the human's character before the flood is the same as the one that marks the creature after the flood. That irony suggests that God's plan for restoring ideal intimacy for the creatures by destroying the world and starting over with Noah fails. Thus, the Yahwist poses a major theological question with the primeval saga: When the creatures broke intimacy on a world-wide scale, God destroyed the world and started over, promising the security of nature as God's part in the new age. But the creatures broke intimacy again. Now what will God do?

Gerhard von Rad suggests that the primeval saga is a theological etiology for Israel. The Yahwist's answer to the question lies in the Abraham saga. This point is confirmed by the position of the Abraham saga following the primeval history. Gen 12:1–3 carries a promise to make Abraham a great nation. But the focus of the promise comes in v 3: God will bless Abraham. And through relationship with Abraham, all the families of the earth will gain blessing. That blessing contains the key for restored intimacy among all of God's creatures. Through the blessing from Abraham, all the families of the earth experience restored intimacy with God, with nature, and with each other.

But the Yahwist does not resolve the problem with the patriarchal theme. At this point, at least in J, it is necessary to observe that the weight of the patriarchal stories does not rest on a promise for progeny or land, not even on the good news of the blessing. To the contrary, the patriarchal stories focus on strife in the family that denies restoration of intimacy for Abraham and blessing for his family members (von Rad, 1972:23). And without intimacy in Abraham's own family, the promise for blessing for all the families of the earth appears subverted. Not even the covenant with Abraham, a covenant that should secure intimacy between Abraham's family and God, overrides the dominant strife that breaks the family apart. Moreover, the broken intimacy is not healed until reconciliation of the family by physical reunion in the Joseph story describes a new day of family unity. For the Joseph story, a commitment to a common future, a commitment to work together in the present for that future, creates a new family intimacy (Coats, 1983).

But that perception belongs to the Joseph story. For the Yahwist, the problem of broken intimacy is not so easily resolved. Following the Joseph story, J paints a scene depicting the family relationships in tragic proportions, parallel to the tragedy J paints following the flood. The pericope in Gen 50:15–21 shows the family members to be as untrustworthy as ever. And the fragments of intimacy, won so laboriously in the family struggles described by the Joseph story, disappear behind brotherly duplicity.

The scene opens in v 15aα with a designation of timing, crucial for the deception that follows. The brothers observe that their father is dead. They can now no longer enjoy his protection. "Perhaps Joseph will hate us and bring back on us all the evil which we did to him." That sentence alone shows that reconciliation is not yet complete in the Yahwist's portrait of the family. Brothers cannot trust the brother. But the gambit developed by the brothers to meet the crisis shows even more sharply that the intimacy of the family has not changed. Without defining the means of communication, the text notes that the brothers deliver a message to Joseph about a scene from the past. The father had left a command for Joseph before he died. Indeed, the verb describing the report of the message is the same as the verb describing the act of the dead father. "They commanded Joseph saying: 'Before he died, your father commanded saying. . . .'" And the content of the message directs Joseph to forgive the brothers for their act that had broken the intimacy of the family. But in fact, no such scene appears in any of the Jacob tradition. The Yahwist creates the impression that the brothers have manufactured the message in order to gain the forgiveness of Joseph and to secure their own position in the court of the pharaoh. And with Jacob dead, no means for verification of the request would be available. Intimacy in the family of Jacob, intimacy between Joseph and the brothers, proves to be as elusive as ever.

Vv 19–21 report that in spite of the apparent deception and the corresponding broken intimacy, Joseph responds favorably. V 17b notes that Joseph wept. This element picks up the weeping motif from the Joseph story (Gen 43:30; 45:1–2, 14) (Coats, 1976:44).[6] And the speech in vv 19–21a contains motifs reminiscent of an oracle of salvation: "Do not fear. For am I in the place of God? You intended evil against me. God intended good in order that he might act to preserve many people as he has done today. Now, do not fear, for I will provide for you and your children." The speech ends, and a narrative comment qualifies the event: "He comforted them and spoke to their heart." The scene thus depicts some intimacy. The opportunity exists. The brothers have but to seize the occasion. Joseph has committed himself to them. And indeed, the expression, *wayĕdabbēr ʿal libbām*, connotes some intimacy. Yet how can these brothers develop a trustworthy and intimate lifestyle? The Yahwist depicts the opportunity, as in Genesis 6–9. But realization of this potential intimacy eludes the principals. For the patriarchal generation in the Yahwist's description, restored intimacy cannot be found. The covenant with Abraham seems as impotent as the covenant with Noah (Coats, 1976:80-92).[7]

The Joseph story fits into the gap between patriarchs in Canaan and Israelites in Egypt. It serves the storyteller as a tool for reporting the move from Canaan to Egypt. And in fact, the Joseph story itself accounts for reconciliation in the family. Yet, the Yahwist undercuts that account of reconciliation. And the process intensifies the form-critical problem of the Hexateuch, the transition from the patriarchal theme to the exodus theme. What now is the relationship between the patriarchal theme of narratives with its promise for reconciliation and the exodus theme? For the Yahwist, the promise for reconciliation with the patriarchal families finds no fulfillment, Thus, with the gap between patriarchs and exodus, the Yahwist poses the same question: What will God do now? Creatures lost intimacy in the Garden. And God established a covenant with Noah as a new creation. But intimacy did not return. So God established another covenant, now with Abraham. But still intimacy does not return. For the Yahwist, the new answer lies with Moses. And the center of the new answer is a new covenant, the event of intimacy between God, Moses, and the people at Sinai.[8]

NOTES

[1] For a critique of Noth's procedure, see Polzin. He objects to the goals in Noth's work for finding the origins of Pentateuchal traditions and, thus, for the disintegrative results of the procedure. But the method of procedure as an analytical tool is productive apart from the assumptions about the origins and independence of particular themes. The structure of the Pentateuch-Hexateuch does, in fact, reveal the four "themes" of tradition identified by Noth. That they might have been originally independent of each other is another question.

[2] For other evaluations of the credo hypothesis, see Huffmon.

[3] Some comment is necessary here about the term "theme." The term can be misleading since a "theme" may be a general word, a motif, a topic that might appear in many different formal modes. Noth apparently used the term in such a general and imprecise manner, for the exodus "theme" would comprise not only the narratives of the Pentateuch about Israel's escape from bondage but also many allusions to the escape outside the Pentateuch. Thus, Hos 11:1, for example, would be a part of the exodus theme of traditions. The term, in this case, functions for a traditio-historical survey. Without denying the merits of this broad usage, I will limit the use of the term for this paper to a form-critical role, a reference to a unit of narrative composed from homogeneous traditions, but with an explicit beginning and an explicit ending. Moreover, the material encompassed by these two points can have a recognizable structure to mark its unity, such as the system of stations in the wilderness itinerary as the pattern of structure for the wilderness theme.

[4] See also Coats (1981). In keeping with my suggestions about intimacy as a key in the Yahwist's treatment of the patriarchs, I would argue that the primary fruit of God's blessing for the patriarchs, and through them for all the families of the earth, is intimacy—intimacy with God, with nature, and with fellow creatures.

[5] Von Rad recognizes the problem but dismisses it since, he feels, the patriarchal traditions are represented apparently in the earliest credo. Yet, he must work around the problem by suggesting that the credo scheme alludes to the "patriarchal period." That caveat is not adequate

for evaluating the role of the patriarchal traditions in the credo, in Genesis, and in the larger structure of the Pentateuch and Hexateuch.

[6] The motif anticipates reconciliation. But it is not yet the act of reconciliation. In fact, it is an ironic twist in the search for reconciliation, for weeping implies pain.

[7] Reconciliation and restored intimacy clearly dominate the final scenes of the Joseph story. But for the Yahwist, reconciliation is not simply restoration of the old order. Reconciliation remains unfulfilled for the Yahwist, a hope that points beyond the limitations of this stage in the tradition to newer stages.

[8] Yet, would the incident with the golden calf not reduce even this event to the same shambles of broken intimacy apparent in the patriarchal traditions in Genesis?

WORKS CONSULTED

Beyerlin, Walter
    1965   *Origins and History of the Oldest Sinaitic Traditions*. Trans. S. Rudman. Oxford: Basil Blackwell.

Coats, George W.
    1972a   "A Structural Transition in Exodus." *VT* 22:129–42.
    1972b   "An Exposition for the Wilderness Theme." *VT* 22:280–95.
    1972c   "The Wilderness Itinerary." *CBQ* 34:135–52.
    1976   *From Canaan to Egypt. Structural and Theological Context for the Joseph Story*. CBQMS 4. Washington: Catholic Biblical Association.
    1981   "The Curse in God's Blessing: Gen 12:1–4a in the Structure and Theology of the Yahwist." Pp. 31–42 in *Die Botschaft und die Bote*. Ed. Jorg Jeremias and Lothar Perlitt. Neukirchen: Neukirchener.
    1983   *Genesis*. FOTL I. Grand Rapids: Eerdmans.
    1985   "An Exposition for the Conquest Theme." *CBQ* 47:47–54.

Davies, G. I.
    1974   "The Wilderness Itineraries. A Comparison Study." *Tyndale Bulletin* 25:46–86.
    1983   "The Wilderness Itineraries and the Composition of the Pentateuch." *VT* 33:1–13.

Huffmon, H. R.
    1965   "The Exodus, Sinai, and the Credo." *CBQ* 27:101–13.

Noth, Martin
    1972   *A History of Pentateuchal Traditions*. Trans. Bernhard W. Anderson. Englewood Cliffs: Prentice-Hall.

Polzin, Robert M.
    1977   "Martin Noth's *A History of Pentateuchal Traditions*." Pp. 174–201 in *Biblical Structuralism. Method and Subjectivity in the Study of Ancient Texts*. Philadelphia: Fortress.

Rad, Gerhard von
    1966a   "The Form Critical Problem of the Hexateuch." Pp. 1–78 in *The Problem of the Hexateuch and Other Essays*. Trans. E. W. Trueman Dicken. Edinburgh: Oliver and Boyd.
    1966b   "The Theological Problem of the Old Testament Doctrine of the Creation." Pp. 131–43 in *The Problem of the Hexateuch and Other Essays*.

1972　　*Genesis. A Commentary.* Rev. ed. Trans. John H. Marks. OTL. Philadelphia: Westminster.

Weiser, Artur
1961　　*The Old Testament: Its Formation and Development.* Trans. S. Rudman. Oxford: Basil Blackwell.

Wolff, Hans Walter
1966　　"The Kerygma of the Yahwist." *Int* 20:131–58.

II
Narrative Tricks

THE REPORTED STORY: MIDWAY BETWEEN ORAL PERFORMANCE AND LITERARY ART

Antony F. Campbell, S.J.
Jesuit Theological College, Parkville

ABSTRACT

This paper sets out to argue the beginnings of a case for the possibility that some of the Old Testament narrative texts contain neither the record of the oral telling of a story nor the skilled fashioning of a story as a work of literary art but, instead, provide the report of a story. Such a reported story would contain the basic elements of character and plot as well as key details but would pass over much that could be easily supplied from the storyteller's imagination. Beyond the theoretical possibility, the case has to be argued for the existence of such reported stories in the Old Testament text. To escape the subjectivity of intuitive judgment, argument is based particularly on the absence of elements necessary to the proper unfolding of the plot, elements which are significant but easily supplied or developed. Examples discussed are 1 Sam 18:20-27; 19:11-17; 22:6-19; 2 Sam 3:12-16. The possible recording, in such reports, of variant ways of telling the same basic story is also noted. Examples discussed are 1 Sam 19:1-7; 20:1-42; 24:1-22 (RSV). A particularly evident setting for the reported story would be a major written narrative composed of a considerable number of stories which needed to be condensed from their full oral potential (for example, the Story of David's Rise). Another setting would be as aide-mémoire for other storytellers. The intention of the reported story, as literary genre, would be to communicate the gist of a story so that it might be recalled or retold.

This paper emerges from a combination of three factors: intuition, commonsense logic, and everyday observation. The intuition is simply a storyteller's conviction, after working with the text of 1-2 Samuel for a while, that no storytellers worth their salt would be able to tell some of the stories the way they are in the text.[1] In exciting areas, they are too bare, too bald; they cry out for embellishment. Commonsense logic says that, as well as the simple telling of a story and the skilled fashioning of a story as a work of literary art, there is also the possibility of reporting what a story is about. Everyday observation makes it clear that the report of a story, telling what it is about, has its place in our narrative conventions—people do it. But the question of literary competence arises and our ability to know the conventions of another culture.[2] We may recognize a phenomenon in our own culture or in another, which then opens the possibility that such a phenomenon existed in the culture of the Old Testament; it is a further step to demonstrate that it did.

A reported story—the outcome of reporting what a story is about—would provide the basic elements from which the full narrative of a story can be developed but would fall short of actually telling the story. The basic elements include characters and plot, key details which impart color or significance and memorable lines or exchanges. In the telling of a story, all these must be introduced and unfolded in the appropriate sequence demanded by the plot.[3] In the report of a story, the sequence is less significant; the obvious or the ordinary can be left out, since they can be supplied easily from the storyteller's imagination.

The argument for the existence of reported stories in the Old Testament narrative texts must proceed in two stages. It is necessary, first, to establish the likelihood that there is such a thing as the reported story in Old Testament narrative. After that, there is the second stage of assessing which texts should be assigned to this category. The purpose of this paper is to argue for the strong likelihood that there are reported stories in the Old Testament text and to point to some of the implications of this for literary critical exegesis. Ths subsequent task of making the inventory of such stories lies beyond the present scope.

The intuitive criteria of "too bare, too bald, cries out for embellishment" are subjective and assume a fair knowledge of the Old Testament's narrative conventions. A surer argument for the existence of the reported story is the recognition that there are texts in the Old Testament in which elements required for the appropriate sequential unfolding if the plot are absent. The gist of the story is communicated and the possibility is there for fuller development, but the sequence in the text is incomplete, being marked by evident gaps. These gaps can easily be filled in with a little exercise of imagination; but until they have been filled in, the story has not been told—it has merely been reported.

An excellent example of what is meant is the dummy-in-the-bed story, involving the strategem by which Michal saved David's life (1 Sam 19:11–17). A central feature, imparting color to the story, is the delaying tactic which made it possible for David to escape from Saul and certain death: "Michal took an image and laid it on the bed and put a pillow of goats' hair at its head and covered it with the clothes" (v 13). The sole purpose of the dummy is to gain time for David to get clear of the city, once his absence has been noted by the guards Saul has posted. Yet, at the appropriate place in the sequence of the story, the dummy is completely neglected: "And when Saul sent messengers to take David, she said, 'He is sick'" (v 11). If the storyteller had intended to portray Michal as able to put off Saul's minions with the simple affirmation that David was sick, there would have been no need for the elaborate description of the dummy. When the dummy is finally mentioned, in v 16, it is too late for delay; once the soldiers enter the room to seize the bed, it is solely a matter of discovery. The time for the use of the dummy was when the soldiers first arrived: they are being held off, they are being stalled, they are simply permitted a glimpse of the sick man in his bed before being sent back to King Saul. Instead, there is no dialogue at all between Michal and the soldiers, just her statement, "He is sick"; yet the scene cries out for some clever exchanges, building up the tension, pitting the quick-witted woman against her father's soldiery. The decisive criterion is that the very logic of the central feature of the story demands its expansion at this point.[4] There is a gap, and it has been left unfilled. The elements for filling it are provided, but are not exploited. The story is not so much told as reported.

Once this observation has been made, a number of other features in the text may be noted which cry out for embellishment; they enhance the likelihood that 1 Sam 19:11–17 is indeed a reported story. No explanation is given why Saul was ready to wait until morning (v 11a). Michal's opening line to David is brief beyond belief: "If you do not save your life tonight, tomorrow you will be killed" (v 11b). If distilled succinctness were the essence of the art, this would be brilliant—but is that its aim here?[5] Would a storyteller pass up the opportunity to have Saul's daughter tell David a few things about the character of her father? "So Michal let David down through the window" (v 12a)—no details at all. No indication is given whether it was morning when Saul's messengers came (v 14) or, if they came during the night, why their change of plan. When the messengers come again, there is no dialogue at all nor any indication that Michal was taken by them to Saul (v 16). Finally, Michal's concluding line to her father is as brief as was her opening line to her husband.[6] These features, taken together with the central failure to exploit the device of the dummy, constitute a reasonable case for considering this text a reported story.

A few other cases of stories, within the larger context of the Story of David's Rise, may be noted briefly which have similar gaps in their narrative sequence. In the story of David's bride-price for Michal (1 Sam 18:20–27), the MT refers to a deadline (v 26b), which has not been mentioned earlier. While there are other explanations, the possibility of a reported story is worth considering; the text is certainly susceptible of considerable expansion.[7] In the story of the slaughter at Nob (1 Sam 22:6–19), Saul's complaint of conspiracy against him, including Jonathan and David (v 8), calls for a previous exposition. While the facts are provided in earlier stories, neither in those nor in this one is it said how Saul came to know of them; it is hardly covered by v 6. Clearly, information has been given to Saul from somewhere. Beyond this, the transition to v 9 is abrupt; no mention is made of the forces at Doeg's disposal in the slaughter (vv 18–19), which can hardly have been presented as an individual effort. There are traditio-historical complications in this material (See Stoebe:411–16). But there is also the possibility that much of it is in the form of a reported story. Finally, we may note the episode of the return of Michal to David (2 Sam 3:12–16). Evidently the agent in Michal's return is Abner; the condition (v 13b) demands evidence of Abner's goodwill and his power to deliver what he promises. Yet in vv 14–16a, Abner is completely in the background, only to reappear again in v 16b. Again, the reported story makes good sense, without the need for literary critical solutions.[8]

Before turning to a second aspect, we should look at the setting in which the need for such reported stories would have arisen. Storytellers, surely, learned their art and enriched their repertoire by listening to stories being told—the oral performance. The compiler of the Story of David's Rise, however, was more than an accomplished storyteller with an extensive repertoire. Depending on how one views it, the Story of David's Rise is either brilliant propaganda or a brilliant reflection on human experience and the working of the divine will (See, for example, McCarter, 1980b:489–504). What is significant is that its subject matter is an extensive collection of stories, some thirty of them or more. It is mainly through the organization and arrangement of these stories that the impact of the Story of David's Rise is made (See, especially, Rendtorff). If all of these were to be told in full, one would certainly have a very lengthy text. It is essential for the Story of David's Rise that some of the component stories be reported, rather than told at length. The setting of a narrative which expounds an understanding of history, distilled from a number of stories, is exactly what one would expect to give rise to the literary genre of the reported story. A further extension of this setting would be the composition of what might be termed an aide-mémoire for other storytellers. The intention of a reported story is to communicate the gist of a story, so that it can be recalled or retold. This is quite different from telling or writing a story for edification, education, or entertainment.

There is a second phenomenon which, strictly speaking, is unrelated to the question of the reported story, but which makes particularly good sense in connection with it: the appearance within a narrative text of indications of variant versions of basically the same story. While these apparent expansions might be considered as simple contamination from the other versions, in the hypothesis of a reported story they make eminent sense as reminders of other themes which can be introduced or of other ways in which a story can be told.[9]

For example, in 1 Samuel 20, there is quite a long story about the carefully prearranged code by which Jonathan is to alert David, should Saul turn out to be hostile toward him. We need to note, from the outset, that the story is really only concerned with the eventuality of Saul's hostility (cf. v 10). If Saul were well disposed, Jonathan could come out and meet with David without any precautions. The precautions are necessary only in the event that Saul is ill-disposed and that, therefore, Jonathan is likely to be followed by Saul's men in order to discover David's hiding place. The code is carefully prearranged. The only problem with the story is that the code is not observed. After carefully arranging for a secret code (vv 20–22), Jonathan adds a different code (v 38), and he and David openly meet and embrace anyway, making any secret code quite unnecessary (vv 41–42). In the traditional understanding, either one is confronted with an example of quite confused storytelling, or there has been serious contamination of the story from other versions.

Once 1 Samuel 20 is looked at as a report of a story, with due note taken of a couple of optional variations, a very different picture emerges. I would like to propose that one basic story is being reported, with brief notes indicating two possible variations on the theme. Basic to all three is the presumption that Saul is hostile to David and so will have Jonathan followed in an attempt to discover David's whereabouts and kill him. The stories and planning of their action are based on this contingency. The first optional variation is noted in vv 20–22. The sign is basically visual; the arrows are to be shot to the side of David's hiding place, presumably either falling short of it or landing beyond it. The words do not add any specific content; they merely specify the code and emphasize the assumed visual message: if the arrows fall short of you, come back, all is well; if the arrows fall beyond you, be off.[10]

The second optional variation is noted within vv 36b–39. In this version, after the agreed code has been employed (v 37b), a clever piece of stage business transforms the audible aspect of the sign into an actual and direct message: "Hurry, make haste, stay not" (v 38). It is apparently shouted to the boy (literally: "after the boy"); it is in fact destined for David.[11] While it can be presented as Jonathan's inventiveness, in fact it renders the earlier code unnecessary. The two are not mutually exclusive, but do offer a basis for two ways of telling the story.

All that is left is to determine the sense of the basic story, without either of these optional variations. Jonathan goes out in the morning with his young attendant. If there is to be neither visual nor audible sign with the arrows, what is the purpose of the lad's accompanying Jonathan? I suggest that the attendant was included in order to create the impression that Jonathan was simply going out for some archery practice, thus defusing any anxieties Saul's men might have had about his going off alone. And so Jonathan got away into the country, and once well clear of the city he sent the boy back (v 40). He was then free to meet David and confirm the danger that threatened David's life. If anyone should be doubtful about the plausibility of this basic version of the story, I will take the liberty of appealing to Josephus for support, according to whose version David went off with the lad, "seemingly for exercise" (*hōs gymnasomenos*)—i.e., for archery practice (*Jewish Antiquities* VI,239).

So, I would submit, there were three possible variants of this story in circulation: one where the attendant functioned simply to allay the suspicion of Saul's watchmen; another in which the security was so tight that only a primarily visual signal could be given, in proximity to a known hiding place (cf. 1 Sam 19:3; 20:19); the third in which a clever ruse was adopted where an order shouted at the attendant was in fact a concealed message, directed to David. 1 Samuel 20 need not, then, be the outcome of incompetent redaction, nor the result of contamination by inattentive copyists; rather, it may be a careful report of a story, including reminders of the possible variants. In an oral performance, a storyteller might choose whichever version was most appropriate to the audience, the mood, or the time available.[12]

A couple of other stories, within the Story of David's Rise, which show similar possibilities may be mentioned briefly. first, in 1 Sam 19:1–7, v 3a presumes a conversation that is secretly overhead ("I will go out and stand beside my father in the field where you are"), while in vv 3b and 7 the conversation is to be reported to David. Contamination from the story of 1 Samuel 20 is possible. But it makes good sense to see the motif in v 3a as a deliberate indication of a variant version of the story, in which the conversation takes place near David's prearranged hiding place and so is overheard rather than reported later (So Hertzberg:165–66; McCarter, 1980a:321–22). Second, 1 Samuel 24 provides traces of considerable complexity. There is a marked awkwardness in vv 4–7 (RSV) (See McCarter, 1980a:383–84, 386–87). There is a most admirable admonition against harming Saul (vv 6–7, RSV), but it comes after David had had his chance to do so, i.e., when he snipped off the skirt of Saul's robe (v 4b, RSV). The difficulty is most simply resolved by recognizing indications of two versions: one in which Saul strayed into a cave where David and his men were, and in which David resisted the incitement to kill his enemy; the other in which the motif of cutting off a piece of Saul's cloak was introduced, so as to attach the cave story to vv 8–22 (RSV) and fashion a story parallel to that of chap. 26. The second version is indicated by the insertion of vv 4b–5 (RSV) in the middle of the story of Saul in the cave, between the incitement from David's men and David's reply. A further awkwardness supports the suggestion of combined motifs. As the story stands in chap. 24, there is an inherent improbability in David's emerging from the cave, waving a piece of Saul's robe in his hand, while apparently three thousand of Saul's chosen troops stand passively looking at the man who is the object of their expedition. The need to establish a safe distance and the security of night is emphasized in chap. 26, but neglected here. It is compounded by the tension between the portrayal of Saul looking back toward the worshipful David in 24:8 (RSV) and the use of the recognition of the voice motif in 24:16 (RSV, cf. 26:17).[13] Skilled telling of this version of the story would be required to cope with these anomalies plausibly. This aspect may point to the presence of a reported story here.

The central interest of the proposal made in this paper is not so much to point out the possible ways in which variants of a story might have been represented, but rather to draw attention to the literary genre of the reported story, which may be present in a number of our texts. The idea of a reported story obliges us to reflect on the limited nature of the knowledge we have about the oral performance of Old Testament stories. It is probable that in relatively few cases do we have what might be called a transcription of the oral performances of a story. And the cases where whole stories are clearly works of literary art are not overwhelmingly numerous. The reported story may account for a considerable number of our texts.

In my understanding, such reports appear to pass over lightly what might easily be left to the storyteller's imagination or memory. On the other hand, they may swell in some detail on key aspects of the story. We need to be aware of this distinction, in order to have a better grasp of the skills of Israelite storytelling. Those parts of the story which are passed over in matter-of-fact fashion may reveal nothing of the way the Israelites told their stories; those parts which are dwelt on in more loving detail, on the other hand, may give a clearer notion of how a skilled Hebrew storyteller functioned.

NOTES

[1] By my observation, while the assumption is never explicit, a narrative text is usually treated as though either it reproduced the oral version of a story or was composed as the written version of a story. P. Kyle McCarter, for example, speaks of 1 Sam 19:11-17 as "a fast-paced and entertaining story" (1980a:326). Once the conviction that the text actually is a complete story has been recognized as an assumption, McCarter's comment may be rendered with much more accuracy: the report outlines briefly and sketchily a story with evident potential for entertainment.

J. P. Fokkelman, discussing the division into scenes, writes that the scene "regularly coincides with an independent story, and I suspect that it reflects the phase of the original, oral recounting" (9). How much is implied here depends on the weight given to "reflects"; it appears to bring the original text, now a scene, into close association with the original, oral recounting.

An important survey of recent anthopological literature on oral storytelling is provided by Burke O. Long.

[2] See, for example, the discussion in John Barton (11-16, 26-29).

[3] The extreme example is provided by the analysis of the sequence of functions in fairy tales, by V. Propp. See also the comments of T. Todorov (116-19).

[4] H. W. Hertzberg, in dealing with this passage, has allowed his imagination to fill in the details which are not in the text but would obviously be supplied by a storyteller. So he can say: "Her deception of the messengers with the help of the teraphim and the readiness of the messengers, indeed of Saul himself, to be deceived, is narrated with furious joy and put to the discredit of the first king" (167). A more careful reading of the text reveals that the "deception of the messengers with the help of the teraphim" is in the unnarrated scene between v 14 and v 15; the readiness to be deceived and the furious joy might all have been part of a telling of the story, but they have to be read into the text we have. Josephus has his version of the unnarrated scene: "and she showed them the bed all covered up, and by the quivering of the liver which shook the bedclothes convinced them that what lay there was David gasping for

breath" (*Jewish Antiquities* VI,217). LXX may have resolved the difficulty very subtly. Its "and they said" in place of "and she said" (v 14b) implies that the soldiers sent word back to Saul, which allows for the possibility that they have been deceived by the dummy (cf. Stoebe:358).

[5] Succinctness can be characteristic of Old Testament storytelling (e.g., Genesis 4; 22), but it need not be (e.g., 2 Samuel 11–12). In this case, it has to be decided whether it is due to literary art or literary genre. Robert Alter is rightly attentive to the elements of urgent compactness in the story, but does not advert to the implications of the failure to exploit the story's central and most colorful feature—the dummy in the bed (119–20).

[6] For further reflections on what is left unsaid here, see Stoebe (360–61).

[7] For other explanations, see McCarter (1980a:316), Stoebe (353).

[8] See the discussion in McCarter (1984:114–15). Alter notes: "The remarkable suggestiveness of the Bible's artistic economy could scarcely be better illustrated" (122). It may well be that the literary genre of reported story is sometimes responsible for such artistic economy.

[9] Note the comment by Long: "If we assume that oral literature lay behind a given text, and recognize that a performer may produce two or more distinct versions of a piece on different occasions, then such differences might persist in the written document" (194).

[10] In this version, the concern of v 10 has been forgotten. If Saul were favorably disposed toward David, there would be no need for concealment or signals.

[11] There is one assumption made in the conflation of the stories. V 36a belongs to the version to be discussed in a moment. The present participle here, "which I shoot," may well reflect a continuous process as Jonathan walks into the country. In v 36b, it is assumed that they have reached the appointed tryst, in David's vicinity. The textual variations between multiple arrows, three arrows, and one arrow may reflect the influence of the different versions of the story.

[12] McCarter's treatment is along classical lines: "vv 11–17 interrupt the flow of our narrative and seem to have been inserted, along with vv 23, 20–42, by the hand that joined the history of David's rise to the subsequent material—probably the Josianic historian (1980a:344). The intention was to show that the survival of Saul's house was the direct consequence of David's loyalty to Jonathan (ibid.). McCarter passes over the variation in v 38 in silence. Presumably, it is felt to lie within the legitimate license of the storyteller.

More important is the question of the transmission of material like vv 11–17 and 40–42. It is not likely that either passage would be handed down independently of the main story, especially if a period of several centuries is envisaged. It is more probable that they were handed down as a variant version of the story. If fact, only vv 40–42 have a bearing on the plot of the story, since they render the system of signals patently unnecessary. The question then is whether they have been added by a later redactor whose interest in David's loyalty to Jonathan overrode any concern for the story's plot, or whether they have been added as a pointer to a variant version of the story with a marked change in the plot.

[13] Alter comments: "Perhaps he asks this out of sheer amazement at what he has just heard, or because he is too far off to make out David's face clearly, or because his eyes are blinded with tears, which would be an apt emblem of the condition of moral blindness that has prevented him from seeing David as he really is" (37). While this may be a legitimate approach to the text as we have it now, when it is viewed in conjunction with the other factors—the accompanying soldiery and the unevenness in the cave scene—it has to be taken seriously as evidence of the nature of the text.

WORKS CONSULTED

Alter, Robert
    1981   *The Art of Biblical Narrative*. New York: Basic Books.

Barton, John
    1984   *Reading the Old Testament: Method in Biblical Study*. London: Darton, Longman and Todd.

Fokkelman, J. P.
    1981   *Narrative Art and Poetry in the Books of Samuel.* Vol. I. *King David.* Assen: Van Gorcum.

Hertzberg, Hans Wilhelm
    1964   *I & II Samuel.* Trans. J. S. Bowden. OTL. Philadelphia: Westminster.

Long, Burke O.
    1976   "Recent Field Studies in Oral Literature and Their Bearing on OT Criticism." *VT* 26:187–98.

McCarter, P. Kyle, Jr.
    1980a   *I Samuel.* AB 8. Garden City: Doubleday.
    1980b   "The Apology of David." *JBL* 99:489–504.
    1984   *II Samuel.* AB 9. Garden City: Doubleday.

Propp, V.
    1968   *Morphology of the Folktale.* 2d ed. Austin: University of Texas.

Rendtorff, Rolf
    1971   "Beobachtungen zur altisraelitischen Geschichtsschreibung anhand der Geschichte vom Aufstieg Davids." Pp. 428–39 in *Probleme biblischer Theologie: Gerhard von Rad zum 70 Geburtstag.* Ed. H. W. Wolff. Munich: Chr. Kaiser.

Stoebe, Hans Joachim
    1973   *Das erste Buch Samuelis.* KAT 8/1. Gütersloh: Gerd Mohn.

Todorov, Tzvetan
    1977   *The Poetics of Prose.* Ithaca: Cornell University.

SPATIAL FORM IN EXOD 19:1-8a AND IN THE LARGER SINAI NARRATIVE

Thomas B. Dozeman
Calvin College

ABSTRACT

Spatial form devices are defined as "techniques ... which ... subvert the chronological sequence inherent in narrative." I have two aims in this article: the first is to describe how redactors have employed spatial-form techniques in their construction of the canonical form of Exod 19:1-8a, and the second aim is to assess the effect that spatial-form devices have on the reader, who seeks to interpret the promulgation of law within the larger Sinai narrative.

I. The Problem

The so-called Sinai narrative (Exodus 19-34) is really a mixture of narrative and legal materials. This combination creates a series of repetitions which have caused problems for modern scholars in interpreting the canonical form of the text. Wellhausen illustrates two central problems that confront the reader of the Sinai narrative. First, he argues that the legislation in the Sinai narrative was a "monstrous growth." In the present form of the Sinai narrative, law-codes are inserted at Exod 20:2-17 (Decalogue), Exod 20:23-23:33 (Book of the Covenant), Exodus 25-31 (Priestly Legislation), and in Exod 34:11-26 (The Legislation of Covenant Renewal). Wellhausen concludes that the legislation is intolerable because "the course of history is interrupted" (1957:342). Second, Wellhausen also extends this criticism to the narratives themselves. He notes how pentateuchal narrative changed from a "natural movement" and "consistent sequence" in Genesis to a "labyrinth of stories" in Exodus 19-34, which did not "naturally progress." The primary problem in the progression of the narratives according to Wellhausen is that the repetitive trips by Moses up the mountain "for the same purpose" interrupt the sequence of the story (1899:81).

The two problems of interpretation addressed by Wellhausen are interrelated. First, his claim that law "interrupted history" (i.e., narrative) is a problem of chronology in the present construction of the story. The insertion of long sections of legislation make it difficult for the reader to maintain any chronological framework for the narrated events. Second, his assessment that the frequent trips by Moses up the mountain were "for the same purpose" points to a problem of causality in the sequence of events. The recurrence of this motif in conjunction with the repeated promulgation of law appears to halt action at several points in the story. These two features of the Sinai narrative could be described as a problem of temporal sequence.

II. Spatial Form

The recurrence of law and the repetitive movement of Moses on the mountain are spatial-form devices in the present construction of the Sinai narrative. Spatial-form devices are "techniques ... which ... subvert the chronological sequence inherent in narrative." This definition is expanded further:

> We read narratives one word after another, and in this sense all narratives are chronological sequences. But the ... arrangement of events within this linear flow of words often departs in varying degrees from strict chronological order. Also, portions of a narrative may be connected without regard to chronology through such devices as image patterns, leitmotifs, analogy, and contrast. "Spatial form" is simply the general label for all these different narrative techniques (Smitten and Daghistany:15–16).[1]

The characteristics of narrative in which spatial-form devices are prominent are clarified when contrasted to *Bildungsroman*—narrative predicated on temporal sequence (Mickelsen:65–67). *Bildungsroman* maximizes the temporal sequence of a story, so that the progression of the narrative is clearly forward toward the consequences of action. Here characters and setting are subordinated to chronology and plot, with the result that the reader is swept along from one event to the next until resolution is reached (Mickelsen:65). Spatial-form devices in narrative, by contrast, minimize temporal sequence to suspend the forward momentum of the story. Instead, characterization and setting predominate over chronology and plot. The resulting structure of narrative in which spatial-form devices predominate has been likened to an orange. Like an orange, such a narrative is structured into individual pieces—similar segments of equal value—in which the movement is circular, focused on the single subject, the core. Scenes, therefore, are often juxtaposed to each other to provide a different perspective on the same core event, with the result that temporal sequence is often replaced by characterization, slow pace, lack of resolution, and repetition. Thus, when spatial-form devices predominate in narrative, the reader is forced "to project not so much forward ('what happens next') as backward or sideways" in order to uncover the progression of the narrative (Mickelsen:64–65, 67).

The distinction between the "labyrinth" of stories in the Sinai narrative and the "natural movement" of the stories in Genesis noted by Wellhausen illustrates the contrast between spatial form and *Bildungsroman* within biblical narrative. In the family stories of Genesis, genealogy underscores temporal sequence by providing the framework for characters and setting, which ensures that the action moves forward to follow the exploits of each promised heir. In the Sinai narrative, by contrast, temporal sequence is subordinated everywhere to characterization and setting. Thus, the primary focus in Exodus 19-34 is on the interrelationship of characters—Yahweh, Moses, and Israel—within the narrowly defined setting of Mount Sinai.

The emphasis on characters and setting in the Sinai narrative affects both chronology and plot. Chronology is almost entirely suspended in Exodus 19-34, while the temporal references that do occur function more to mark significant events than to provide a clear sequence for actions.[2] Thus, for example after the opening temporal clauses (Exod 19:1), the reader is told that theophany required three days preparation and began on a new day (Exod 19:10-11, 16), that the covenant ceremony commenced on a new day (Exod 24:4b), that Moses required seven days preparation to receive plans for the tabernacle on the mountain (Exod 24:16b), that twice he stayed there forty days (Exod 24:18b; 34:28a) with the latter trip also commencing on a new day (Exod 34:4b), and that Israel's worship of the calf (Exod 32:5, 6) and Moses' intercession for them after the event (Exod 32:30) also began on a new day.[3]

Second, action throughout Exodus 19-34 is subordinated to lengthy discourse by characters (primarily Yahweh), who are, for the most part, stationary. Thus, for example, Yahweh is situated at the top of the mountain, while Israel is located at its base. Moses is the most active character, but even his movement is vertical and circular in the setting of the mountain. As Wellhausen noted long ago, the repetitive movement of Moses appears to interrupt rather than to provide sequence to the story.

The aim of this article is to describe how redactors have employed spatial-form techniques to construct the canonical form of the Sinai narrative. The focus of this study will be Exod 19:1-8a, which serves as the introduction to the narrative.[4] An examination of this unit will provide specific illustrations of how redactors have emphasized the setting of Mount Sinai by shaping the narrative around the movement of Moses. Finally, the introductory role of Exod 19:1-8a for the subsequent promulgation of law will provide clues to interpret the movement of Moses in the larger Sinai narrative as a spatial-form technique, which is meant to provide narrative context for the distinct legal codes that now function as one Torah in the canonical form of the text. It is beyond the scope of the present study to anchor this redaction in a particular *Sitz im Leben*.

III. Exod 19:1-8a

Exod 19:1-8a is composed of at least three distinct traditions: the priestly itinerary in Exod 19:1-2a (Coats; Cross:310-17); a preexilic tradition concerning the Mountain of God in Exod 19:2b–3a;[5] and a deuteronomic Proposal of Covenant in Exod 19:3b–8 (Noth:157 and Perlitt:167–91). Spatial-form devices provide the primary means by which redactors have interrelated these independent units of tradition. The central role of spatial-form devices in providing the canonical shape to these diverse traditions becomes evident immediately in the opening verses of the Sinai narrative.

A. *The Priestly Itinerary*

The priestly itinerary in Exod 19:1–2a immediately confronts the reader with a problem in narrative logic. The expected temporal sequence of this itinerary (when compared to the other itinerary notices in Exodus[6] and to the summary of Israel's travels in Numbers 33[7]) should read:

> Israel journeyed from Rephidim,
> and they came to the wilderness of Sinai,
> and they camped in the wilderness
> on the third "month". . . .[8]

This form of the itinerary follows a logical sequence in the order of events. Redactors, however, have disrupted the expected temporal sequence so that the priestly itinerary is now organized by two repetitions, which emphasize the time and the setting of the narrative with two temporal clauses and two notices of Israel's arrival at the wilderness of Sinai. These disruptions of the expected temporal sequence force the reader to "project not so much forward ('what happens next') as backward or sideways" in order to uncover the progression of the narrative. The text reads:

> On the third month (*bahōdeš haššĕlîšî*) after the people of Israel had gone
>   forth out of the land of Egypt
> On this very day (*bayyôm hazzeh*)
> they came (*bw'*) to the wilderness of Sinai
> And they journeyed from Rephidim
> And they came (*bw'*) to the wilderness of Sinai
> And they camped in the wilderness (Exod 19:1–2a).

A closer examination of these repetitions will illustrate the effect of spatial-form devices on the reader. The first repetition immediately disrupts the chronology of the Sinai narrative with the juxtaposition of the two temporal clauses. The opening temporal clause makes a general reference to the third month, which is clearly located in the past tense of narrative time. Israel's arrival, therefore, is associated with their previous exodus from Egypt and thus placed within a chronology of past events, which are being recounted by the narrator. The second temporal clause, however, makes reference to a specific day (*bayyôm*) in contrast to the more general reference of "the third month," while the use of the nearer demonstrative "on *this* day," as opposed to the more remote demonstrative, "on *that* day," also contrasts to the past tense of narrative time that was established with the opening temporal clause. The result is that instead of harmonizing with the first temporal clause to emphasize that Israel arrived at the wilderness of Sinai on "that very month" (i.e., the third month after they left Egypt), the reference to a specific day in the second temporal clause not only disrupts chronological sequence, but also switches from anterior action to emphasize a present day in relation to the reader.[9]

The juxtaposition of contrasting temporal clauses forces the reader to suspend the forward momentum of the narrative already in the opening verse of the story in order to determine the exact time of Israel's arrival. The additional contrast of time between the two temporal clauses and their affects on the reader raise a further question concerning whose day is being narrated in the promulgation of the Torah on Mount Sinai.

Dislocation of temporal sequence continues with the second repetition, which emphasizes the setting of the Sinai narrative. Here, Israel's approach to the wilderness of Sinai is reported both before and after the notice of their departure from Rephidim:

> they came (*bw'*) into the wilderness of Sinai
> and they journeyed from Rephidim. . . . (Exod 19:1b*b*)
> and they came (*bw'*) to the wilderness of Sinai (Exod 19:2a*b*).

The result of this arrangement is that the reader must once again suspend the forward momentum of the narrative, which, in turn, draws attention to the wilderness of Sinai as the setting of the story.

The present organization of the priestly itinerary around repetition rather than temporal sequence illustrates the use of spatial form. Once repetition has become the organizing feature of the itinerary, it also provides the basis for linking the priestly itinerary with the preexilic Mountain of God tradition in Exod 19:2b–3a by creating yet a third repetition (Van Dyke Parunak:525–48, esp. 529ff.)

B. *The Mountain of God Tradition*

The Mountain of God tradition in Exod 19:2b–3a describes an unnamed mountain as the location where Israel camps and where Moses ascends to God. This unit most likely functioned as an introduction to a preexilic account of Elohim's appearance to Israel at a cosmic mountain, which now continues later in Exodus 19.[10] The text reads:

> Israel camped (*ḥnh*) there (*šām*) before the mountain (*hāhār*)
> but Moses ascended to God (*hā'ĕlōhîm*) (Exod 19:2b–3a).

The linking of this tradition with the priestly itinerary is accomplished by the repetition of the verb "to camp" in the closing line of the priestly itinerary (Exod 19:2a*c*) and in the opening line of the Mountain of God tradition (Exod 19:2b):

And they camped (*ḥnh*) in the wilderness (Exod 19:2a*c*)
And Israel camped (*ḥnh*) there (*šām*) before the mountain (*hāhār*) (Exod 19:2b).

The combination of these distinct traditions in the canonical form of the Sinai narrative affects the interpretation of the preexilic Mountain of God tradition, since the emphasis on the setting in the priestly itinerary now supplies a more specific location for the unnamed Mountain of God (*hāhār*) as being in the wilderness of Sinai. The reference to the wilderness in the final line of the priestly itinerary (Exod 19:2a*c*) further reinforces such an interpretation. This general reference to the wilderness still maintains its connection to the more specific wilderness of Sinai in the previous sentence that it always had in the priestly itinerary, but it now also acquires the additional function of associating the wilderness of Sinai (which was emphasized in the previous repetition) with the unnamed Mountain of God in following sentence.[11] Thus, *šām* ("there") in Exod 19:2b must be read in the context of the wilderness of Sinai, so that the mountain, which Moses ascends in Exod 19:3a, is now most naturally interpreted as Mount Sinai.[12]

Spatial-form techniques have subverted temporal sequence and momentarily stopped action in the introduction to the canonical form of the Sinai narrative (Exod 19:1–3a) in order to emphasize the setting. The reader, in turn, has been forced "to project not so much forward ('what happens next') as backward or sideways" to uncover the progression of the narrative. The introduction to the Sinai narrative now progresses in the following manner according to the three repetitions: temporal notices (Exod 19:1a*a*, a*b*), markers of Israel's arrival at the wilderness of Sinai (Exod 19:1b, 2a*b*) and encampment before the Mountain of God (Exod 19:2a*c*, 2b). A number of scholars have pointed out that the wilderness of Sinai in the priestly itinerary suggests a wilderness region rather than a specific mountain.[13] The previous analysis reinforces this conclusion, yet it also demonstrates how the linking of the wilderness of Sinai with the unnamed Mountain of God lays the foundation for the important role that Mount Sinai will play as the location for the revelation of Torah in the canonical form of the Sinai narrative.[14]

C. The Deuteronomic Proposal of Covenant

Scholars have provided four reasons why Exod 19:3b–8 is a distinct unit of tradition. Its content suggests a "compositional integrity of its own" (McCarthy:155). The style of the unit conveys the parallelism of poetry rather than narrative (Patrick:146–47). The vocabulary is distinct (McCarthy:156). And finally, the function of Exod 19:3b–8 in anticipating the concluding of the covenant also separates it from the surrounding material (Noth:154).

A rhetorical analysis of Exod 19:3b–8 illustrates how the pericope is dominated by divine speech with the Proposal of Covenant (Knutson:191–94), and, furthermore, how the entire unit is also organized around verbs of speech:

Speech of Yahweh:	*qr', 'mr* in Exod 19:3b
	'mr, ngd in Exod 19:4
Speech of Moses:	*qr'* in Exod 19:7
Speech of Israel:	*'nh, 'mr* in Exod 19:8

The pericope completes a full cycle in the process of communication with a beginning, middle, and end. It begins with the Proposal of Covenant to Moses in Exod 19:3b-6. The middle is reached when Moses conveys the Proposal of Covenant to Israel, and they respond favorably in Exod 19:7-8a. The pericope ends when Moses brings the word of the people back to Yahweh in Exod 19:8b (Perlitt:168; McCarthy:155 n. 6).

The primary role of verbs of speech gives the pericope a sense of indefiniteness (Zenger:57-58). The only reference to setting in Exod 19:3b-8 occurs in the opening verse when we are told simply that Yahweh spoke from the mountain (*min-hāhār*).[15] Even with the placement of Yahweh on the mountain, Moses and the people of Israel are not clearly located in the setting. This is illustrated by following the movement of Moses in the pericope. His placement in relation to Yahweh and to the people is not defined. He does not ascend the mountain at the beginning of the pericope, but is merely given a message for the people.[16] After Yahweh's speech, the approach of Moses to the people is also not spelled out. He merely brings (*bw'*) the word of Yahweh to them in Exod 19:7a, and then returns (*šwb*) their response to God (Exod 19:8b) (Zenger:58-59). The reader is given no clues to locate Moses at anytime in this pericope. He functions here less as a mediator who maintains distance and clear boundaries between Yahweh and Israel, and more as a prophet or teacher who simply brings the word of Yahweh to the people. The prophetic role of Moses is reinforced in Exod 19:4 when he is addressed by Yahweh with the commissioning formula "Thus you will say to . . ." (Muilenburg:354).

However, additional rhetorical features are superimposed on the deuteronomic Proposal of Covenant through the larger canonical context: First, the more specific setting of Mount Sinai that was created through the combination of the priestly itinerary and the Mountain of God tradition in Exod 19:1-3a must now also be carried through Exod 19:3b-8. The address of Yahweh to Moses "from the mountain" in Exod 19:3b, therefore, must now be interpreted as the mountain in the wilderness of Sinai—Mount Sinai. In addition, once spatial-form techniques stop the action and emphasize the setting of Mount Sinai, the juxtaposition of the deuteronomic Proposal of Covenant in Exod 19:3b-8 to Exod 19:1-3a allows for the introduction of characters within the setting. Thus, in the canonical form of the Sinai narrative, Israel, Moses, and Yahweh are introduced in rapid succession in relation to Mount Sinai:

Israel camped there before the mountain
but *Moses* ascended to God
And *Yahweh* called to him from the mountain (Exod 19:2b-3b*a*).[17]

Here, characters are juxtaposed to each other vertically, which defines their interrelationships spatially in the context of Mount Sinai (Rivard:339). By emphasizing the setting, spatial-form techniques have provided the narrative context not only to clearly locate characters within the setting but also to explore spatial relations between characters, where Yahweh and Israel are separated by Mount Sinai and must communicate through Moses. Lotman concludes that "the language of spatial relations (within narrative) turns out to be one of the basic means for comprehending reality." He explains further that "the structure of the space of a text becomes a model of the structure of the space of the universe" (217–18). If we apply Lotman's analysis of spatial relations to the Sinai narrative, then the spatial-form techniques in the opening verses of Exodus 19 acquire an even clearer purpose. Emphasis on the new setting of Mount Sinai points beyond geography to envision a cosmic mountain on which characters are clearly located: Yahweh is associated with the mountain top, Israel is at the base, while Moses moves vertically between them.

Redactors have been able to expand the role of Moses to include the function of a priestly mediator by locating all three characters within the setting of Mount Sinai. The additional role of Moses as a mediator in the canonical form of the text is achieved by accentuating his vertical movement between Yahweh and Israel. The ascent of Moses to God in Exod 19:2b to receive the Proposal of Covenant forces the reader to interpret his approach (bw') to the people in Exod 19:7 as a descent, while his return ($šwb$) of the people's response to Yahweh in Exod 19:8b must also be read as an ascent to Yahweh. Thus, in the canonical form of the Sinai narrative, Moses resembles a mediator, who maintains distance and clear boundaries between Yahweh and Israel, in addition to his previous role as the commissioned prophet or teacher of deuteronomic law.

The vertical movement of Moses as the mediator on Mount Sinai even becomes the primary structuring device in the canonical form of the Proposal of Covenant. His movement between Yahweh and Israel establishes a certain symmetry between events at the summit of Mount Sinai and at its base. The symmetry of the pericope is maintained by the repetition of the verb "to call" (qr', Exod 19:3b, 7ab) and by the repetition of the divine Proposal of Covenant at the summit of Mount Sinai (Exod 19:3b–6) as recounted speech by Moses at the base of the mountain (Exod 19:7b). This structure can be illustrated in the chart on page 95.

Thus, the movement of Moses as mediator provides structure to the canonical form of the Proposal of Covenant and reinforces the spatial relations among characters: Israel, Moses and Yahweh around Mount Sinai. But the restructuring of the deuteronomic Proposal of Covenant around the vertical movement of Moses also forces a new boundary to this pericope in

Moses is on the mountain with Yahweh in Exod 19:3-6 which separates into three parts:
(1) Moses ascends (*'lh*) to God (Exod 19:3a)
(2) Yahweh calls (*qr'*) to Moses (Exod 19:3ba)
(3) Yahweh delivers a Proposal of Covenant to Israel (Exod 19:3bb-6)

Moses is at the base of the mountain with Israel in Exod 19:7-8a, which follows the same pattern as Exod 19:3-6:
(1') Moses descends (*bw'*) to the people (Exod 19:7aa)
(2') Moses calls (*qr'*) to the elders (Exod 19:7ab)
(3') Moses repeats the Proposal of Covenant (Exod 19:7b)
(4) The people accept the Proposal of Covenant (Exod 19:8a)

---

its present canonical context. The return (*šwb*) to Yahweh in Exod 19:8b of the people's acceptance must be read as an ascent by Moses, which begins a new scene. The boundaries of the introductory scene in the canonical form of the Sinai narrative, therefore, consist of Exod 19:1-8a.

In summary, the reader is forced continually to halt the forward momentum of Exod 19:1-8a because redactors utilize spatial-form techniques as a means for linking distinct traditions. Redactors first disrupt the temporal sequence of the introduction to the Sinai narrative by organizing the priestly itinerary and the Mountain of God tradition around three repetitions, which emphasize the setting of Mount Sinai. Then, once spatial-form devices stop action, the further addition of the deuteronomic Proposal of Covenant allows for the introduction of characters within the setting. The vertical juxtaposition of Israel, Moses, and Yahweh in the context of Mount Sinai establishes the spatial relations among characters, while the movement of Moses on Mount Sinai in Exod 19:1-8a reinforces those spatial relations by becoming the primary structuring device within the pericope. The result is that in the canonical form of Exod 19:1-8a, the divine Proposal of Covenant is clearly located at the summit of Mount Sinai, where it is given to Moses, alone, and then mediated to Israel at the base of the mountain.

IV. The Movement of Moses and Law: From Spatial Form to Canonical Function

The present structure of Exod 19:1-8a provides clues to the larger structure of the canonical form of the Sinai narrative. The repetitive movement of Moses on Mount Sinai between Yahweh and Israel continues to mark the boundaries of successive scenes, which then provides the context for the promulgation of distinct legal codes by Yahweh on the cosmic mountain. In each scene, therefore, Moses is described at the outset as being on the mountain alone with Yahweh where he receives the revelation of law, and also as approaching Israel with the legislation. Thus, the canonical form of the Sinai narrative follows the progress of Moses up and down the mountain as he mediates each successive legal code to Israel. Moses completes six full cycles of travel between Yahweh on the mountain top and Israel at the base, which can be outlined as follows:

Exod 19:1–8a (*Proposal of Covenant*—Exod 19:3b–6)
   A. Moses on Mount Sinai: Exod 19:3–6
      Exod 19:3a ("Moses ascended [*'lh*] to God")
   B. Moses at the base of Mount Sinai: Exod 19:7–8a
      Exod 19:7a ("Moses approached [*bw'*] . . . the people")
Exod 19:8b–19 (*Theophany*)
   A. Moses on Mount Sinai: Exod 19:8b–13
      Exod 19:8b ("Moses returned [*šwb*] the words of the people to Yahweh")
   B. Moses at the base of Mount Sinai: Exod 19:14–19
      Exod 19:14 ("Moses descended [*yrd*] from the mountain to the people")
Exod 19:20–20:20 (*Decalogue*—Exod 20:2–17)
   A. Moses on Mount Sinai: Exod 19:20–24
      Exod 19:20 ("Yahweh descended [*yrd*] on the top of Mount Sinai . . . and Moses ascended [*'lh*]")
   B. Moses at the base of Mount Sinai: Exod 19:25–20:20
      Exod 19:25 ("Moses descended [*yrd*] to the people")
Exod 20:21–24:11 (*Book of the Covenant*—Exod 20:23–23:33)
   A. Moses on Mount Sinai: Exod 20:21–24:2
      Exod 20:21 ("Moses drew near [*ngš*] to the thick darkness where God was")
   B. Moses at the base of Mount Sinai: Exod 24:3–11
      Exod 24:3a (Moses approached [*bw'*] . . . the people")
Exod 24:12–32:35 (*Priestly Legislation*—Exodus 25–31)
   A. Moses on Mount Sinai: Exod 24:12–32:14
      Exod 24:12 ("Yahweh said to Moses, 'Ascend [*'lh*] to me' ")
   B. Moses at the base of Mount Sinai: Exod 32:15–29
      Exod 32:15 ("Moses descended [*yrd*] from the mountain")[18]
Exod 34:1–35 (*Legislation of Covenant Renewal*—Exod 34:11–26)
   A. Moses on Mount Sinai: Exod 34:1–28
      Exod 34:4 ("[Moses] ascended [*'lh*] Mount Sinai")
   B. Moses at the base of Mount Sinai: Exod 34:29–35
      Exod 34:29 ("When Moses descended [*wayĕhî bĕredet*] from the mountain")

The movement of Moses on Mount Sinai not only provides structure to the Sinai narrative, but also becomes a spatial-form device, itself, in the canonical form of the text. The repetitive trips by Moses up the mountain often interrupt the progression of the narrative. Problems in temporal sequence begin with the opening scene, when Moses functions in an office of mediation to which he is only later appointed (Exod 19:9a).[19] But even the appointment of Moses as mediator in the second scene disrupts the narrative logic, for we expect a divine speech directed to the people in response to their acceptance of the Proposal of Covenant.[20] Then the narrative is stopped completely in Exod 19:20 when Moses ascends the mountain in the midst of theophany only to have Yahweh negate earlier commands that Israel would ascend Mount Sinai at the sound of trumpets. The result of this unexpected ascent by Moses is that Yahweh promulgates the Decalogue to Moses alone.[21] Finally, we have already seen from Wellhausen's assessment of the narrative that these dislocations of temporal sequence continue in the following scenes (Exod 20:21; 24:12; 34:1) as Moses repeatedly ascends the mountain for the same purpose of receiving still more legislation.

Thus, instead of establishing a clear temporal sequence to the Sinai narrative, the repetitive movement of Moses creates scenes that are juxtaposed to each other much like the segments of an orange. Moses' ascents provide the narrative context for the promulgation of distinct legal codes, which are now all anchored in the one revelation on Mount Sinai. Each scene, therefore, now provides a different perspective on the same core event, with the result that the canonical form of the Sinai narrative appears to be a series of images of the same thing: the revelation of Yahweh on Mount Sinai and the giving of Torah there. The repetitive movement of Moses is one of the central devices which allows for the promulgation of the distinct legal codes within this one revelation of God.

The movement of Moses, as a spatial-form device, forces the reader "to project not so much forward ('what happens next') as backward or sideways" to uncover the progression of the Sinai narrative. But the effect of spatial-form techniques on the reader does not end at this point, for the promulgation of law by Yahweh on Mount Sinai is an additional spatial-form device. Long sections of legislation, which correlate with the movement of Moses on Mount Sinai, suspend temporal sequence for chapters at a time. Throughout these extended divine discourses on law, the reader repeatedly loses a sense of the past, present, and future of narrated time. But this loss of narrated time serves a canonical purpose, for the result is that the reader's time becomes the significant moment for interpreting the promulgation of Torah "on this day."[23]

NOTES

[1] For further reading on spatial form in narrative see also Wellek and Warren (212–25), Todorov (1977:108–19, 1980:41–47).

[2] Childs (1979:170) also notes the subordination of chronology within the book of Exodus in general and in the Sinai narrative in particular, which leads him to conclude that the interest of the writer "falls on certain specific moments within the history."

³ Additional support for interpreting temporal references in the Sinai narrative as a means for emphasizing significant events rather than for providing chronological sequence is their stylized arrangement in the narrative. For example, the two forty-day stays on the mountain by Moses clearly balance each other (Exod 24:18; 34:28). Furthermore, the appearance of Yahweh in Exodus 19 is balanced by Israel's construction of the golden calf in Exodus 32, with both events being structured into a three-day period with the time-words *māhār* (Exod 19:10; 32:5, 6, 30) and *bayyôm/hayyôm* (Exod 19:10, 16; 32:28, 29). See De Vries (73) on the function of *māhār* as marking the quality of an event. He concludes that this word can signify a "decisive manifestation of Yahweh's will and power."

⁴ On the introductory function of Exod 19:1–8a see Noth (154) and Childs (1974:360).

⁵ Exod 19:2b–3a has been judged to be a unit of older tradition for five reasons: (1) the subject change from "sons of Israel" in Exod 19:1 to "Israel" in Exod 19:2b (Wellhausen, 1899:96); (2) also the verb changes from plural in Exod 19:2a to singular in Exod 19:2b (Zenger:57); (3) a doublet of content between Exod 19:2ag and Exod 19:2b (Noth:157); (4) the reference to God as Elohim in Exod 19:3a could be a proper name rather than an appellative (Rudolph, 1938:42); and (5) the reference to the mountain as *hāhār* evokes the older Mountain of God tradition from Exod 17:6; 18:5 (Booij:17).

⁶ Exod 12:37; 13:20; 14:1; 15:22, 27; 16:1; 17:1a. For more detailed analysis of the vocabulary of the itinerary notices see Coats (136–38).

⁷ Num 33:15 reads, "They [Israel] journeyed from Rephidim, and they camped in the wilderness of Sinai." See Cross (309–17) for an interpretation of Numbers 33 as the source document for the wilderness itinerary.

⁸ This sequence corresponds to Exod 16:1, which also includes a temporal reference at the end of the itinerary notice.

⁹ Solutions for harmonizing the two temporal clauses have gone in two directions. (1) One avenue of interpretation argues that *baḥōdeš* in this instance was originally intended to be read as "new moon" and thus designates a specific day (Noth:155). But the syntax suggests the more general reference to "month" (Gen 7:11; Num 9:22). As Dillmann (191) points out, we would expect *bĕ'eḥād laḥōdeš* for a reference to a specific day (see Gen 8:5; Exod 40:2; Num 1:1, 18; 29:11). (2) An even more unlikely solution would be to interpret *bayyôm hazzeh* in a general sense, and thus not referring to a specific day (Keil:489).

¹⁰ The Mountain of God tradition continues in Exod 19:10–11a, 12a*a*, 13b–5a. See Gressmann (180 *et passim*) who argues that these units are one tradition, consisting of a third version of theophany within the Elohist tradition. Compare also Rudolph (1938:42–44) and Zenger (67) for a similar division, but with different tradition-historical evaluations.

¹¹ The complete designation of the "wilderness of Sinai" in Exod 19:2a*b* accounts for the abbreviated reference to "wilderness" in Exod 19:2a*c*. Thus there is no reason to conclude as Zenger (57) does that Exod 19:2a*c* is redactional because it does not refer specifically to the wilderness of Sinai.

¹² On the effect of this linking in the present form of the text Cassuto's (225) conclusion is instructive: "Only this is clearly to be inferred from the passages (Exod 19:1–2), that the mountain called in this section Mount Sinai is the same as the one named in chapter iii 'the mountain of God' and Horeb. . . .'"

¹³ See, for example, Clifford (109) who concludes that "this exclusively Priestly use (wilderness of Sinai) . . . does not associate a mountain with Sinai. . . ." In addition, reference to the wilderness of Sinai is confined to priestly tradition: Exod 19:1, 2; Lev 7:38; Num 1:1, 19; 3:4, 14; 9:1, 5; 10:12; 26:64; 33:15, 16.

¹⁴ The implication of this analysis would suggest that the account of a revelation of law on Mount Sinai is a late tradition-historical development within priestly tradition. A complete analysis of this thesis is beyond the scope of the present study. See Booij (21), who suggests that perhaps "a mountain-of-God tradition has been shaped 'Sinaitically' " in the present form of the Sinai narrative.

[15] The LXX^B reads *ek tou ouranou* ("out of heaven") as the place from which Yahweh called to Moses in Exod 19:3b. Rudolph (1938:432 n. 2) suggests a mistake for *orous* ("mountain"), which is the preferred reading. But the matter is complicated by the reference to heaven in Exod 20:22, which parallels Exod 19:3b-4 in form and vocabulary. At the very least this raises the question of whether Exod 19:3b always included the reference to the mountain or originally located Yahweh's speech from heaven as in Exod 20:22. The location of heaven for Yahweh's speech also corresponds with deuteronomic parenesis in Deut 4:36.

[16] Driver (168) writes, "in xix. 3a Moses 'goes up' into the mountain, but in v. 3b he is apparently below, and the natural sequel to 'went up' in v. 3a would be, not 'came' in v. 7. . . ." See also Perlitt (168) and Zenger (58).

[17] An additional effect of the present canonical context of the Mountain of God tradition and the deuteronomic Proposal of Covenant is that if Elohim did indeed function as a proper name in the older Mountain of God tradition, such a reading is no longer possible. In its present context, Elohim must be read as an appellative followed by the proper name Yahweh.

[18] Moses also ascends Mount Sinai in Exod 32:31 to make atonement for the people. But Yahweh's rejection of Moses' offer of atonement stops this cycle prematurely, which leads to the intercession of Moses for the presence of Yahweh in Exodus 33. No legislation is promulgated in this section; rather the intercession of Moses sets the stage for the legislation of covenant renewal in Exodus 34.

[19] McCarthy (157) writes about the opening scene: "That Moses should act as mediator in virtue of his general position is easy enough to accept. That he should be described as so acting in a special capacity to which he is then specifically appointed immediately afterwards seems impossible."

[20] The problem in narrative logic here concerns both a change in theme, from covenant to the coming of Yahweh, and a change in the object of Yahweh's discourse, from Israel (Exod 19:3b-6) to Moses (Exod 19:9a). See Perlitt (168) and Childs (1974:368).

[21] Childs (368) summarizes the general assessment of this section by past scholars as being "a dismal anticlimax which disturbs the ongoing movement of the chapter."

[22] This effect of spatial-form devices corresponds with Childs' (1979) description of canon as literature which is not limited to the historical past, but shaped in such a way as to be read continually in the present.

WORKS CONSULTED

Booij, Th.
    1984   "Mountain and Theophany in the Sinai Narrative." *Bib* 65:1–26.

Cassuto, Umberto
    1967   *A Commentary on the Book of Exodus.* Jerusalem: Magnes.

Childs, Brevard S.
    1974   *Exodus.* OTL. Philadelphia: Westminster.
    1979   *Introduction to the Old Testament Scripture.* Philadelphia: Fortress

Clifford, Richard J.
    1972   *The Cosmic Mountain in Canaan and the Old Testament.* HMS 4. Cambridge: Harvard University.

Coats, George W.
    1972   "The Wilderness Itinerary." *CBQ* 34:135–52.

Cross, Frank M.
    1973   *Canaanite Myth and Hebrew Epic. Essays in the History of the Religion of Israel.* Cambridge: Harvard University.

De Vries, Simon J.
1975   "The Time Word *māhār* as a Key to Tradition Development." *ZAW* 87:65–79.

Dillmann, August
1880   *Die bücher Exodus und Leviticus*. Kurzgefasstes exegetisches Handbuch zum Alten Testament 12. Leipzig: S. Hirzel.

Driver, S. R.
1929   *The Book of Exodus*. The Cambridge Bible. Cambridge: Cambridge University.

Eissfeldt, Otto
1966   *Die Komposition der Sinai-Erzählung Exodus 19–34*. Sitzungsberichte der Sächsischen Akademie der Wissenschaften zu Leipzig 113/1. Berlin: Akademie.

Gressmann, Hugo
1913   *Mose und seine Zeit*. FRLANT 18. Göttingen: Vandenhoeck & Ruprecht.

Keil, C. F.
1861   *Die Bücher Mose's*. Biblischer Commentar Erster Band Genesis und Exodus. Leipzig: Dörfflung und Franke.

Knutson, J. B.
1975   "Literary Genres in PRU IV." Pp. 191–94 in *Ras Shamra Parallels II*. AnOr 50. Rome: Pontifical Biblical Institute.

Lotman, Jüri
1977   *The Structure of the Artistic Text*. Michigan Slavic Contributions 7. Ann Arbor: University of Michigan.

McCarthy, Dennis J.
1963   *Treaty and Covenant: A Study in form in the Ancient Oriental Documents and in the Old Testament*. AnBib 21. Rome: Pontifical Biblical Institute.

Mickelsen, David
1981   "Types of Spatial Structure in Narrative." Pp. 63–78 in *Spatial Form in Narrative*. Ed. Jeffry R. Smitten and Ann Daghistany. Ithaca: Cornell University.

Muilenburg, James
1959   "The Form and Structure of the Covenantal Formulations." *VT* 9:347–65.

Noth, Martin
1962   *Exodus*. Trans. J. S. Bowden. OTL. Philadelphia: Westminster.

Patrick, Dale
1977   "The Covenant Code Source." *VT* 27:145–57.

Perlitt, Lothar
1969   *Bundestheologie im Alten Testament*. WMANT 36. Neukirchen-Vluyn: Neukirchener.

Rivard, Richard
1981   "Pour une Relecture d'Ex 19 et 20: Analyse Semiotique d'Ex 19, 1–8." *ScEs* 33:335–56.

Rudolph, Wilhelm
    1935   "Der Aufbau von Exodus 19–34." Pp. 41–48 in *Werden und Wesen des Alten Testaments*. BZAW 66. Berlin: Töpelmann.
    1938   *Der Elohist von Exodus bis Joshua*. BZAW 68. Berlin: de Gruyter.

Smitten, Jeffrey R. and Ann Daghistany
    1981   "Editor's Preface." Pp. 13–14 in *Spatial Form in Narrative*. Ed. J. R. Smitten and A. Daghistany. Ithaca: Cornell University.

Todorov, Tzvetan
    1977   *The Poetics of Prose*. Ithaca: Cornell University.
    1980   *Introduction to Poetics*. Theory and History of Literature 1. Minneapolis: University of Minnesota.

Van Dyke Parunak, H.
    1983   "Transitional Techniques in the Bible." *JBL* 102:525–48.

Wellek, René and Austin Warren
    1977   *Theory of Literature*. 3d ed. New York: Harcourt Brace Jovanovich.

Wellhausen, Julius
    1957   *Prolegomena to the History of Ancient Israel*. Trans. Menzies and Black (from the 1883 ed.). New York: Meridian.
    1899   *Die Composition des Hexateuchs und der historischen bücher des Alten Testament*. 3d ed. Berlin: Georg Reimer.

Wildberger, Hans
    1960   *Jahwes Eigentumsvolk*. ATANT 37. Stuttgart: Zwingli.

Zenger, Erich
    1971   *Die Sinaitheophanie: Untersuchung zum jahwistischen und elohistischen Geschichtswerk*. Forschung zur Bibel. Würzburg: Echter Verlag Katholisches Bibelwerk.

THE INSTITUTIONAL MATRIX OF TREACHERY IN 2 SAMUEL 11

Joel Rosenberg
Tufts University

ABSTRACT

Readers of the David and Bathsheba story are accustomed to seeing the story as an episode of personal failing that, for all its critical timing and historical reverberation, bears little intrinsic relation to the political events and social order described in 2 Samuel and 1 Kings 1–2. Historians, for their part, use the stories in Samuel and Kings to reconstruct political history, but at the expense of the material's narrative subtlety, which is seen as but an incidental bonus in the text's unfolding as history. This essay shows how the physical and logistical details set forth in the opening lines of 2 Samuel 11 form a portrait of the institutional history of Israel during the monarchic revolution. Every detail of the king's interaction with his servants; his court's relation to the distant battlefield; his relation to the institutions of holy war and mercenary combat; his sense of protocol and priorities; his manner of conveying and receiving information; and his vulnerability to manipulation, public scrutiny, and court gossip—each helps to build a tragic situation in which David is the criminal, and the nation both his accomplice and his victim. The study thereby seeks to show, by means of literary analysis, the role of story in a political history, and why institutional factors must be accorded special weight in exegesis.

Historians inquiring into the Davidic history frequently preface their efforts with some words of praise for the anonymous court historian of the so-called "Succession Document" (comprising, at a minimum, 2 Samuel 11– 1 Kings 2). This praise has certain recurring motifs: Wellhausen, for example (262) speaks of events "faithfully reported," Alt (268) of a "heightening of the historical conscience," Pfeiffer (357–59) of "historicity" and "strict objectivity," Sellin (163) of "true-to-life portrayal," and Bright (163) of "eyewitness flavor."[1] Alt, to be sure, also speaks of an author "who conceals rather than reveals," and Wellhausen, most engagingly, of "a naiveté which is almost malicious," but all observers cited here more or less assume a close and inevitable association between historical verisimilitude and literary artfulness. The literary artist is seen as the humble servant of events, not the agent by whose mediation the events were constituted as "events" in the first place. An analogous assumption underlies the frequent attribution of the story's authorship to a contemporary and intimate of—indeed, eyewitness to—the events narrated, which more or less takes for granted that it is the presence or access of the writer to the events that constitutes what is most significant, interesting, or usable—in short, from the historian's perspective, most "reliable"—about the court history.

The assumption is, of course, belied by the historians themselves when they get down to using the source for their discussions. For they do not talk, when at their best, about the influence of the court scandals, of David's tragic chastening, of the play of domestic feuds and intrigues, and the like, on Israel's early monarchic history. They talk, rather, about institutional relations; about military, diplomatic, and geographical factors; about socioeconomic and class conflict; about structural and political contradictions; about confederate and royal ideologies and the shifting balance of power. Yet most of this, somehow, they have learned from the text, and this indebtedness is not always properly accounted for.

A reverse kind of blind spot is encountered in the growing literary study of the court history, where the institutional domain has generally receded behind the play of psychological ambience, of personal moral choice, of the clash of will and the persistence of obsessions. Fokkelman speaks of symmetries, of ternary principles, and karmic justice; Perry and Sternberg of narrative irony and narrational gaps; Conroy of microcontextual narrative patterns, Gunn of art and entertainment. We need the physiognomies of the text these investigators provide, but, amid a flurry of charts and diagrams, one often misses a sense that our text is, after all, weighing and assessing real history. It thus makes sense of Israel's past in a manner that our modern historians have, if often for the wrong reasons, justifiably considered congenial to their own.

* * *

The pivotal figure in Israel's institutional history is, obviously enough, King David, to whom more pure narrative space is accorded than any other biblical character, including even Moses. Although he is not Israel's first king (and, given the typology of rulership in the era of the Judges, perhaps not even the *second*), he is the first to succeed in establishing a royal dynasty, and, as such, the figure through whom the presuppositions of dynastic institutions are anatomized. In Israel of the eleventh and tenth centuries B.C.E., as our text unfolds its history, the merits of dynastic leadership seem by no means self-evident or widely appreciated. Yet the parochial forces behind this resistance to monarchy maintain only the most muted presence in the books of Samuel and project their unresolved social tensions and political contradictions onto the figure of the judge or king, who, as in the mythological archetypes available to Israel from the Near Eastern milieu, served as a kind of paradigmatic man, a symbol of the body politic and expression of its will. David and his household so command the center of our attention in 2 Samuel that we are inclined to forget that this "center" is framed with care into a relation of texts. In that 1 Samuel 8 — the story of Israel's demand for a king in the days of Samuel and Saul — makes kingdom a project of the king's subjects, reflection on the fate of kingship in Israel must be seen as the vehicle of a reflection on Israelite society as a whole.

If David is the pivotal figure in that reflection, the David-Bathsheba episode in 2 Samuel 11 is pivotal to our understanding of his reign — not simply because Bathsheba is the dynastic mother, a status that (like Sarah's as ancestral mother) is to be clarified only at the end of a long narrative cycle, but because the melodrama of David's illicit affair is the occasion of a whole complex of routine gestures and messages, of terrain traversed and terrain avoided, of verbal choices and verbal slips, that do more to explain Israel's institutional changes than even the sober and discursive pen of the historian.[2] I want to illuminate here a part of that process and ask, in particular, if, indeed, it is verisimilitude and factuality that lie at the heart of the text's literary artfulness, or if another kind of process is at work.

* * *

The story opens with a curious textual ambiguity, seemingly only a problem for so-called "lower" criticism, but which, intentionally or otherwise, conveys a perplexity crucial to the story's unfolding:

It happened at the turning of the year, at the time when kings/agents go forth [to battle] . . . (2 Sam 11:1).

The consonantal text reads "agents"(*mal'ākîm*), but the Masoretic vocalization reads "kings" (*mĕlākîm*), the latter being the most widely accepted reading.[3] While it seems unwise to accord conflicting versions of a biblical word *equal* weight, the fact that the ambiguity exists at all suggests that conflicting interpretive pressures (what Barthes in another context called *pressions de lisibilité* [24]) may themselves have helped shape the history of the text. This is, after all, the first place in the Bible that a leader of Israel stays off the battlefield in time of war,[4] and the question of the role of agents in the conduct of kingly business returns again and again throughout the story (and, indeed, throughout the court history). Since a king, as defined in 1 Samuel 8, is *himself* an agent of the people, and his exit to battle a constitutive moment of his authority,[5] we find ourselves with an oddly convoluted inversion of kingly function in the king's preference of agents to represent him. In this transition to a sedentary monarchy, the agent within the king and the king within the agent seem at war with each other, a struggle indeed analogous to the opposition of consonantal and spoken text, the *kĕtîb* and the qĕrê. (Similarly, if Joab's literal taking of Rabbat-Ammon in 2 Sam 12:26 be thought of as a kĕtîb, the king's symbolic possession of the city in vv 27–31 constitutes quite literally a qĕrê.) The contradiction, at any rate, is borne out further by the details that immediately follow:

> ... that David sent Joab, and his servants with him, and all Israel, and they laid waste to the Ammonites, and laid siege upon Rabbah. David stayed in Jerusalem (1 Sam 11:1).

The inversion is made clear by the apparent hierarchy: Joab, second (or first) in command; his servants, i.e., the professional elite guard and largely foreign mercenary troops that had comprised David's extra-Israelite power base since his exile from Saul's court;[6] only last is "all Israel," namely, the tribal muster that comprised the oldest institution of warfare in ancient Israel, and that made the battle a specifically Israelite battle in the first place. It is unclear here who is hiring whom to do what. The pointed reference to David's remaining in Jerusalem, in any case, makes clear to us that war is being conducted in a very different way from that of the archaic tribal muster, with whose dynamics (and defects) we are familiar from the Song of Deborah (Judges 5). The rational and bureaucratic mode of statecraft that is David's specific innovation has better uses for the king than the charismatic and warlord functions that elevate a man to kingship in the first place. The advantages of a sedentary monarch are both practical and symbolic: as strategist, the king can move troops and materiel with greater freedom and suppleness than his location amid the heat of battle would permit. And, as symbol of the unity and continuity of the territorial state, the king's immobility creates a semantic and mythological bulwark of immense psychological value against any enemy, especially one like King Hanun of Ammon, whose challenge had specifically represented an attack on the legitimacy of the Cisjordanian ruler (2 Sam 10:1–5).[7]

David's genius as a monarch is shown here to consist of his overcoming a certain literalism of kingly function that had plagued both the reign and mental tranquility of Saul. Saul, to be sure, is shown anticipating the kingly style of David in certain important ways: by his movement within a cloud of agents, henchmen, and informers; by his responsibility for orchestrating the instrument of war; and by his establishment of the rudiments of a court and dynasty. But Saul's power rested, as the beginning of his reign suggests (1 Sam 11:5–13; cf. 10:9–13), in his personal military prowess and in the vagaries of prophetic inspiration. Both his reputation and his mind begin to come apart with the inevitable rise of younger rivals (like David, and, indeed, like his own son Jonathan) from within the ranks. Saul remains a kind of prisoner to the typology of judgeship. "Is Saul also among the prophets?" The obscure gnomon that appears in an etiological context in 1 Sam 10:9–13 and 1 Sam 19:18–24 hauntingly expresses Saul's inability to control the conditions of his own inspiration and ecstasy and serves as a kind of emblem for the curiously hybrid and unrealized nature of his kingship. David's public career remains largely untroubled by such imperatives. Strategy, deceit, and a certain aloofness from the sweat of battle characterize his reign. Whereas Saul has staked his legitimacy in a kind of frenzied effort to reduplicate his early successes on front after front, David discovers that a king's success can be predicated on the deeds of others. If the king does not have to be everywhere, he does not have to be anywhere but his home base.[8]

Thus far, at any rate, 2 Samuel 11 proceeds on the level of institutional history: the office of king and the conduct of war form the principal subject of the opening verse. Yet the outcome of the battle against the Ammonites (along with David's symbolic assumption of the mantle of military success) is not recounted until 2 Sam 12:26-31. If the pattern of parenthetic interpolation, which we know to be common to biblical narrative in general, holds true here, the ensuing tale of personal intrigue will comment in some way on the institutional and military history that forms the framework. This is borne out, though it might not seem that way initially, by what follows:

> And it happened one evening that David arose from his couch and went for a walk atop the roof of the King's house, and he saw from the rooftop a woman bathing. The woman was very beautiful. David inquired about the woman, and was told "Why, that's Bathsheba daughter of Eliam [and] wife of Uriah the Hittite." So David sent agents and summoned her, and she came to him and lay with him—she had just formally ended her monthly impurity—and she returned home (2 Sam 11:2-4).

A fairly ramified web of assumptions underlies these spare, rapid, almost calligraphic details. The otiose king is portrayed neither in ceremonies of state (as in numerous psalms) nor at work with his palace councils, but in distinctly private, and perhaps pointedly unflattering forms of leisure: napping, strolling, running after his eyes.[9] We note that he is not called "the King," nor "King David," but simply "David," yet the rooftop he treads rests on "the King's house," a tension in terminology that hints of one between man and role. Indeed, a certain relational instability inhabits the narrative at this point, suggested by the ambiguous preposition *mēʿal*, which can mean both "atop" and "from atop." Is it David's position ("He saw from atop the roof a woman bathing") or the woman's ("He saw a woman bathing atop [her] roof") that is referred to here?[10] Even the narrative voice takes on a suggestive ambiguity amid this description. We have not been explicitly apprised of David's thoughts about what he sees, but the narrative caesura effected by the phrase, "The woman was very beautiful," creates a voice that is neither purely narratorial nor purely the words of David's thoughts. Momentarily, all attention is focused exclusively on the spell exerted by the bathing woman. This typologically resonant phrase[11] transports us briefly into the cadences of the morality fable, yet the social context that frames it gives it special meaning.

We next learn that "David sent and inquired...," which can admit initially of two interpretations: either he summoned someone to the rooftop to gaze at the woman with him and to tell him who she was, or he sent a messenger to the woman's house to ask for her name. Either way, the ease with which aides are ever present to the king's (and, for that matter, to David's) bidding is masked only by the minimal way in which this court background is represented: informers, spies, and gossipers abound in the palace milieu, but their faces and names are obliterated; their discourse is a ubiquitous murmur cradling the action of the story's named figures, threatening their privacy and reverberating their deeds. Yet this is the very milieu on which the king's political and military success is founded. When the Arameans under Hadadezer, for example, mass troops at Helam (2 Sam 10:15–16), the text reports: "David was informed of it" (v 17). Indeed, one could do a fruitful comparison of the contexts in which the verb *lĕhaggîd* appears throughout the Saul and David histories.[12] Israel's dependence on informers in and around the Syro-Phoenician borders is a security policy not unique to the twentieth century (see Levanon:35). The Ammonite king Hanun, the man who had begun the conflict between Israel and an Ammonite-Aramean league, may have had good reason to fear David's legates as spies, or known of David's reputation for obtaining intelligence. The answer David now seeks, at any rate, from one of his anonymous informants, is clear in its essentials: "Why, that's...!"—a style of exclamation suggesting the former of the two alternatives mentioned earlier, namely, that someone is guessing the woman's identity from the king's vantage-point. The exclamation is then followed by Bathsheba's patronymic and her husband's name. The information, presumably helpful to David, is a double-edged sword: the king himself is a prisoner of his own network of gossip, as the unfolding of the story will make clear.

Now, it might strike us that "Uriah the Hittite" seems a curious way of designating one with a clearly Yahwist name, unless, to be sure, it is a Hebraization of a Hittite name.[13] The Hittite presence in David's Jerusalem, while disputed (cf. de Vaux, 1978:134–36), is quite plausible, and it might be quite appropriate that Uriah, as a member of the entrenched aristocracy that antedated David's conquest of the city would, in good Canaanite fashion, have sought the protection and patronage of the new strong man of the region, much as the Hittites of Hebron had paid homage to David's typological ancestor Abraham in his day and intertwined their interests with his (see Levanon:37; 2 Sam 23:39; 24:18–25; 2 Chron 11:10, 41; 21:18–25). The "Yahwism" of Uriah's name can be seen as a tactfully patriotic concession to the winds of change. Uriah's position as one of David's *gibbōrîm* ("strongmen") (see 2 Sam 23:8ff.; 1 Chron 11:10ff.) should cause us to modify somewhat the picture of Uriah as a humble foot-soldier that the general drift of 2 Samuel 11 encourages us to assume.[14] One whose name is accompanied by a designation as foreigner and whose dwelling is located so near "the king's house" is very likely a prominent member of royal-military circles, one well-enough known to the king's courtiers, if not to the king himself, that his naked wife seen from an adjacent rooftop would trigger astonishment of a rather precise nature.

David now sends "agents"—again, a conspicuous choice of words that suggests a cloak of secrecy.[15] The agents fetch Bathsheba; we are not told by what means, nor do we learn of the woman's reactions, nor of the nature of the blandishments, threats, or other inducements that motivate her to lie with David. The simplicity and rapidity of the action at this point suggest that her resistance, if any, was minimal, or perhaps (within the scope of this chapter, at least) irrelevant.

The general appearance of the woman as passive and acquiescent at this stage of the court history stands in sharp contrast to her boldness at the end of the history, when her decisive intervention throws the dynastic succession to her son Solomon (1 Kings 1). Only by hindsight, blurred by the passing of nearly twenty turbulent years, do we recall the Bathsheba of 2 Samuel 11; only then, much belatedly, do we wonder about her assertiveness in the first encounter. By then, of course, her boldness may owe itself to other factors: her years of (unreported) experience of court life, the clear favor that Solomon occupies in David's eyes, or the enfeeblement of the aged king. So again there is no clear clue to her behavior in the adultery episode. In any case, the dispatching of "agents" is a detail conforming to the larger pattern of the king's reliance on agents for the conduct of state business. The adultery with Bathsheba is thus shown as a byproduct of more or less the same apparatus that enabled David to know in advance of Aramean troop movements, and matters of similar strategic import.

The seemingly parenthetic annotation "—she had just formally ended her monthly impurity—," as commentators observe, sets the framework for the action which follows: if Uriah had left for battle prior to or during Bathsheba's isolation from conjugal relations, her later pregnancy (1 Sam 11:5) cannot be attributed to him unless he can be brought home and somehow induced to cohabit with her (e.g., Perry and Sternberg:271–76). David now embarks on such a plan. His first interchange with Uriah takes only two verses, but again a number of institutionally weighted factors are brought to bear in these compressed sentences:

> Uriah came to him. David asked about the welfare of Joab, the welfare of the people, and the welfare of the war. David said to Uriah: "Go down to your house, and wash your feet." Uriah went out from the king's house, and the king's provisions went out after him (vv 7–8).

The priorities of protocol in David's amenities are similar to the palace-downward hierarchy presented in the story's opening verses (with the notable absence of Joab's "servants," the elite military body to which Uriah belongs, and with the notable addition of "the war," as if political disorder itself were somehow part of the ranks). No specific conversation is recorded at this point, although we must assume that more detailed words would have been exchanged, and that the three subjects mentioned delineate the main parameters of their discussion, in the order of their importance to David. Because, with one exception, the thoughts and words of Uriah are nowhere recorded in the story (and David's thoughts, while deducible from his words, are not stated by the narrator), we have no idea of the specific tone, tenor, and tensions of their conversation. We have no idea of whether Uriah was used to serving this function as bearer of battlefield tidings, whether David routinely asked the questions he asks here, or whether both men were struggling through an uncomfortable encounter. Yet we do know something of David's preoccupations at this point, without being informed directly. Our awareness of context supplies a new meaning to David's words that may or may not be perceived by Uriah.[16]

It is worthwhile here, however, to concentrate not so much on speculation about Uriah's thoughts, but on the relation between what David's words mean and what they purport to mean. We see here that the split between "David" and "the king" can again be observed, even if David is, in a sense, hiding behind "the king" (as when we are told: "the king's provisions went out after him"). David relies at this moment on a certain kind of kingly chatter, which *sounds* like a gracious king bestowing rest on his hardworking and loyal messenger. It is of course in David's interest that these words not be perceived by Uriah as too obtrusive or jarring (one can well imagine a thoroughly neutral and uneventful official conversation preceding this invitation, a conversation from which David hopes to glide imperceptibly into the hidden agenda). Yet the words jar, if only because they are the first direct discourse of the exchange, and because they cannot avoid intruding one half-clause too far ("and wash your feet") into the delicate intangibles of Uriah's domestic life, in order to press upon Uriah a trajectory of action that David hopes will lead further. In a sense, it may not even matter to David whether the action proceeds further. Uriah's return to his house is all that matters; the appearance that he has come home to resume all normal domestic activities is sufficient to sow the appropriately neutralizing rumor on the winds of gossip.

At this point, however, David makes a fateful miscalculation, for which his command of protocol and his assumptions about Uriah have not prepared him. In a story where such a clear division was made from the start between the elite guard and the Israelite muster, David would have no particular reason to believe that members of the respective bodies would observe the same religious code in respect to war duties and their suspension. He, more than anyone, knows what a mixed multitude he has created through his years of isolation from Israelite institutions and through his gradual incorporation of Philistine, Canaanite, and Hittite elements into his ranks. While David was particularly sensitive to the semantic nature of his actions and restraints concerning religious sensibilities, we may assume that he would have displayed a certain liberal courtliness (out of the same instincts for tact and expedience) toward his marginal Israelites and adopted Yahwists. We have other examples of David's worldly pragmatism and his cavalier attitude toward religious ritual (see 2 Sam 13:20-23; also 1 Sam 21:6 and McCarter, 1980:365; Brueggemann:7-8). So it makes perfectly good sense at this point that he assume it within the prerogatives of the monarch to grant such dispensations, even where they might contradict the practices and institutions of Israelite holy war.[17] For this reason, David is caught by surprise in what follows:

> Uriah lay down at the gate of the king's house, with all his master's servants. He did not go down to his house. They reported to David: "Uriah did not go down to his house." David said to Uriah: "Haven't you come from a journey? Why didn't you go down to your house?"
> Uriah said to David: "The Ark and Israel and Judah are dwelling in makeshift dwellings (or: in Succoth), and my master Joab and the servants of milord are camping on the face of the field — and I should go to my house to eat and drink, and lie with my wife?! On your life, as your soul lives, I shall not do this thing!" (vv 9-11).

There could be no clearer expression of the clash between cultural codes. The king's appeal to the common sense propriety of resting from a journey in wartime presupposes an essentially secular use of the instrument of war, whereas Uriah's reply presupposes the confederate standard of the holy war: the highest symbol of authority is the Ark; the tribal muster is mentioned next, conspicuously ordered by region ("Israel and Judah"); they dwell in booths (or, a term with both historical and ritual resonances: "in Succoth"); only last is "my master Joab and milord's servants"—the ambiguity of the "milord" (Joab or David?) suggests to us both the king's remoteness from the core and Uriah's sincere grounds for doubt about David's presence to the events at all. Uriah's name turns out to be Yahwist, after all. In the heart of the imperial phalanges we find an orthodox Israelite, quietly observing the wartime soldier's ban against conjugal relations (cf. 1 Sam 21:4-7). The significance is double: it compounds the enormity of David's crime (violating a marriage is bad enough; violating a marriage under sacred conjugal suspension is a particularly cruel and nasty offense); and it attests to the vitality of the confederate faith that it could take root amid the ranks of those structurally the most independent from the confederate polity.

*   *   *

I will leave us at this point in the story, focused on David's astonishment, for we have here a particularly ripe and pregnant moment amid which to assess our critical dilemma: is the story meaningful to us because it illuminates an institutional juncture, or is that juncture meaningful to us because it reaches us through the devices of story? We need, perhaps, a mode of inquiry that gives no privileged position to the one or the other of the two alternatives. In the textual example I have focused on here, we have seen that the art of storytelling is no mere decorative adjunct to a lived experience that is now being faithfully "reported." Rather, it is the currency of thought itself, the agent by which the raw events of political history are constituted as "history" in the first place. Through the motions and turns of the narration, the key issues and contradictions in Israel's political evolution are distilled for the reader's active input and interpretation. We see that hardly a moment in the text elapses without communicating something fundamental about Israel's institutional history, so that the story, far from being reportage with an aim of verisimilitude, is a kind of cipher or parable of larger realities. That such a process can be shown to exist in a text which has long been held to be the most fact-like and circumstantial of the Hebrew Bible's narratives should cause us to modify radically the view of Israel's literary history that had rested on the cornerstone of the "eyewitness" connection. Once that questionable edifice begins to come apart, David's astonishment may, in some sense, mirror our own.

NOTES

[1] Cf. also von Rad (1966:166–204, esp. 193).

[2] One wishes, in a way, for a treatment that combines the perspectives of Perry and Sternberg with that of Moshe Garsiel (100ff.), who justly faults Perry and Sternberg for their inattention to institutional factors, but who sacrifices in the process their subtler grasp of the text's manner of ellipsis and indirection. Thus, what Perry and Sternberg have portrayed as an isolated moral failing on the king's part in his staying home from battle, Garsiel shows to represent a pivotal institutional change: the necessity of preserving the king's (dynastic) person as political figurehead, which is summarized etiologically in 2 Sam 21:15–17. Yet Garsiel, for his part, overlooks the general subordination of this "dynastic" etiology to the story's moral and psychological themes.

[3] So MT[MSS], LXX (*eis ton chairon tēs exodias ton basileōn*), OL, Tg., Vg, and 1 Chron 20:1; cf. also Josephus *Ant.* 7:120, RSV, et al. But see Syriac. Fokkelman, preferring the MT as *lectio difficilior*, reads "envoys," with reference to the diplomats sent by David in 2 Sam 10:2. Hertzberg (303, 305), reading "kings," places the verse as the closing verse of the account of the Ammonite war in 2 Samuel 10. McCarter (1984:284–85) refers the "kings" to the Aramean coalition of 2 Sam 10:6–2 Sam 11:1 thus marking the turning of one year since their original sally in defense of the Ammonites.

[4] On the role of the king/judge in Near Eastern and Israelite holy war, see, among others Frankfort (36–60); de Vaux (1965:100–104); Ishida (6–25); Halpern (1–109); von Rad (1969); Smend; Miller.

[5] See 1 Sam 8:20; cf. 11:4–7. On the affiliation of royal investiture with procession into battle, cf. Halpern (132), who reads Isa 51:9; 52:1–2; Ps 93:1, and Job 40:10 as presuming a military context. See Ishida (47–48), who stresses the importance of the tribal leadership in securing a charismatic warrior-king in the era of Samuel and Saul. See Alt (258), on Saul's role in raising and leading troops. The narrative significance of David's remaining sedentary and in Jerusalem

⁶ Alt (248, 264). Cf. 1 Sam 22:1-2 (400 men, recruited from among the discontented of the land); 23:13; 27:2-28:3; 30:9 (600 men, now having the character of a mercenary army). Cf. 2 Sam 10:6.

⁷ On the background of David's relation to Hanun and his father Nahash, see Hertzberg (203-4; McCarter (1984:273-74); and Fokkelmann (42), who associates David's homage to the house of Nahash the Ammonite with the latter's enmity toward Saul, in connection with the events told in 1 Samuel 11.

⁸ It follows that the king need not be an ecstatic, since the display of his transported state is no longer the chief instrument for the raising and rallying of troops, as outlined classically for the "judge" pattern in Judg 3:7-11, esp. v 10 (but cf. 3:26 where the sounding of a ram's horn seems to substitute for this element). See also Judg 6:34; 11:29; 13:25; 14:6, 19; 15:14; and Boling (31-83). McCarter (1980:187) views the prophetic pattern as a form-critical category influential in the shaping of Israelite tradition—so, too, Birch (55-68, esp. 61-66) and Richter (13-29)— without, apparently seeing in it an institutional basis appropriate to the period of judges, a matter made more explicit by Halpern (114). See Halpern's allusion to the rarity of reference to prophetic inspiration in connection with Israel's kings (found only in 2 Sam 23:2, and perhaps in 1 Kings 3:5ff.). While David, at his public debut in 1 Sam 17:38ff., can be said to be "inspired" in a colloquial sense of the term, the episode is notable for the conspicuous absence of prophetic ecstasy and for the emphasis on common sense and cunning.

⁹ I borrow this last expression from Num 15:39. The unguarded or compromised posture of a king, prince, military leader, or hero is a frequent motif: see Judg 3:15-25; 4:17-21; 5:24-27; 9:52-55; 16:15-21; 2 Sam 2:23; 3:27, 32-34; 4:5-8, etc.

¹⁰ Compare textual variants: OL^{L15}: *per porticum;* Tg.^{MSS}: *'l 'ygr'*; Vg.: *ex adverso super solarium suum.*

¹¹ See permutations of this and similar expressions in Gen 12:11, 14; 24:16; 26:7; 29:17; 39:6; 41:2, 4, 18; Deut 21:11; 1 Sam 16:12; 17:42; 25:3; 2 Sam 13:1; 14:7; 1 Kings 1:3, 4; Esth 1:11; 2:3, 7, etc.

¹² See 1 Sam 14:33; 17:31; 18:20, 24; 19:19, 21; 23:7, 13; 24:2; 27:4 (all instances of reporting to Saul); 1 Sam 15:12 (to Samuel); 1 Sam 18:26; 23:1, 25; 25:12; 2 Sam 2:4; 3:23; 6:12; 10:5; 17:21, etc. (to David); 2 Sam 19:2 (to Joab); 1 Kings 1:51 (to Solomon).

¹³ Such as the more identifiably Hittite name "Araunah"—Hitt. *a-ra-u-wa-ni,* "freeman, aristocrat"—in 2 Sam 24:18ff. On the name "Araunah," see Rosen (318-20); Hertzberg (414n.); McCarter (1984:507 n. 20, 512, comment on 2 Sam 24:18).

¹⁴ See, especially, Uriah's retort to David in 2 Sam 11:11, which, despite its unusual frankness toward a superior, bespeaks more the foot-soldier than the professional officer (see my discussion further on), as does his ready obedience in verse 14 in conveying an order he apparently is not authorized to unseal.

¹⁵ The legates that had been sent on David's *public* mission to Ammon in 2 Sam 10:2 were called "his servants," not "his agents." Compare Saul's use of "agents" (which, given David's reputation would likely have been secret operations) in 1 Sam 19:11, 14, 15, 16, 20, 21 (bis), and David's use (which, given his precarious position at that time, would have likely been secret) in 1 Sam 25:14. See also Judg 11:17, where a context of secrecy is presumed, even though the line itself is spoken by "agents" in what appears to be a forthright delegation (see vv 11, 14) to the Ammonite king Nahash. There seem to be several contexts of the word "agents": as a secret delegation to a more powerful person, where the sender is outlawed or out of favor (so Num 2:26; Judg 11:17, et al.); as a lawful but perhaps confidential communication where the sender proposes an alliance or beneficial assistance (so, e.g., 2 Sam 2:5; 5:11); as an aggressive action, where the legal or moral grounds of the sender's demand is questionable (so, Num 22:5, the Saul actions cited above, and David's in 2 Sam 3:14 and 11:4). There is, in general, an undertone of covenant rhetoric (recital of favors past) in what often seems to be a request for return of good

(*ṭôbâ; ṭôb*) for good, kindness (*ḥesed*) for kindness, amid a general absence of *de jure* alliance.

[16] On the complicated question of Uriah's awareness of the circumstances, see esp. Perry and Sternberg (271-76).

[17] Marcus (165-66) argues with some justification that no legal basis can be found for arguing that a ban on cohabitation was in effect for soldiers home from the battlefield (see Deut 23:10-15; Josh 3:5; 1 Sam 20:6; also Exod 19:10, 15 – all instances where an anticipated theophany required ritual purity, and so presumably only in the area of the theophany *per se*). But this argument from silence is clearly contradicted by Uriah's retort, where it is made clear that he still considers himself *on* duty, and subject to the battlefield regimen. See McCarter (1984:286-87), who connects the cadences of Uriah's retort with David's own statement in 2 Sam 7:1, and with the oath attributed to David in Ps 132:3-5:

> I will not enter the shelter of my house
> I will not lie on the cushions of my bed,
> I will not let my eyes have sleep, or my eyelids slumber
> until I find a place for YHWH, a dwelling place for Jacob's Bull.

WORKS CONSULTED

Alt, Albrecht
    1968   "The Formation of the Israelite State" (1930). Pp. 225–309 in *Essays on Old Testament History and Religion*. Trans. R. A. Wilson. Garden City: Anchor Books.

Barthes, Roland
    1974   "The Struggle with the Angel: Textual Analysis of Genesis 32:23-33." Pp. 21–33 in R. Barthes, F. Bovon, et al. Eds. *Structural Analysis and Biblical Exegesis*. Trans. Alfred M. Johnson, Jr. PTMS 3. Pittsburgh: Pickwick.

Birch, Bruce C.
    1971   "The Development of the Tradition of the Anointing of Saul in I Sam 9:1-10:16." *JBL* 90:55-68.

Boling, Robert C.
    1975   *Judges*. AB 6A. Garden City: Doubleday.

Bright, John
    1952   *A History of Israel*. 1st ed. Philadelphia: Westminster.

Brueggemann, Walter
    1972   "On Trust and Freedom: A Study of Faith in the Succession Narrative." *Int* 26:3-19.

Conroy, Charles C.
    1978   *Absalom Absalom! Narrative and Language in 2 Sam. 13-20*. AnBib. 81. Rome: Pontifical Biblical Institute.

Fokkelman, J. P.
    1981   *Narrative Art and Poetry in the Books of Samuel*. Vol. I. *King David*. Assen: Van Gorcum.

Frankfort, Henri
    1948   *Kingship and the Gods: A Study of Ancient Near Eastern Religion and the Integration of Society and Nature*. Chicago: University of Chicago.

Garsiel, Moshe
    1975   *The Davidic Kingdom: Studies in History and Reflections on Historiography.* Tel Aviv: Society for Biblical Studies. (in Hebrew).

Gunn, David M.
    1978   *The Story of King David: Genre and Interpretation.* JSOTSup 6. Sheffield: JSOT.

Halpern, Baruch
    1981   *The Constitution of the Monarchy in Israel.* HSM 25. Chico: Scholars.

Hertzberg, Hans Wilhelm
    1976   *I & II Samuel.* Trans. J. S. Bowden. OTL. Philadelphia: Westminster.

Ishida, Tomoo
    1977   *Royal Dynasties in Ancient Israel. A Study on the Formation and Development of Royal-Dynastic Ideology.* BZAW 142. Berlin and New York: de Gruyter.

Levanon, Avraham
    n.d.   *Joab: A Study in the Book of Samuel.* Jerusalem: Moses and Jacob Levanon Memorial Association (in Hebrew).

Marcus, David
    1986   "David the Deceiver and David the Dupe." *Prooftexts* 6:163-71.

McCarter, P. Kyle
    1980   *I Samuel.* AB 8. Garden City: Doubleday.
    1984   *II Samuel.* AB 9. Garden City: Doubleday.

Miller, Patrick D., Jr.
    1973   *The Divine Warrior in Ancient Israel.* HSM 5. Cambridge, MA: Harvard University.

Perry, Menahem and Meir Sternberg
    1968   "The King Viewed Ironically: On the Narrator's Devices in the Story of David and Bathsheba." *Hasifrut* 1:263-92 (in Hebrew).

Pfeiffer, Robert H.
    1948   *Introduction to the Old Testament.* New York: Harper & Row.

Rad, Gerhardt von
    1966   "The Beginning of Historical Writing in Ancient Israel." Pp. 166-204 in *The Problem of the Hexateuch and Other Essays.* Trans. E. W. Trueman Dicken. Edinburgh: Oliver and Boyd.
    1969   *Die heilige Krieg im alten Israel.* 5th ed. Göttingen: Vandenhoeck & Ruprecht.

Richter, Wolfgang
    1970   *Die sogenannte vorprophetischen Berufungsberichte.* FRLANT 101. Göttingen: Vandenhoeck & Ruprecht.

Ridout, G. P.
    1971   "Prose Compositional Techniques in the Succession Narrative." Ph.D. dissertation, Graduate Theological Union, Berkeley.

Rosén, Haiim B.
  1955   "Arawna—nom hittite?" *VT* 5:318-20.
Sellin. Ernst
  1968   *Introduction to the Old Testament.* Rev. George Fohrer. Trans. David Green. Nashville: Abingdon.
Smend, Rudolf
  1970   *Yahweh War and Tribal Confederation.* Nashville: Abingdon.
Vaux, Roland de
  1965   *Ancient Israel: Social and Religious Institutions.* New York: McGraw-Hill.
  1978   *The Early History of Israel.* Trans. David Smith. Philadelphia: Westminster.
Veijola, T.
  1979   "Salomo—der erstgeborene Bathsebas." Pp. 230-50 in *Studies in the Historical Books of the Old Testament.* Ed. J. A. Emerton. VTSup 30. Leiden: Brill.
Wellhausen, Julius
  1957   *Prolegomena to the History of Ancient Israel.* Trans. Menzies and Black (from the 1883 ed.). New York: Meridian.

III

Feminist Criticism of Biblical Narrative

THE HARLOT AS HEROINE: NARRATIVE ART AND SOCIAL PRESUPPOSITION IN THREE OLD TESTAMENT TEXTS

Phyllis A. Bird
Garrett-Evangelical Theological Seminary

ABSTRACT

The narrator as artist works within a historically determined social world in which shared understandings of language, gestures, roles, etc. create the repertoire of symbols and senses employed in literary creation. Full appreciation of narrative art consequently requires both literary and social (historical) criticism. This essay attempts to combine the two methodologies by examining the interrelationship of narrative art and social presupposition in three texts having a harlot, or assumed harlot, as a major actor (Gen 38:1-26; Josh 2:1-24; 1 Kgs 3:16-27). Two questions guide the investigation: (1) What is the image of the harlot assumed in the text? and (2) How does that image or understanding affect the construction or narration of the story? The study argues that each of the texts requires as its presupposition a view of the harlot as a marginal figure in the society, tolerated but despised, and that fundamental ambivalence toward the harlot's role is not resolved by any action of the harlot, either in literature or life.

A desire for brevity and alliteration in the title has led me to overextend the meaning of the term "heroine." It is intended here as a cover term for three cases in which a harlot (or assumed harlot) plays a major role in a biblical narrative. My aim in this article is to explore the role of social presupposition in narrative construction or story telling, using the case of the harlot, or prostitute,[1] as an example. I am convinced that literary art and social presuppositions are so interrelated in any literary work that adequate interpretation requires the employment of both literary criticism and social analysis. Neither alone suffices. Each makes assumptions about the other, often leaving them unrecognized and uncriticized. Here I want to focus on their interrelationships.

Narrative art, in whatever form and whatever degree of sophistication, depends upon highly selective and purposeful use of language and images. The narratives of the Hebrew Bible, especially those contained within the Pentateuch and Deuteronomistic History, represent a particularly compressed and selective form of story-telling art, in which individual terms or figures must carry far more weight of suggested meaning than in the more expansive and nuanced prose of the modern novel, or even of the novella (ancient or modern). Thus, when a designation such as *zônâ* is attached to a name or a figure, a picture is called up in the reader's or hearer's mind and a range of meanings, attitudes, and associations on which the narrator may draw in constructing or relating the story. The twofold question I want to address in this article is (1) what was the image and understanding of the *zônâ* assumed in each of the narratives? and (2) how was that image or understanding employed by the narrator, or how did it influence the construction or narration of the story?

In my analysis I have set aside the question of historicity, insofar as this was possible without violating the terms of the narrative. That is, I have not made a judgment about the historical claims made by any of the narratives. Each of the narratives I shall examine is presented as the account of a historical event, and historical experience may dictate much of the terms of each narrative. But each is also clearly a literary work that has been shaped in its presentation by social and literary considerations. It is to these that I wish to direct my attention.

In the space alotted to me I can neither give a full literary analysis of each narrative nor a complete portrait of the harlot as she is presented in the biblical texts and other relevant records from the ancient Near East. While I will draw from time to time on a broader study in progress,[2] I will concentrate my attention in this article on the information supplied by the three texts or required for their understanding. My procedure will be to comment on those features of the portrait of the harlot that have significance for the particular text under consideration and thus to compose and develop the picture as I move through the three texts. I will begin, however, with a brief preliminary sketch, summarizing those traits or elements that are essential to the portrait of the prostitute in Israelite society. My treatment of the individual cases will attempt to explain and defend that sketch.

First, definition and terminology. A prostitute, or harlot, is a woman who offers sexual favors for pay (Gagnon:592; cf. Gebhard:75–81).[3] In the Hebrew Bible she is normally designated by the single term *zônâ*, a Qal participle from the root *znh*, used either alone, as a substantive, or attributively.[4] Her social status is that of an outcast, though not an outlaw, a tolerated, but dishonored member of society. She normally has the legal status of a free citizen; where she is a slave, or is otherwise legally dependent, it is not because of her occupation. As a free citizen she may seek the legal protection of the state, and as a woman who is not under the authority of a husband, she may have rights of legal action (e.g., signing contracts) not possessed by other women, except hierodules and widows without male guardians. She is typically contrasted to the "normal" woman, i.e., the married woman, from whom she is separated spatially and symbolically, through distinctive dress[5] and habitat. The places and times of her activity maintain distance between her and the married woman. She is a woman of the night, who appears on the streets when honorable women are secluded at home. She approaches strangers and businessmen by the roadside and in the public squares, and she lives in the shadow of the wall, on the outskirts of the city, where the refuse is dumped.[6]

Prostitution is not a universal phenomenon, nor can it properly claim to be the world's oldest profession (Gebhard:76). But it *is* characteristic of urban society, and more specifically of urban patriarchal society. It is a product and sign of the unequal distribution of status and power between the sexes in patriarchal societies, which is exhibited, among other ways, in asymmetry of sexual roles, obligations, and expectations. This may be seen in the harlot's lack of a male counterpart. Female prostitution is an accommodation to the conflicting demands of men for exclusive control of their wives' sexuality and for sexual access to other women. The greater the inaccessibility of women in the society due to restrictions on the wife and the unmarried nubile women, the greater the need for an institutionally legitimized "other" woman. The harlot is that "other" woman, tolerated but stigmatized, desired but ostracized.

A fundamental and universal feature of the institution of prostitution wherever it is found is an attitude of ambivalence. The harlot is both desired and despised, sought after and shunned. Attempts to show changes in attitudes toward prostitutes over time or from one culture to another founder on this point. Despite considerable historical and cultural variation in attitudes, the harlot is never a fully accepted person in any society.[7] What a man desires for himself may be quite different from what he desires for his daughter or wife. One of the earliest and clearest expressions of that fundamental attitude of ambivalence toward the harlot is found in the Gilgamesh Epic. As Enkidu is about to die, he looks back over his life in the civilized world, recalling its pain, and he curses the harlot who initiated him into that world from his former carefree life among the beasts of the steppe. The curse is an aetiology of the harlot as outcast and despised.[8]

> Come, prostitute,[9] I shall establish (your) status,[10]
> a status that shall not end for all eternity.
> . . . .
> May [your lovers] discard (you) when sated with your charms,
> [May those whom] you love [despise(?) . . .] your favors(?).
> . . . .
> [Dark corners] of the street shall be your home,
> The shadow of the city's wall shall be your station,
> [Men shall piss there in front of] your feet,
> The drunken and thirsty shall slap your face.

But Shamash, overhearing Enkidu's curse, chides him, reminding him of the fine clothes and food that he had enjoyed and of his companionship with Gilgamesh. All this was the harlot's gift, for which he should be grateful. Enkidu acknowledges the right of Shamash's argument and counters his curse with a blessing. The blessing is an aetiology of the harlot as desired.

> May [your lover(?)] (always) return(?) (to you) [even from far away places]
> [Kings, prin]ces, and nobles shall love [you].
> No one shall slap his thighs (to insult you)
> [Over you the old man will] shake his beard.
> [... the young(?)] will unloose his girdle for you.
> [So that you shall receive from him(?)] lapis and gold.
> [May he be paid] back (who) pissed in front of you,
> [May his home be emptied(?)], his filled storehouse.
> [To the presence of] the gods [the priest] shall let you enter.
> [On your account] a wife will be forsaken, (though) a mother of seven.

I. *Genesis 38:1-26*

Let us turn now to the biblical narratives. Genesis 38 stands as an independent tradition unit within the Joseph story. It recounts a complex story concerning Judah, with a number of aetiological motives. The centerpiece of the chapter, however, and the bulk of the narrative is a fully developed story in itself with its own internal dynamics in which aetiological elements are lacking or play a minor role (cf. Skinner; von Rad; Speiser; Westermann).

The scene is set in the Judean Shephelah in the period before the Israelite settlement, a time when Israel's ancestors lived side by side with the people of the land and intermarried with them, apparently without censure. "At that time," the narrator informs us, "Judah went down from his brothers" and sojourned with an Adullamite named Hirah, marrying a Canaanite woman, who bore him three sons (vv 1-5). For the eldest, Er, Judah selects a wife named Tamar,[11] a woman of the region. But Er dies at the hand of God as does the second son, Onan, who refuses to fulfill the duty of the levirate toward his brother's widow (v 8). Judah, now fearful of losing his only remaining son, sends Tamar home to her father's house, instructing her to remain a widow until the third son, Shelah, grows up. And as a dutiful daughter-in-law she goes, a widow, yet "betrothed" and therefore not free to remarry. Judah in his anxiety has sealed her fate, for he intends her widowhood to be permanent.

With Tamar's dismissal, attention is turned to Judah. Years pass and his wife dies. And when his mourning is over, he sets out with his friend Hirah to attend to the shearing of his flocks at Timnah in the hill country (v 12). The report of Judah's journey is a signal to Tamar, who has perceived her father-in-law's design and is unwilling to accept the fate he has determined for her. His journey provides an opportunity for Tamar to act. But the meaning of her action and her intention in it is not spelled out by the narrator, who simply reports as an observer and thus elicits the reader's speculation. "She put off her widow's garments," he says, "covered herself with a 'veil' and wrapped herself in it (*wattĕkas baṣṣāʿîp wattitʿallāp*) and sat at the entrance to Enaim, which is on the road to Timnah" (v 14).[12]

The language is deliberately opaque and suggestive. The narrator does not say that Tamar dressed as harlot. That is the inference that Judah makes — and is intended to make — but the narrator leaves it to Judah to draw the conclusion. "When Judah saw her, he thought her to be a harlot because she had covered her face" (*wayyaḥšĕbehā lĕzônâ kî kissĕtâ pānê(y)hā*) (v 15).[13] His action is presented as following naturally from that inference: "[So] he went over to her by the roadside" and propositioned her. And Tamar, in keeping with her assumed role, asks what her favors are worth to him (v 16). Judah offers her a kid from his flock, but Tamar demands a pledge until he is able to send it, specifying his signet, cord, and staff, which he gives her. With the essential negotiation completed, the critical action begins: "He lay with her and she conceived by him" (v 18b). The scene concludes with the note that she departed, removing her veil and resuming her widow's garments (v 19). How are we to understand this scene of entrapment and why does it succeed? Tamar, the victim of her father-in-law's injustice, has been denied the means of performing her duty toward her deceased husband and for achieving a sense of womanly self-worth in bearing a child. Her bold and dangerous plan aims to accomplish that end by the agency of the man that has wronged her.[14] It satisfies both duty and revenge. It is not a husband she wants, but an heir for Judah, and so she approaches the source. It is intercourse she wants, not marriage. Her plan works because of the role she has chosen to accomplish this end. The features of the story that make it work involve commonly held presuppositions concerning the prostitute, some peculiar to the Israelite/Canaanite setting of this story, others widely shared.

First, Judah is needy and therefore vulnerable. At the point where the critical action begins, he is depicted as recently bereaved and hence in need of sexual gratification or diversion. The notice about his wife's death is certainly meant to provide this motivation. He is also a traveler, away from home, desiring entertainment and free to seek it in a strange place. Prostitution is typically offered (and often organized) as a service to travelers, a tourist attraction. Attention is directed to the activity rather than the actor(s). The act is basically anonymous; anyone can provide the service. In this case, that common aspect of anonymity is reinforced by a custom of concealment of the face — at least in public — and apparently also in the execution of the encounter. (A dimly lit room would have aided concealment, though it is unclear from this account just where the union took place). The harlot's veil is a specific feature of this story and an essential prerequisite for the construction of the tale, or at least for this plan of action. It cannot be universalized, however.[15] Tamar's position is probably just as telling as her garb. A lone woman sitting by the road without apparent business would probably be enough to suggest the wares she was selling.

The climax of the narrative comes, as the text says, "about three months later" (or, at the end of the first trimester), when it is reported to Judah that his daughter-in-law Tamar has "played the harlot" (zānĕtâ) and "moreover . . . is with child by harlotry" (hārâ lizĕnûnîm, v 24). Now the English translation which I have quoted from the RSV contains a word play that is absent in the Hebrew, or it sharpens a word play that is not focused in the original. The translation of the verb zānâ as "play the harlot" is, I think, mistaken (Bird, 1981), but it points to an important socio-linguistic consideration in the language employed to describe Tamar's disguise and her crime. The English translation acknowledges that Tamar "played the harlot" when, in fact, no one but the reader knows that that is literally true. What the Hebrew means in its use of the verb and the qualifying noun zĕnûnîm is that Tamar, who is bound by her situation to chastity, has engaged in illicit intercourse, the evidence of which is her pregnancy. The Hebrew word zānâ, like its Arabic cognate, covers, I believe, a wide range of extramarital sexual relations, including both fornication and adultery, although its biblical usage appears focused on the activity of the unmarried woman.[16] In any case, when Judah hears this report of his daughter-in-law's unfaithfulness, his response is an immediate unconditioned sentence: "Bring her out and let her be burned!" (v 24).

If the word play in the English translation is overdrawn, the Hebrew use of the common root znh in two critical scenes of the narrative is still worthy of note and explanation. A striking contrast is created through use of the same root to describe two situations which occasion very different reactions from Judah. When he perceives that the woman by the road is a zônâ, his response is a proposition; when he hears that his daughter-in-law has zānâ-ed, his response is a sentence of death. He embraces the whore, but would put to death the daughter-in-law who "whored." The irony on which the story turns is that the two acts and the two women are one, and the use of etmylogically related terms as the situation-defining terms strengthens the irony. The essential difference between the two uses is the socio-legal status of the woman involved. In the first instance, the term zônâ describes the woman's position or profession (prostitute) as well as the activity on which it is based. Thus, it serves as a class or status designation. In the second instance, the verb describes the activity of one whose socio-legal status makes it a crime. The activity is the same in both instances, as the common vocabulary indicates, namely, non-marital intercourse by a woman. In one case, however, it appears to be licit, bearing no penalty; in the other it is illicit, bearing the extreme penalty of death.

This anomaly is explained by the differing social positions of the actors. What is outlawed for the one by her status as a "married" woman is allowed to the other by her status as an unmarried but non-virgin woman, but not without penalty. The harlot's act is not penalized, I would argue, because her role or occupation is. The harlot is a ˈ ind of legal outlaw, standing outside the normal social order with its approved roles for women, ostracized and marginalized, but needed and therefore accommodated.¹⁷ A stigma is always attached to her role and her person, however desired and tolerated her activity. But she does not bear the stigma alone, although only she is legally ostracized; she passes a measure of it on to her patrons. The cost to the man is admittedly slight and may he understcod in different ways, from contamination to humiliation or intimidation. For the harlot not only demands a price, she controls the transaction, as is so well illustrated in our narrative (is this to be understood as a reversal of the normal sex roles?). There is a degree of opprobrium about the whole affair, and a degree of risk for the man, who may be trapped, duped, or "taken." Thus, ambivalence pervades the whole relationship and is, as I argued earlier, a fundamental feature of the institution.

In my analysis of the narrative plot and of the harlot's role within it I omitted a scene which has heavily influenced most discussions of this chapter and is frequently made the central point. The scene is important to our understanding of the narrative, and of the harlot, but it has been over-interpreted and misinterpreted, I believe, precisely because insufficient attention has been given to narrative art in its analysis.

When Judah sends back the kid by his friend the Adullamite and attempts to reclaim his pledge, the friend cannot find her and so inquires of the men of the place (MT: "her place"): "Where is the *qĕdēšâ* who was at Enaim by the wayside?" They reply, "There has been no *qĕdēšâ* here" (v 21). Hirah then returns to Judah, repeating their answer verbatim.

What are we to make of this shift in terms? Have we misread Tamar's action? Did she intend to represent herself as a hierodule, a cultic "prostitute," who might be understood to have some particular association with festivals of the yearly cycle such as sheepshearing? I think not, though it is conceivable that at some stage in the development of this story such an association might have been made. The substitution of terms in this passage is not accidental, and the interchange must indicate some kind of association between the two figures. But there is no justification for the common collapse of the two nor for assuming that the word hierodule is the determining designation for understanding Judah's action.¹⁸

The term *qĕdēšâ* is confined to the interchange between Hirah the Adullamite and the men of the place. Two possible factors might affect this usage: first, the designation of the woman as a hierodule¹⁹ might reflect the narrator's view of Canaanite usage, for it occurs only in the conversation of non-Israelites; second, it is language used in public speech. Judah's original action was prompted by a private assessment: "he thought her to be a harlot" and acted accordingly. But the search for the shady lady requires public inquiry. The decisive clue to the substitution of terms is given, I believe, in Judah's response to Hirah's report. "Then let her keep the things as her own," he says, *"lest we be laughed at"* (lit. "lest we become an object of contempt"). But what might be the reason for contempt or ridicule? A sacred act of lovemaking with the hierodule of a Canaanite cult? Hardly, for the people of the place are understood to be Canaanites and would find no cause for contempt in that. Being outwitted, and more specifically "taken," by a common prostitute? Surely.

Here the issue of opprobrium surfaces. Judah, a man of standing, who has surrendered his insignia to a prostitute in a moment of weakness, does not go back in person to retrieve his goods, but sends a friend, a man of the region, to inquire discreetly of the local inhabitants. Hirah knows how to handle the situation; he uses a euphemism — comparable to our substitution of the term "courtesan" for the cruder expression "whore"— (a substitution of court language in the latter instance, cult language in the former). Here we have an example, I think, of a common contrast between private, or "plain," speech (which may also be described as coarse) and public, or polite, speech (which may also be described as elevated).[20] Such an interchange of terms does not require that the two have identical meanings, especially since euphemism is a characteristic feature of biblical Hebrew usage in describing sexual acts and organs. A foot or a hand is not a phallus, though both terms are used with that meaning. And a *qĕdēšâ*, I would argue, is not a prostitute, though she may share important characteristics with her sister of the streets and highways, including sexual intercourse with strangers.[21]

II. *Joshua 2:1-24*

The story of Rahab in Joshua 2, like the story of Tamar in Genesis 38, is a distinct literary unit, with its own tradition, clearly set off from the surrounding material. While the history of the Rahab story, in both its literary and pre-literary stages, is more complex than the Tamar story, and while an attempt has been made to integrate the tale into the now dominant account of the miraculous fall of Jericho, the narrative in Joshua 2 can still be analyzed as a discrete literary unit, and the apparent duplication or displacement in the narrative which has taxed many interpreters does not substantially affect my analysis. Only the Deuteronomistic editing, which is both obvious and limited, constitutes a reinterpretation of the tradition that represents a significant literary variant.[22]

The account opens with the sending of two spies from the Israelite camp at Shittim and closes with their return. The spies are instructed by Joshua in the first verse of the chapter to "see the land"[23] (i.e., the land West of the Jordan), which Israel is poised to attack. In the concluding verse, the returned spies report that "Yahweh has given the whole land into our hands; and moreover all the inhabitants of the land are fainthearted because of us"

(RSV; NEB "panic stricken," v 24). That language, augmented by the Deuteronomistic editor in the reference to the peoples' response,[24] presupposes the institution or ideology of holy war, in which an assurance of victory is required from Yahweh before the battle can take place. But the assurance which the spies offer is given without consultation of a priest or other oracle, by spies whose mission has been simply to spy out the land. We might assume then that the assurance of victory is an inference from what they have seen. But what lies between the opening and closing sentences is no acoount of a secret reconnoitering of the land, as commissioned, but the account of a single encounter in Jericho, the spies' first stopping place across the Jordan, an encounter from which they escape only by the skin of their teeth, or more precisely, by a lie and a cord. The key figure in their escape and in their knowledge of the land and its inhabitants is the harlot Rahab. In the present form of the story, she is both savior and oracle.

Commentators invariably discuss the role and reputation of Rahab. Two questions shape that discussion: (1) was Rahab a hierodule? and (2) why would the Israelites consort with a prostitute, who is portrayed as a heroine, without apparent censure of her profession or role? Some commentators claim to find a cult legend at the root of the tradition, an aetiology of a sanctuary or of a class of sacred prostitutes which persisted in later Israel (*inter alia*, Gressmann, 1922:136; Hölscher:54–57; Mowinckel:13–15). Even those who can find nothing in the present story to support a cultic identification feel constrained to observe that the term *zônâ* may designate either a sacred or a secular prostitute and is thus ambiguous, leaving either interpretation as a possibility (e.g., Soggin:36; Boling:144; Miller and Tucker:31). The question of Rahab's profession is prompted in part by wonder at her role in the tradition, in which the stigma normally attached to prostitutes is perceived as lacking. Either, it is argued, she cannot have been a common prostitute, or the status of the prostitute must have been higher in Canaanite society, for she appears in the story as a fully accepted member of the society.

In contrast to these opinions, I shall argue that nothing in the story suggests a hierodule and that, conversely, an understanding of Rahab as a harlot is essential to the story. I shall also argue that her portrayal as a heroine in no way cancels the negative social appraisal attached to her role as a harlot.

The narrator begins the account of the spies' mission with a deliberately suggestive lead sentence. "Go, view the land," the spies are instructed, and the report of their action immediately follows: "and they went and came to Jericho[25] and entered the house of a harlot (*bêt- 'iššâ zônâ*), whose name was Rahab, and slept there (*wayyiškĕbû šammâ*).[26] The place should probably be understood as an inn or public house, but the narrator clearly wishes to focus attention immediately on the connection with Rahab and especially on her occupation. Thus the designation *'iššâ zônâ* precedes the name as the determining expression following the noun "house." The language is obviously meant to suggest a brothel, and the following verb, *šākab*, reinforces that suggestion.[27]

The association of prostitutes with taverns or beer houses is well attested in Mesopotamian texts,[28] and it may be surmised that a similar association is assumed in our passage.

> As a prostitute he took her in from the street (and) supported her, as a prostitute he married her but gave her back (as separate property) *her tavern (Ana ittišu* VIII ii 23–25 [CAD, Ḫ:102a]).

> When I sit at the entrance of the tavern I (Ishtar) am a loving prostitute[29] (SBH 106:51–53 [CAD, Ḫ:101b]).

Indirect testimony to this association comes from §110 of the Laws of Hammurabi, which decrees death for the *nadītu* who enters a tavern.[30] Since the *nadītu* belonged to a class of hierodules who were bound by a rule of chastity and normally cloistered, the kind of activity associated with the place is apparent. In our passage, the "house" is identified as Rahab's and is clearly not her family home, since her parents and siblings must be brought into *her* house in order to be saved (v 18).[31] In view of her profession, then, it is reasonable to view the house as her place of business.

The narrator's words about the spies' approach to their task tantalizes the reader and elicits speculation about the spies' motive and plan. How is this action meant to serve their mission? What exactly do they think they will do there? Do they hope to obtain information by sleeping with a loose, and presumably, loose-tongued woman? Do they mean to bargain for intelligence from a business woman who will sell anything for a price? Or do they simply hope to overhear the talk of local citizens and travelers who have gathered there or engage them in unguarded conversation over a pitcher of beer? Whatever their precise plan of action may be, they have chosen a natural place to begin their reconnaissance of the land. For the inn, or public house, or brothel, provides them both access and cover. It is a resting place for travelers and a gathering place for all sorts of persons seeking diversion and contacts; strangers will not be conspicuous here and motives will not be questioned. The proprietor's status also makes the harlot's house a logical point of entry, for, as an outsider in her own community, the harlot might be expected to be more open, perhaps even sympathetic, to other outsiders than would her countrymen.

But if the spies have chosen their point of entry wisely, they have not gone unobserved. The king of Jericho has been informed of their entry and whereabouts and sends immediately to Rahab, requesting that she hand over the men who have entered her house. Instead, she hides the spies and shrewdly diverts the king's men with a false report. Here again the ambiguous language of entry/intercourse is employed, first by the king's messengers who command: "Bring out the men who were going in to you (*habbāʾîm ʾēlayik*), who entered your house (v 3)"; and then by Rahab, who acknowledges:

"They did indeed come in to me (*bā'û 'ēlay*, v 4).".³² Thus sexual innuendo is not confined to the opening verses but pervades the whole first scene as an element of narrative intention. Rahab's action, however, contradicts the expectations aroused by the suggestive language, leaving the reader to speculate about her intentions.

At the end of the opening sentence the reader is meant to ask: why did the spies go to a harlot's house and what did they do there? At the end of the first scene the reader is left with the question: why did Rahab do what she did? The story has given us no reason to believe that there was any previous relationship between the two parties. What then can explain her action? The reader must speculate — and is invited to do so by the construction of the narrative. But the modern reader must speculate without the "feel" for the situation possessed by the ancient audience. Multiple motives and factors may be involved, either originally or as the result of editorial reinterpretation. Rahab's response may represent hostility to the king and his cohorts. Perhaps she has been harassed before about her establishment and its clients. If dangerous aliens are found on her premises, she will surely be penalized. Her action may then be interpreted as self-interest, an effort to save her own neck, and/or her business and reputation. Or is a connection to be seen in class affinity or class interest? Are we to understand her act as that of a social outcast among her own people protecting the representatives of an outcast people, an outcast people on the move, that may offer her a new future? I must admit that I find no element in the story to suggest the latter understanding, but I will leave the matter open. In the present form of the narrative, the question of Rahab's motivation is answered in the following scene. In an eloquent speech, enhanced by the Deuteronomist, Rahab reveals to the spies, whom she has concealed on the roof, the meaning and purpose of her action. She has come to strike a bargain, and now she presents her terms; *ḥesed* for *ḥesed*, she requests, my life for yours. By her act of protection, here described as an act of *ḥesed*, she has established a bond of obligation with the spies. Now she seeks their protection when they shall be in a position to give it, an act of *ḥesed* on their part, since they are now morally obligated, though not legally bound (Sakenfeld:64–70). Her speech begins with a confession of Yahweh's mighty acts toward Israel and concludes with a request for an oath of assurance from representatives of Yahweh's people.³³ The scene ends with the spies' oath.

In the final scene, Rahab enables the spies to escape by letting them down through a window in the wall, in which she ties a scarlet cord as a sign to the attacking Israelites, so that they will recognize and spare her house. The outcome of this encounter — viz. the saving of all who were in the harlot's house — is reported in chapter 6, with the aetiological note that Rahab "dwelt in Israel to this day" (6:25).

This account supplies us with further information about the harlot in Israel's understanding and corroborates features noted in other ancient Near

Eastern texts and in comparative studies. She lives on the outer periphery of the city, where other outcast and low caste groups or professions are commonly located in the ancient city. Her house in the wall (near to the city gate?) would be readily accessible to travelers and easily located. Was the red cord a permanent sign of an ancient red light district, or only specific to this narrative?[34]

It has been argued on the basis of this story that no censure or stigma was attached to the harlot in early Israel—or in Canaanite society—in contrast to later Israel. But this argument misreads the story. The entire account depends upon Rahab's marginal status, in both Canaanite and Israelite societies. Her descendants, persisting in later Israel, form a distinct group, the strange tolerance of which is "explained" by the aetiology of the harlot's loyalty. And it is only because she is an outcast that the men of Israel have access to her (an "honorable" woman would not meet alone with strange men). The narrator has drawn upon popular understanding of the harlot's profession and reputation in the construction of the story and deliberately elicits that understanding in his opening words which place the whole of the subsequent action in a harlot's house. The associations that operate in this story are many and complex, and may never be fully determined by the modern reader, but understanding requires some attempt at specification.

The prostitute's low social status and low reputation are essential, and related, features. The reader does not expect anything from her, or at least not anything of moral strength, courage, or insight. For she is the lowest of the low, and, as Jeremiah's search illustrates, Israel did not expect much from the lowly (Jer 5:4-5). The harlot is viewed as lacking in wisdom, morals, and religious knowledge. Her low status and despised state must be due either to unfortunate circumstance or personal fault, and neither, I think, would elicit much sympathy or charity from an ancient audience. The harlot may be a victim, but she is commonly viewed as a predator, preying on the weakness of men, a mercenary out for her own gain, an opportunist with no loyalty beyond herself, acknowledging no principle or charity in her actions.

These attributes in an enemy may serve the Israelite spies well, though the game they would play with her is a risky one. The story requires no positive assessment of the harlot, no counter to the common portrait, to explain the initial action of the spies, nor, I have suggested, to explain Rahab's action in saving them. For although the harlot lacks wisdom in the popular view, she lives by her wits. She is a shrewd and calculating operator, and men must beware her tricks. Self-interest (here broadened to include her kindred) still plays an important role in the final form of the story and may have played a larger role in the pre-Deuteronomistic version. But while essential to the construction of the tale, it is not the decisive motive. The present form of the story builds on a reversal of expectations. The negative presuppositions are required precisely for their contribution to that reversal.

Rahab does not act as we expect her to act when she protects the spies. Self-interest alone cannot explain her commitment, for the risk of siding with an unknown force against one's own people is too great to ascribe solely to that motive. Either faith or discernment, or both, is required to explain such unproved loyalty (ḥesed), and for that there is no place in the ruling stereotype of the harlot. But if the harlot as heroine involves a conflict of expectations, it is also a recognizable subtype of the harlot in literature (and presumably also in life), a romantic antitype to the dominant image: the whore with the heart of gold, the harlot who saves the city, the courtesan who sacrifices for her patron.[35] Her action, which is praiseworthy in itself, is the more so for being unexpected and unsolicited. In her display of loyalty, courage, and altruism, she acts out of keeping with her assumed character as a harlot and thus reveals her true character as a person. But this does not normally lead to a change in her status, or a change in attitudes toward harlots. The determining negative image of the harlot is not fundamentally challenged by the counterimage, but maintained. For the harlot is never allowed to become a good wife, but only a good harlot, a righteous outcast, a noble-hearted courtesan, the exception that proves the rule—just as Robin Hood does not define the type of the bandit, but only the antitype.

Rahab is a heroine because she protects the Israelite spies and, as a consequence, contributes to Israel's victory. If the LXX preserves an original variant, she may have been credited originally with enabling the Israelites to breach the wall and hence with handing over her city to the invaders, a motif which is closely paralleled in two classical texts pointed out by Hans Windisch (189–198).[36] In the present form and setting of the story, the deliverance of the city to Israel is attributed to Yahweh's miraculous action, and Rahab's role is that of an oracle rather than an instrument of that action (her deliverance of the spies may be taken as a kind of proleptic sign of Israel's victory). The Deuteronomistic redaction of the chapter has made Rahab's speech the center of the story. Rahab is here the pagan confessor, the one who discerns what others fail to see, and the one who commits her life to the people of Yahweh. She is wiser than the king of Jericho, and also more clever. Like the lowly Hebrew midwives, she outwits the king. Like them, she is bold in rejecting an unrighteous command. Like them, she is given a house and a name in Israel and a story to perpetuate her memory, while the king she opposed remains nameless and forgotten.

The Israelite author has made of the harlot of Jericho a heroine of faith and a friend of Israel. I have assumed that the story depends on a reversal of expectations. Others have argued that it could also be explained by unnoted affinities, by positive expectations that might serve to qualify the predominantly negative expectations of the harlot. A parallel might be drawn by the narrator—and an affinity recognized—between the low or outcast estate of the harlot of Jericho and the low and outcast estate of the band of escaped slaves beyond the Jordan. While Israel's petition to the kings in the

Transjordan was met only by uncomprehending belligerence, their approach to the harlot of Jericho elicits immediate reception and a pledge of support. Rahab knows what the kings do not know, that the Lord is with this outlaw band and no power can stand against them. And so the wise harlot sides with the outcasts whose day is dawning on the Eastern horizon. I find that construction theologically appealing, but I cannot now find historical or literary evidence that would convince me of its plausibility.

The story of Rahab depicts a figure identified with a Canaanite milieu, and a group identified by her name, persisting, anomalously, in later Israel. I find no suggestion of cultic identification either in the narrative of Joshua 2 or in the aetiological note of Joshua 6. It is a clan legend, not a cult legend, memorializing an individual and her family, not a sanctuary or cultic institution. An Israelite lineage, not a class of hierodules, traces its ancestry to this heroine. The harlot designation of its eponym suggests an outcast status for the group, which requires explanation. The story provides the explanation: it was because of the *ḥesed* of Rahab toward our ancestors that her clan dwells among us today.

III. 1 Kings 3:16-27

If the harlot of Joshua 2 and the supposed harlot of Genesis 38 are depicted in Canaanite settings, the existence of prostitution as a recognized institution in Israel is also well attested.[37] Relative incidence is impossible to judge and so are changes in attitudes. If Israelite religion censured the institution, it was still accompanied by the same attitudes of ambivalence displayed in cultures more open to its acceptance. And the basic stereotypes and presuppositions still hold, as we can see from various biblical witnesses. An instructive example from the period of the monarchy is found in the famous story of Solomon's judgment (1 Kings 3:16-27).[38]

The story concerns a case of rival claims brought by two harlots (*nāšîm zōnôt*, v 16) who are described as living together in one house, probably to be understood as a brothel because of the reference to "strangers" in v 18.[39] Both give birth, according to the story, within three days of each other. The women are alone at the time with no others[40] in the house — an unlikely situation in a normal household, but one essential to the story and the case it presents; for as they are harlots and as they are alone, there are no witnesses to the incident they describe, and no husbands or kinsmen to defend the claims of the women or to arbitrate for them. Thus it is a case of one woman's word against another and, more specifically, one harlot's word against another, that is, the words of women whose word cannot be trusted. For the harlot is characterized in the ruling stereotype as a woman of smooth and self-serving speech. One does not expect truth from such as these. And so the case that is presented to Solomon is a case to test the wisest judge. The harlot plaintiffs assure that.

As the case is laid out before the king, the child of the one dies and she substitutes the child of the other for it. Each now claims the living child as her own, and Solomon must judge whose claim is true. Here Solomon's wisdom is displayed, for he does not attempt to discern the truth through interrogation—a hopeless approach with habitual liars. His wisdom lies in recognizing a condition that will compel the truth. The story—and Solomon's action—appeals to another stereotype of the woman, that of the mother, who is bound by the deepest emotional bonds to the fruit of her womb. That bond will not lie. And so Solomon orders a sword to be brought and the child to be divided between the two claimants. At this the true mother reveals herself by relinquishing her claim in order to spare her child.

Again I would argue that the story does not reveal a generally accepting attitude toward harlots, as some have argued, but depends, rather, on their marginal status and their reputation for lying and self-interest. It is these commonly shared presuppositions about the harlot that make this case an ideal test, one by which extraordinary wisdom might be demonstrated. For the audience is meant to see only two prostitutes, but Solomon in his wisdom sees what is hidden by that stereotype, namely, a mother. In this case two counter images operate, which are normally distinct but are here combined in a single figure. The case is built on the one and resolved on the other.

What I have tried to do in these three examples is to draw out the picture of the prostitute that was operative in each and show how it functioned in the narrative. The author has reckoned in each case with the attitudes and presuppositions that would be called forth from his audience by the use of the term zônâ. These presuppositions are, for the most part, subtle and complex and are commonly missed or misread by modern readers who mistake narrative interest for social status, and role in the story for role in life. The harlot heroine, or protagonist, remains a harlot. She is lifted for a moment, as an individual, into the spotlight by the storyteller, but her place remains in the shadows of Israelite society.

NOTES

[1] I use the terms interchangeably, adopting "harlot" because of its use by the RSV (on its misuse, see below). Cf. Setel (89–91) for a usage that distinguishes the terms.

[2] I am currently engaged in a book-length study of the harlot and the hierodule in Old Testament and Ancient Near Eastern literature and society. (I use the term hierodule as a provisional class designation for all types of cult-related women, without regard to their particular duties, activities or status.) While the two figures, or classes of women, are commonly identified and even exchanged in interpretive literature, beginning with the Old Testament's polemical treatment of Canaanite religion and culture, there appears to be little or no evidence of confusion or interchange in the primary ancient texts. In her popular treatment of the origins of prostitution, Gerda Lerner rightly criticizes the confusion of the two classes by most authorities as well as the attempt to derive secular prostitution from sacred sexual service (238–45); but she falls

prey to the same confusion in her own treatment of the Mesopotamian *ḫarimtu* ("prostitute") (244-46). This essay does not permit discussion of the important but complex question of the relationship between the harlot and the hierodule or assessment of Lerner's arguments, which are based on secondary sources and misconstrue critical Mesopotamian texts.

³ Male prostitution, which was homosexual, appears to have been a limited phenomenon and is poorly attested in our sources (cf. Gebhard:80). It is not considered in this article.

⁴ I have discussed the problems of the translation and use of this term and the related verbal forms in an unpublished paper (Bird, 1981). Some of the issues are treated in the discussion of the Tamar story below.

⁵ See Gebhard (76); cf. also the following texts:

> She is not a wife, she is a *ḫarimtu* [prostitute] (JEN 666:14, Nuzi [CAD Ḫ:101b]).
> A *qadištu* [hierodule] whom no husband has married (must go) bareheaded in the street, must not veil herself.
> A *ḫarimtu* [prostitute] must not veil herself (KAV 1 v 66, Ass. Code § 40 [CAD Ḫ:101b; cn. G:152b]*).

In the latter case, both the harlot and the unmarried hierodule are prohibited from wearing the veil, which is the distinguishing garb of the married woman. The preceding clause requires the married hierodule to veil herself on the street.

*CAD Ḫ:101b mistakenly connects the two clauses cited, understanding the *qadištu* as a class of *ḫarimtu*. Cf. Meek (183).

⁶ On the harlot's habitat, note the following:

> If a man's wife has not borne him children but a harlot (from) the public square (Lipit-Ishtar Code §27 [Kramer 1955:160]; cf. §32).
> If someone regularly approaches a *ḫarimtu* at a streetcrossing (CT 39 45:30, SB Alu [CAD Ḫ:101b]).

Cf. also Sjoberg (133-37) and Oppenheim (41).

⁷ Attempts to compare attitudes and incidence of prostitution in Canaanite and Israelite society or in different periods of Israelite history are futile, because the data do not permit statistical comparison and because the different literary genres in which the references are preserved display quite different pictures of the harlot and attitudes toward her (e.g., Proverbs offers practical advice to men, stressing the pocketbook, while Priestly legislation is concerned with the harlot as ritually unclean and her contacts as defiling).

⁸ The translation and interpretation of the following texts from the Gilgamesh Epic (VII, iii, 6-22 and iv, 1-10) is based on Oppenheim (40- 41) and Speiser (1955:86-87). Cf. Tigay (170-72).

⁹ The term *šamḫatu*, which is interchanged with *ḫarimtu* ("prostitute") in the texts relating to Enkidu and the harlot, is treated as a proper noun by Tigay (171). Speiser translates "harlot-lass" (1955:74-75) or simply "lass" (86), noting the etymological meaning "pleasure girl" (74 n. 23).

¹⁰ Oppenheim's rendering of the phrase *ši-ma-tu lu-šim-ki*, conventionally translated "I will decree (your) fate."

¹¹ Heb. "Palm," a fertility symbol. The symbolism in the text is far richer and the literary art more subtle and complex than my limited analysis is able to convey.

¹² The location is uncertain (cf. ancient Versions, and commentaries), but unnecessary for our analysis.

¹³ The "veil" may have been understood immediately by the hearers as a harlot's apparel, but it is more likely that the term is meant to be more general in its application and more ambiguous in the author's use. By suggesting, but not specifying, a harlot's garb, the narrator makes of her act both an act of concealment and an act of invitation.

¹⁴ Tamar is legally helpless; therefore she must move outside the law to accomplish what duty (for her the higher "law") demands of her.

15 It is useless to argue from the Middle Assyrian Laws (cf. n. 5) to practices in Canaan/Israel, since dress is a matter of local or regional custom. Restrictions or prescriptions in dress are generally meant to distinguish the married or betrothed woman from all other classes of women, saying, in effect, "hands off!" That the harlot was not always veiled in Israel is suggested by Jeremiah's reference to the "harlot's brow" (Jer 3:3).

16 According to Wehr, Arabic *zanā* has the meaning "to commit adultery, fornicate, whore." Cf. *zinan:* "adultery, fornication;" *zinā':* "adultery, fornication;" *zānin:* "fornicator, adulterer;" *zāniya:* "whore, harlot, adulterous." See Mernissi (24–25). While the activity designated by this root is usually understood as illicit, that description does not give adequate account of the differences in attitudes and sanctions related to the sex and status of the actors. See below.

17 Susan Niditch has explained this anomalous position of the prostitute by using the term "liminal," as employed by Victor Turner: "That which is liminal is that which is betwixt and between nearly (sic) defined categories. A harlot falls between the two allowable categories for women. She is neither an unmarried virgin, nor a non-virgin wife" (147 n. 13). As a liminal character, outside the social order, Niditch argues, the harlot "belongs to a special class of women who can 'play the harlot' without being condemned." "In effect," she continues, "one could fall between the proper categories and survive, once that outside betwixt-and-between status was itself institutionalized and categorized" (147).

While Niditch's analysis of women's roles and of the harlot's status in ancient Israelite society corresponds closely in substance to my own (made independently in an unpublished paper [Bird, 1980]), I have retained my original characterization of the harlot as a "legal outlaw," because I want to emphasize the ambivalence or conflict in attitudes toward the prostitute and the fact that she is both freed and constrained by her position.

18 Von Rad's interpretation is, unfortunately, typical of this type of reasoning, which invariably appeals to Herodotus: "Tamar . . . does not pretend to be a harlot as we think of it, but rather a married woman who indulges in this practice [sacrifice of chastity in the service of the goddess of love], and Judah too thought of her in this way" (354–55). Cf. Astour (185–96).

19 There is no justification for RSV's translation of "harlot" here.

20 Speiser (1964:300) is one of the few commentators who has recognized this. See now Alter (9).

21 Whatever the reasons for the identification of these two marginal classes of women, it is essential to maintain the linguistic distinctions made in the Hebrew. See n. 2 above.

22 Noth's analysis (1953) remains basic. See also Boling; Soggin; Gray 1967; and Hertzberg. On the question of sources, see further Tucker (13–14) and Mowinckel (33–34).

23 Omitting "and Jericho" with LXX, Noth (1953:24) and NEB, as displaced from the following clause (where LXX reads it) or secondarily introduced to explain the following account, which concerns only Jericho.

24 *wĕgam-nāmōgû kol-yōšĕbê hā'āres mippānênû* (24b) is a Deuteronomistic phrase that picks up the words of Rahab's speech: *wĕkî nāmōgû kol-yōšĕbê hā'āres mippĕnêkem* (9bβ), the main piece of Deuteronomistic composition in the chapter (Tucker:70).

25 See n 23. Cf. LXX, which reads Jericho here, but also has a longer text.

26 There is no justification for RSV's "lodged," which eliminates the double entendre in the Hebrew. It rests, however, on ancient precedent; the Old Greek eliminated the sexual intimation by employing *kataluein:* "lodge" (Liddell-Scott), a verb that normally represents the Hebrew root *lwn/lyn* in LXX and is used only here to translate *škb* (Hatch-Redpath).

27 *Bêt zônâ* may be a technical term for a brothel. Cf. Jer 5:7, "they committed adultery and trooped to the harlot's house *(bêt zônâ)*"; Ezek 16:41, *wĕśārĕpû bāttayik bā'ēš . . . wĕhišbattîk mizzônâ:* "they shall burn your houses . . . ; I will make you stop playing the harlot" (the whole section, beginning in v 35, is addressed to Israel as a harlot). If *bêt zônâ* is a technical term, then the insertion here of the word "woman" into the construct may represent a weakening of the term in the direction of an individual's house: it was the house of a woman who was a harlot—or a promiscuous woman. It is difficult to judge the force of *'iššâ zônâ*, which appears as a frequent

variant of *zônâ* used alone. But however the compound term is interpreted, its use to identify the house can only be understood as provocative. See vv 3 and 4 and n. 31 below.

The qualifying term *zônâ* is not used again in chapter 2. This is in keeping with the author's style in describing the roles of the main figures when they are first introduced (*'ănāšîm měraggĕlîm* and *'iššâ zônâ*, v 1) and thereafter referring to them simply as "the men" and "the woman." The qualifying role designations are employed again in chapter 6, where the characters are reintroduced.

²⁸ See Jacobsen and Kramer 1953:176, l. 106, and 184 n. 68. Cf. also Bergmann:2-3; Falkenstein:118-19; and CAD A 473 (*aštammu*).

²⁹ *ḫa-ri-im-tum ra'imtum*. A variant, written as a gloss, *šarraqitum:* "a female thief," gives testimony to the low repute of the place and of the classes associated with it.

³⁰ The term here is *É-KURRUN(NA)* = *bit-kurrunim*(?): "tavern, ale-house" (cf. Driver and Miles), which may be distinguished from the *É-EŠDAM* = *aštammu* "inn." Jacobsen and Kramer (1953:184-85 n. 68) argue that the latter should he understood as "Gasthaus mit Herberge" rather than "bordello," even though it was typically frequented by and owned by the *ḫarimtu* ("prostitute"). They see it as "the social center of the state or village . . . a place in which the inhabitants would typically gather for talk and recreation after the end of work" (185 n. 68).

³¹ I take the references to her *bêt-'āb* in 2:12, 18 as ancient expansions of the basic story, belonging to the aetiological motif that comes to expression now in 6:17, 22-23, 25. A distinction must be made between her house and her "father's house" (= family or lineage). The latter survives, the former does not.

³² The Old Greek lacks the suggestive first clause in v 3. MT may be conflate, but the echoing language of v 4 is assumed by all of the Versions and thus is firmly fixed in the tradition.

³³ The oath has been commonly understood in recent literature as a covenant oath (e.g., Boling:147 n. 12). But there is no reference here, or in chapter 6, to a covenant, despite recognizable similarities between this story and the story of the Gibeonites. The oath here functions as a guarantee that the spies will honor their promise to Rahab to spare her family when they take control of the city.

³⁴ The initial reference to the cord in the phrase, "a strand of *this* scarlet cord" (v 18), suggests that it is already known and associated with the house (though it could also be understood as something brought by the spies). One may surmise that a sign, originally associated with the house in one capacity, has been reinterpreted in the story, giving it a new meaning and function.

³⁵ The motif is widespread. I have been given examples from Chinese as well as European literature. For a parallel from Classical literature, see below.

³⁶ Windisch argued that the Rahab story should be seen as one example of a type in which a city is delivered from its enemies (external or internal) by a prostitute and the memory of her action is perpetuated by aetiological legend. His two Classical parallels include a Roman and a Greek legend, the former concerning a prostitute of Capua who remained loyal to Rome when the city fell to Punic invaders, the latter a hierodule of Abydos (referred to as both *hetaira* and *pornē* in the account) who enabled her countrymen to retake the city from enemy occupation.

Windisch notes a common attitude displayed in the transmission of the two stories that honor a common prostitute. As Christian and Jewish interpretation have traditionally shown embarrassment over Rahab's profession and the absence of censure in the biblical narrative, a similar attitude is evident in the Roman tradition in which wonder was expressed at the Senate's action (granting freedom and restoration of possessions) on behalf of a woman of low repute. In the case of Rahab, tradition elevated her by suppressing knowledge of her occupation or making her a convert, allowing her to be a heroine only as an ex-harlot (Windisch:188-192).

³⁷ The term *zônâ* is used in the following texts relating to the period of the monarchy or later: Lev 21:7, 14; Deut 23:19; 1 Kings 3:16; Isa 1:21; 23:15, 16; Jer 3:3; 5:7; Ezek 16:30, 31, 33, 35, 41; 23:44; Hos 4:14; Joel 4:3; Micah 1:7, 7; Nah 3:4; Prov 6:26; 7:10; 1 Kings 22:38; Prov 23:27; 29:3.

[38] This story has long been recognized as having the character of popular tradition or folk tale and constituting a distinct literary unit. See Gressmann; Gray, 1970:114-16, 127-29; Noth, 1969:44-48; and Montgomery:108-10.

[39] Presumably prostitutes withdrew from active work during advanced stages of pregnancy. Unfortunately, we know virtually nothing about the working conditions of prostitutes in ancient Israel, means of contraception that may have been employed, or arrangements for raising (or disposing of) children. From the story of Jephthah we learn that although he was the son of a harlot, he was apparently raised in his father's household or was at least recognized by his father as a son and potential heir (Judg 11:1-2). The prohibition of priests from marrying harlots (Lev 21:7, 14) implicitly recognizes the practice by others. One may surmise that a man might marry a harlot who had borne him a child, especially a son.

[40] The Hebrew is $z\bar{a}r$ (v 18), meaning "stranger," one outside the family. It may be assumed from the fact that they were harlots living together that there would be no husbands present, or other members of a normal family. The use of the word "stranger" here refers, presumably, to clients.

WORKS CONSULTED

Alter, Robert
    1981   *The Art of Biblical Narrative*. New York: Basic Books.

ANET =
    1955   *Ancient Near Eastern Texts Relating to the Old Testament*. 2nd ed. Ed. James B. Pritchard. Princeton: Princeton University.

Astour, M. C.
    1966   "Tamar the Hierodule. An Essay in the Method of Vestigal Motifs." *JBL* 85:185-96.

Bergmann, Eugen
    1964   "Untersuchungen zu syllabisch geschriebenen sumerischen Texten." *ZA* 56:1-43.

Bird, Phyllis A.
    1980   "Harlot and Hierodule: Images of the Feminine in Old Testament Anthropology and Theology." Unpublished Essay, Bunting Institute Colloquium, Radcliffe College, Cambridge.
    1981   "'To Play the Harlot': An Inquiry into an Old Testament Metaphor." Unpublished Essay, Perkins School of Theology, Southern Methodist University, Dallas.

Boling, Robert G.
    1982   *Joshua*. AB 6. Garden City: Doubleday.

CAD =
    1956   *The Assyrian Dictionary of the Oriental Institute of The University of Chicago*. Chicago: Oriental Institute, University of Chicago.

Driver, G. R., and John G. Miles
    1955   *The Babylonian Laws*. 2 vols. Oxford: Clarendon.

Falkenstein, A.
    1964   "Sumerische religiöische Texte." *ZA* 56:44-129.

Gagnon, John H.
1968   "Prostitution." Pp. 592–98 in *The International Encyclopedia of the Social Sciences*. Vol. 12. Ed. David L. Silk. New York: Macmillan and The Free Press.

Gebhard, Paul Henry
1974   "Prostitution." Pp. 75–81 in *The New Encyclopedia Britannica*. Vol. 15. 15th ed. Chicago: University of Chicago.

Gray, John
1967   *Joshua, Judges and Ruth*. NCB. Greenwood, SC: Attic.
1970   *I and II Kings. A Commentary*. 2d ed. OTL. Philadelphia: Westminster.

Gressmann, Hugo
1907   "Das Salomonische Urteil," *Deutsche Rundschau* 130:212–28.
1922   *Die Schriften des Alten Testaments in Answahl*, I/2. Göttingen: Vandenhoeck & Ruprecht.

Hertzberg, Hans Wilhelm
1953   *Die Bücher Josua, Richter, Ruth*. ATD 9. Göttingen: Vandenhoeck & Ruprecht.

Hölscher, Gustav
1919/20 "Zum Ursprung der Rahabsage." *ZAW* 38:54–57.

Jacobsen, Thorkild, and Samuel N. Kramer
1953   "The Myth of Inanna and Bilulu." *JNES* 12:160–71.

Kramer, S. N.
1955   Trans. "Lipit-Ishtar Law Code." Pp. 159–61. ANET.

Lerner, Gerda
1986   "The Origin of Prostitution in Ancient Mesopotamia." *Signs: Journal of Women in Culture and Society* 11:236–54.

Meek, Theophile J.
1955   Trans. "The Middle Assyrian Laws." Pp. 80–88. ANET.

Mernissi, Fatima
1975   *Beyond the Veil. Male-Female Dynamics in a Modern Muslim Society*. New York: John Wiley & Sons; Halstead.

Miller, J. Maxwell, and Gene M. Tucker
1974   *The Book of Joshua*. Cambridge: Cambridge University.

Montgomery, James A.
1957   *The Book of Kings*. ICC. Edinburgh: T. & T. Clark.

Mowinckel, Sigmund
1964   *Tetrateuch-Petateuch-Hexateuch*. BZAW 90. Berlin: Töpelmann.

Niditch, Susan
1979   "The Wronged Woman Righted: An Analysis of Genesis 38." *HTR* 72:143–49.

Noth, Martin
1953   *Das Buch Josua*. 2d ed. HAT I, 7. Tübingen: J. C. B. Mohr (Paul Siebeck).
1969   *Könige*, 1. BKAT 9, 1. Neukirchen-Vluyn: Neukirchener.

Oppenheim, A. Leo
1948   "Mesopotamian Mythology II." *Orientalia* 17:17–58.

Rad, Gerhard von
    1972   *Genesis. A Commentary.* Rev. ed. Trans. John H. Marks. OTL. Philadelphia: Westminster.

Sakenfeld, Katherine Doob
    1978   *The Meaning of Hesed in the Hebrew Bible: A New Inquiry.* HSM 17. Missoula: Scholars.

Setel, T. Drorah
    1985   "Prophets and Pornography: Female Sexual Imagery in Hosea." Pp. 86–95 in *Feminist Interpretation of the Bible.* Ed. Letty M. Russell. Philadelphia: Westminster.

Sjoberg, Gideon
    1960   *The Preindustrial City, Past and Present.* New York: The Free Press.

Skinner, John
    1910   *A Critical and Exegetical Commentary on Genesis.* 2d ed. ICC. Edinburgh: T. & T. Clark.

Soggin, J. Alberto
    1972   *Joshua.* Trans. R. A. Wilson. OTL. Philadelphia: Westminster.

Speiser, Ephraim A.
    1955   Trans. and ed. "Akkadian Myths and Epics." Pp. 60–119. ANET.
    1964   *Genesis.* AB 1. Garden City: Doubleday.

Tigay, Jeffrey H.
    1982   *The Evolution of the Gilgamesh Epic.* Philadelphia: University of Pennsylvania.

Tucker, Gene M.
    1972   "The Rahab Saga (Joshua 2): Some Form-Critical and Traditio-Historical Observations." Pp. 66–86 in *The Use of the Old Testament in the New and Other Essays. Studies in Honor of William Franklin Stinespring.* Ed. James M. Efird. Durham: Duke University.

Wehr, Hans
    1961   *A Dictionary of Modern Written Arabic.* Ed. J. Milton Cowan. Ithaca: Cornell Uhiversity.

Westermann, Claus
    1986   *Genesis 37–50. A Commentary.* Trans. John J. Scullion. Minneapolis: Augsburg.

Windisch, Hans
    1917/18   "Zur Rahabgeschichte (Zwei Parallelen aus der klassischen Literatur)." ZAW 37:188–98.

HIS STORY VERSUS HER STORY: MALE GENEALOGY AND FEMALE STRATEGY IN THE JACOB CYCLE

Nelly Furman

Cornell University

ABSTRACT

Drawing on semiotics and deconstruction, and beginning with the failed seduction scene between Joseph and Potiphar's wife (Genesis 39), the author explores the meaning and function of garments in the Jacob cycle, showing us that these have "her story" as well as "his story" to tell. For the male characters, garments have a fixed meaning and a symbolic value through which they distinguish special relationships. For the men of the Jacob cycle, garments are a means of communication. For the female characters, on the other hand, garments are signifiers open to a variety of meanings. Garments become for the women the channel they use to insert themselves into the exclusively male communicative process. Like the garments, the biblical story can be understood from an androcentric or a gynocentric viewpoint, serving as a metaphor for a patriarchal or a feminist reading.

A text, according to the definition that French semiotician Roland Barthes (73–81) has given the word, is not a literary work or a portion of it, but its conceptualization, that is to say, a reading. Roland Barthes's concept of textuality is often illustrated by the following two metaphors. In the first, the reader is compared to a musician for whom interpretation is an activity, a personal rendition of an original score. Like the musician, the reader proposes a personal understanding of the meaningful aspects of a literary work. Because it is the perception of the reader which creates the text, its coherence is in the eyes of the reader and not in the intentionality of the author(s), narrator(s), or editor(s). The etymology of the word "text" leads us to the second metaphor used to explain the reading process. The Latin noun *textus* means not only text, passage of scripture, but also texture, tissue, structure, and context; the verb *textere* is translated "to construct," "to compose," "to weave." Thus the text is often described as a fabric, a network, or a web. The reader's interest is focused on the materiality of the literary work, the fabric of its narrativity, in other words the processes by which and through which stories are told and understood. The interlacing of narrative threads, the weaving and wavering of plot, the matter in which a yarn is spun create a substratum of meaning structures, supports, or undermines our understanding of the story. Insofar as it examines the systems of signs that allow literary communication to take place, textual criticism belongs to the semiotic enterprise. Understood as a semiotic exercise, textual criticism is a reading process that differs substantially in its practice and presuppositions from classical biblical textual approaches and from traditional notions of formal or textual criticism.

Though any number of narratives, linguistic, or thematic features may be used as heuristic devices for a textual reading, features that describe or refer to interpretation are particularly inviting for the semiotician. Thus, characters that function as interpreters and events that emphasize communicative acts are powerful poles of attraction.[1] In this respect, the seduction scene between Joseph and Potiphar's wife (Genesis 39) beckons the interest of the reader, for it deals with two contrary interpretations of one event, two seemingly antithetical readings. Potiphar's wife gives a willfully misleading explanation, which her husband, nonetheless, believes. They are the first set of narrator-narratee encoded in the text. A differing perception of the same event is suggested by the anonymous biblical narrator and Joseph, both of whom guarantee the existence of another viewpoint.

When Jacob's beloved Joseph was taken to Egypt, he was sold to Potiphar, an Egyptian, an officer of Pharaoh and captain of the guard. Pleased with Joseph, Potiphar makes him overseer of his house. While in Potiphar's employ, Joseph, who, according to the narrator, is handsome, attracts the attention of his master's wife. She tries to seduce him. He rejects her advances and explains his refusal in these terms: "Lo, having me my master has no concern about anything in the house, and he has put everything that he has in my hand; he is not greater in this house than I am; nor has he kept back anything from me except yourself, because you are his wife; how then can I do this great wickedness, and sin against God?" (Gen 39:9–10). However, one day, when Joseph is alone in the house, Potiphar's wife grabs him by his coat and again makes overtures. He runs out of the house leaving the garment behind in her hands. She calls in the men of the household and tells them the following: "See, he has brought among us a Hebrew to insult us; he came in to me to lie with me, and I cried out with a loud voice; and when he heard that I lifted up my voice and cried, he left his garment with me, and fled and got out of the house" (Gen 39:15–16). She later repeats the same story to her husband, and Joseph is imprisoned.

One piece of clothing, two stories. His story versus her story. In this episode, Joseph's piece of attire is the mediating object between divergent desires. Here, one garment suggests a male and a female text, two gender-marked readings.

If we were to listen solely to the words of Potiphar's wife, as the servants and her husband do, without the leading comments of the narrator, the abandoned garment would stand for his desire and her refusal. The narrator, however, lets us know that Joseph had on previous occasions rejected her advances and that her story is fictional, a total fabrication. Whereas the garment represents for Joseph his loyalty to his master, for her the garment becomes a means of manipulation, a strategic device for a successful frame-up. The interpretation she proposes for the presence of the garment shows that explanation is a matter of point of view and further suggests that it is neither the truth nor the falsehood of the story that matters, but its plausibility. Her husband believes her story, and Joseph is sent to prison. For Joseph, the abandoned garment represents his rejection of Potiphar's wife, and therefore his loyalty to his master, and ultimately his obedience to God. George W. Coats (89) points out that in the context of Joseph's relation to power, the abandoned garment shows first of all "a kind of human enlightenment, a commitment to a fellow man because he is a fellow who trusts the relationship, commitment to a relationship because only in that relationship does life make sense."

For Joseph, garments do have a special meaning and do suggest a specific bond between men. His father, Jacob, gives him a long robe with sleeves for he "loved Joseph more than any other of his children, because he was the son of his old age" (Gen 37:3). Joseph's brothers become resentful and their jealousy turns to hatred after Joseph reports on them to their father and then recounts his dreams, which, according to them, predict that they will bow to him. When Jacob sends his favorite son to see if the others are doing well in the pastures, Joseph's brothers conspire to kill him. Reuben, the oldest, succeeds in convincing them to spare the boy's life. They strip Joseph of his robe and put him in a pit. Midianite traders passing by rescue the boy from the pit and sell him to Ishmaelites. Upon discovering that Joseph had disappeared from the pit where they had hidden him, the brothers take Joseph's robe, dip it in the blood of a goat and show it to their father. Joseph's bloodied robe stands in lieu of an explanation, and Jacob understandably concludes that his favorite son has been devoured by a wild beast.

Jacob gave Joseph the robe as a token of his affection for him. Joseph abandons his coat in the hands of Potiphar's wife, his stated reason is his respect for his master. In both cases, a piece of attire represents an emotional link, a trust between men. When the Pharaoh makes Joseph vizier of Egypt, he gives the young Hebrew not only his signet ring but also garments of fine linen and a gold chain (Gen 41:42). Joseph will mark his reconciliation with his brothers by given them ceremonial garments as well as provisions before they leave Egypt (Gen 45:21). For the men, garments express feelings. When overcome with grief, men tear their clothes. Reuben, upon discovering Joseph's disappearance, "rends" his clothes (Gen 37:29), and so does Jacob upon being shown Joseph's bloodied robe (Gen 37:34). Later on, when they are accused of having stolen the divining cup, Joseph's brothers too "rend" their clothes (Gen 44:13). Whether a token of love and respect or a sign of despair and mourning, for Jacob and his sons, garments are symbolic items.

By giving Joseph a long robe with sleeves, Jacob sets Joseph apart from his brothers. Joseph will emulate his father's partiality, for he will give his full brother Benjamin not just one ceremonial vestment, as he gave his other brothers, but "three hundred shekels of silver and five festal garments" (Gen 45:22). By distinguishing among siblings without regard to the order of birth, Jacob sets up a hierarchical order founded on the father's liking for a child, and garments are the distinguishing markers of this new filial order. Joseph's robe establishes a visible link between father and son, the seal of approval for all to see of Joseph's election as favorite son and legitimate heir. Items of clothing are the textual signifiers which, in the latter part of Genesis, support the theme of sibling rivalry and the resulting victory of the youngest. They implement the new hierarchical order of elective dominance in opposition to the "natural" predetermined rule of sovereignty of the first and oldest.

When Rebekah was pregnant with Esau and Jacob, the Lord told her: "Two nations are in your womb, and two peoples, born of you, shall be divided; the one shall be stronger than the other, the elder shall serve the younger" (Gen 25:23). The story of Jacob actualizes the words of the Lord. Esau, the first-born, "came forth red, all his body like a hairy mantle" (Gen 25:25). Jacob first bought Esau's birthright in exchange for some bread and soup. Then, at the urging of Rebekah, Jacob put on his brother's attire. He covered his hands and neck with the skin of kids fetched so that Rebekah could prepare some savory food for him to bring Isaac. Impersonating his brother, Jacob secured Isaac's blessing meant for Esau.

Robert Alter (10–11) reminds us that the midrashic commentators had already noted that the goat and kid established connecting threads between the Judah and Tamar episode and the Joseph story: "The Holy one Praised be He said to Judah, 'You deceived your father with a kid. By your life, Tamar will deceive you with a kid. . . .'" The kids prepared by Rebekah also belong to this network, and Esau's garment now in Jacob's possession provides us with yet another connecting thread between the stories of Jacob and those of Joseph and Judah. Judah Goldin (27–44) attributes the presence of the Judah and Tamar episode, which is embedded in the story of Joseph, to the thematics of fraternal rivalry. Garments, as we have seen, form the textual support of this theme, and they play as well a prominent role in the story of Judah and Tamar.

Tamar, the widow of Judah's eldest son Er, has remained childless because Onan, Judah's second son "spilled the semen on the ground, lest he should give offspring to his brother" (Gen 38:9). We are told that this displeased God, and Onan too was slain. Judah sends Tamar back to her father's house promising to send his last son Shelah to her when the lad is grown up. Time passes. Judah does not honor his promise. Having learned that Judah, now himself a widower, was going to shear his sheep, Tamar takes off her widow's clothes, puts on a veil and sits by the roadside. Judah mistakes her for a harlot and asks to "come into her" (Gen 38:16) She accepts on the condition that she be given his signet, cord, and staff as a pledge of payment for her favors. This time Judah will be true to his word and send her a kid from his flock, but Tamar having taken off the harlot's veil and dressed in her widow's garment again cannot be found by Judah's envoy. Three months later, Judah learns that his daughter-in-law is pregnant by harlotry. He orders that she be burned, but upon being shown the signet, the cord, and staff which he recognizes as his, Judah declares: "she is more righteous than I, inasmuch as I did not give her my son Shelah" (Gen 38:26).

In the first ruse, Tamar simply exchanges two symbolically marked garments: the widow's clothes, which denote the absence of both husband and sexual relations; a harlot's veil, which advertises readiness for intercourse without parental responsibility. As Onan's punishment suggests and Judah's words confirm, the point of the story is not sexuality but fertility to assure the family's line of descent, a significance which the harlot's veil does not imply. Tamar's second stratagem is shrewder. Like Potiphar's wife, Tamar makes pieces of attire serve her own interest and purpose. The signet, cord, and staff were supposed to be the guarantee of payment Tamar was to receive for her favors. Tamar, however, does not use these objects as promissory notes. For her the importance of the signet, cord, and staff resides neither in their value as objects nor as down payment for a pledge; they are desirable only because they function as signatures, as evidence of the identity of the progenitor, as proof in a paternity suit. These objects are not meant simply to reveal her identity; rather their purpose is to establish a link between father and progeny, thereby legitimizing the births of Perez and Zerah. Judah's cord, signet, and staff belong to the same network of signifiers as Joseph's robe or the coat Joseph leaves in the hands of Potiphar's wife. They are the visual markers of a father (or master) and son relationship.

Tamar, like Rebekah, gives birth to twins. While she is in labor, one child puts out a hand to which the midwife attaches a scarlet thread. It is the other child, however, who comes out first. Because the midwife exclaims: "What a breach you made for yourself" (Gen 38:29), the first-born is named Perez, which means "a breach." The second child, the one with the red thread around his wrist, is called Zerah. The birth of Perez and Zerah is emblematic of the Joseph story, for like Zerah, who guides his older brother by widening the birth canal, Joseph as vizier of the Pharaoh directs his older brothers when they come to Egypt to fetch food.

The birth of Perez and Zerah recalls the birth of Esau and Jacob. The two sets of twins form a chiasmus. The "red hairy mantle" which distinguishes Esau, the oldest, becomes the red thread around the youngest's wrist. By wearing Esau's attire, Jacob makes Esau's distinguishing marking—namely, his "red hairy mantle"—his own. Isaac's blessing assures Jacob's superiority over his brother, and the garment becomes the signifier of Jacob's prominence. Similarly, when Jacob gives Joseph a long robe with sleeves, it symbolizes Joseph's superiority; and, when the bloodied robe is returned to Jacob, it signals Joseph's elimination from the line of succession. In Eygpt, his brothers may well bow before him, but it is not Joseph's progeny that will assure the might of the people of Israel. That task, as we know, will be assumed by Judah's descendant, for Reuben, Jacob's oldest, had sexual intercourse with Bilhah, his father's concubine (Gen 35:22), thus revealing himself unworthy of his father's trust. It is therefore fitting that in his blessing to his sons, Jacob should distinguish Judah, his chosen heir, by his red garment, thereby bestowing upon him, albeit metaphorically, the symbolic marker of genuine legacy. Judah, Jacob tells us, "washes his garments in wine and his vesture in the blood of grapes" (Gen 49:11). In Genesis, Jacob's line of descent stops with the description of the birth of Perez and Zerah; the fact that it is not Zerah but Perez who is named in the ancestry of David (Matt 1:3) suggests that the sibling rivalries characteristic of the Jacob cycle continued beyond the events recounted in Genesis. However, since the eventual ascendancy of Perez lies outside the content of Genesis, it plays no part in the narrative processes at work in the Jacob cycle. For Michael Fishbane (38), the power of the Jacob cycle is that "it personalizes the tensions and dialectics which are also crystallized on a national level at later points: the struggle for blessing; the threat of discontinuity; the conflicts between and within generations; and the wrestling for birth, name and destiny." In the Jacob cycle, garments form the subtext which upholds these concerns. From Jacob to Joseph to Judah to Zerah, the red thread establishes an order of filiation, a metaphorical umbilical cord that relates directly, without the mediation of women, father to son to grandson.

As the Judah and Tamar episode illustrates, in such a system what matters is not who bears the child but the identity of the father. In this male-marked genealogy, women have no say. Their role is strictly biological. The womb as the relevant place of origin is superseded by the progenitor's authority, and ranking of siblings becomes a father's prerogative. It is therefore not surprising that Jacob favors Joseph not because he is the firstborn of his beloved Rachel but because Joseph is "the son of his old age" (Gen 37:3).

Following the path of Claude Lévi-Strauss, Judah Goldin (44) reminds us that stories function somewhat like myths for they provide acceptable channels for the expression of discontent:

> The law of God may not be abolished, and besides, for the most part, the society assents to its terms because without these there would be chaos. But the resentments are nonetheless real! How are these to find an outlet? By folktales and folklore. Here no frontal attack is made on the divine law. That is the policy of rebellion. But in stories and fables one turns the order

of the world up side down without giving up the establishment that provides protection. This is the revenge of the weak against the strong.

For Judah Goldin, "the revenge of the weak against the strong" refers to the theme of fraternal rivalry and the triumph of the youngest. In order to be counted once again among Jacob's sons, Joseph uses a personal item as a ploy to force recognition. The silver divination cup he has placed in Benjamin's sack of grain (Gen 44:2) serves as an excuse to get his brothers to stand before him so that he can reveal his identity to them. Joseph's stratagem recalls the ploys of Rebekah, Potiphar's wife, and Tamar, who like him use objects as the mediating device for their own personal ends. Sibling rivalry and the ensuing importance of the father and son bond erase the privilege of rank among wives and reduces women's function strictly to their reproductive role. In such a patriarchal system, women are still needed, but they are nonetheless outsiders. When Rebekah, Potiphar's wife, or Tamar uses a piece of attire for their own personal ends, they do not create a gratuitous disturbance in the order of things. Although in a world under divine guidance their actions can be said to actualize the Lord's will, these actions can also be seen as the expression of women's resentment and rebellion. When Rebekah suggests that Jacob take his brother's place, or when Potiphar's wife tries to seduce Joseph, or when Tamar calls attention to Judah's progeny, their interference breaks up the exclusive father-son dialogue and forces recognition of their presence. It is therefore not surprising that, in the cycle of Jacob, the women use pieces of attire—which are the symbolic markers of the father-son relationship—to reinscribe themselves in the patriarchal system. Their intervention in the sequence of events ruptures the continuum of the narrative and reveals the patterns interwoven in the textual fabric. In the latter part of Genesis, garments have his and her story to tell: as used by men, garments form a communicative channel from which women are excluded; but when used by women, garments function as communicative devices between the sexes. For the men, garments are symbolic markers of filial love and recognition, whereas for the women they serve as a means of self-inscription in a system that neglects them. Christine Garside Allen argues that, in securing for Jacob Isaac's blessing meant for Esau, Rebekah was only carrying out God's wishes. For Allen, it is not Isaac but Rebekah who through her selfless obedience shows herself to be a model of sanctity. "It is tempting," she writes (168–69), "to bring Rebekah into relief by maintaining that Isaac was not a saint. In this way Rebekah would be the necessary link between Abraham and Jacob." Allen's analysis clearly shows that, even if seen as a consecrated deed and interpreted from a psychological viewpoint, Rebekah's deceitful action ultimately disturbs the exclusively male genealogical lineage.

For Isaac, as for Jacob and Judah, garments have a fixed meaning: Esau's tunic and Joseph's robe represent specific individuals, Isaac mistakes the garment for the wearer and thus gives his blessing to Jacob instead of Esau.

As for Judah, he is unable to recognize his daughter-in-law behind the prostitute's veil. Whereas for the men garments have a determined, precise meaning, that is to say, a truth value, for the women clothes are nothing but signifiers open to a variety of meanings; they are items whose function and referential meaning can easily be changed. When Tamar exchanges her widow's dress for the prostitute's veil, she simultaneously calls attention to two social functions of garments: first, their use as symbols in the sexual code; and, second, their use as masks and disguises. When Potiphar's wife points to Joseph's coat at her side as the proof of Joseph's attempt to seduce her, her story is believable because she provides a sexual significance to an item which, in the social context, can have a sexual referential meaning. She also uses Joseph's coat to hide her own sexual desire. Because for women, garments do not necessarily refer to a specific individual or convey solely one message, they are the place of juncture for a multiplicity of meanings, the locus for the expression of divergent desires. For Tamar, as for Potiphar's wife or Rebekah, garments are the means by which they impart their desire to play a relevant role in the patriarchal hierarchy. By pluralizing the meaning of a piece of attire, Rebekah, Potiphar's wife, and Tamar explode and thereby subvert the closure of the patriarchal representational system and symbolic code. Thus, in the latter part of Genesis, the function of garments, as understood by the women of the cycle of Jacob, can serve as the very metaphor for textuality and the deconstructive nature of modern reading practices which Barbara Johnson (3) describes as "a careful teasing out of warring forces of signification within the text." The patterns woven in the biblical narrative take their shape from the filling as well as the warp; the two strands may have different functions, but they are equally necessary to the making of the textual fabric.

Because it can be construed as a representation of different critical approaches, the episode between Joseph and Potiphar's wife (Genesis 39) provided me with a point of entry into the text. Joseph rejects the advances of his master's wife and runs out of the house leaving his coat behind, Potiphar's wife tells her husband that Joseph tried to seduce her; Potiphar believes her and Joseph is incarcerated. Potiphar accepts his wife's explanation because her story does seem plausible, after all. And besides, since for the men in the Jacob cycle garments are a sign of trust and have a symbolic power that lends them even more verity, in the eyes of Potiphar Joseph's "abandoned" coat gives added credence to his wife's words. However, in accepting his wife's explanation as stated, Potiphar ignores the possibility of personal motivation. He is blind not only to his wife's self-serving reasons, but equally blind to what may be his own reasons for wanting to believe her. Potiphar's attitude is an example of a critical perspective that leaves unquestioned both the subjective needs of the storyteller and the conscious or unconscious investment of the interpreter. Yet for each of the characters in this episode, the coat has a special meaning. For Joseph and the biblical narrator, the coat stands as the proof of Joseph's innocence; for Potiphar's wife, it is the reminder of her frustrated desire; for her husband, the evidence of Joseph's guilt. Joseph's coat is the place of juncture for diverging desires; the textual fabric of a narrative is similarly the locus and the product of the interaction of the narrator's and the reader's subjectivities. Not unlike the story told by Potiphar's wife, my version of the stories in the Jacob cycle may be warped, skewed by my feminist and critical concerns. But, on the other hand, the anonymous biblical narrator wages for Joseph's innocence. In siding with Joseph, the narrator embraces the ideological structure which Joseph serves, namely, the male desire for an exclusive bond between men. On the question of family lineage or on the subject of human relationships, the position of the biblical narrator is no more "neutral" than that of the feminist reader.

NOTES

[1] For a discussion of the question of reading and its relation to criticism, see Suleiman.

WORKS CONSULTED

Allen, Christine Garside
    1979   "On Me Be the Curse, My Son!" Pp. 159–72 in *Encounter with the Text: Form and History in the Hebrew Bible*. Ed. Martin J. Buss. Philadelphia: Fortress.

Alter, Robert
    1981   *The Art of Biblical Narrative*. New York: Basic Books.

Barthes, Roland
    1979   "From Work to Text." Pp. 73–81 in *Textual Strategies: Perspectives in Post-Structuralist Criticism*. Ed. Josué Harari. Ithaca: Cornell University.

Coats, George W.
    1976   *From Canaan to Egypt: Structural and Theological Context for the Joseph Story*. CBQMS 4. Washington: Catholic Biblical Association.

Fishbane, Michael
    1975   "Composition and Structure in the Jacob Cycle (Gen. 25:19–35:22)." *JJS* 26:15–38.

Goldin, Judah
    1977   "The Youngest Son or Where Does Genesis 38 Belong." *JBL* 96:27–44.

Johnson, Barbara
    1978   "The Critical Difference." *Diacritics. a review of contemporary criticism* 8:2–9.

Suleiman, Susan R.
    1980   "Introduction: Varieties of Audience-Oriented Criticism." Pp. 3–45 in *The Reader in the Text. Essays on Audience and Interpretation*. Ed. Susan R. Suleiman and Inge Crosman. Princeton: Princeton University.

THE LITERARY CHARACTERIZATION OF MOTHERS AND SEXUAL POLITICS IN THE HEBREW BIBLE

Esther Fuchs
The University of Arizona

ABSTRACT

This article offers a feminist critical reading of motherhood as it is presented in the Hebrew Bible. The method I am suggesting decodes narratives involving male-female relationships as dramatizations of sexual politics. Focusing on increasingly obtrusive association of morality and procreativity in biblical annunciation type-scenes, I suggest that the biblical narrative is legitimating the vulnerable status of barren women by intimating that "good" women eventually become fertile. By repeatedly ascribing to female figures an invincible desire for sons, the biblical narrative creates women in the image of patriarchal desire. Emphasizing the narrative closure encircling the mother figure's (procre)activity with the male figures of the husband and the son, I exemplify how the biblical narrative contains the subversive power of motherhood within the genealogical economy of patriarchy.

The impact of the Hebrew Bible on the present state of sexual politics has been universally recognized by feminist critics.[1] Nevertheless, few of them went beyond the "aetiological" myth of Genesis 2-3 to demonstrate the patriarchal conception of the Bible. While the narrative strategies of androcentric "classics" have been challenged (e.g. de Beauvoir; Millet), while feminist philosophers and theologians worked out critical analyses of biblical patriarchalism (e.g. Daly), and while feminist historians began to document the social status of women in ancient Israel (Bird), not a single consistent analysis of the patriarchal (literary) strategies of the biblical narrative has yet been produced. A possible explanation for this remarkable scholarly gap may lie in the traditional appropriation of the Bible by specialists who defined the Bible as anything but literature. A more reasonable explanation would take into consideration the privileged status of the Bible as the alleged locus of divine revelation. This may illuminate the dominant status of what I might call, for lack of a better word, an appropriative tendency among contemporary feminists, who emphasize what they interpret as antipatriarchal or anticultural currents in the biblical text (e.g., Trible:1–30). In what follows, I would like to exemplify how we might approach the literary strategies of biblical patriarchalism. As a part of a more comprehensive study of the patriarchal determinants of the Bible's presentation of women, the present reading focuses on the mother figure.

Although certain female biblical characters create the impression that "the story belongs" to them and to "chance" as Phyllis Trible puts it (178), I would like to argue that they are the product of the Bible's subtle and effective patriarchal didacticism (178). The "legislative" aspect of female characterization is not unique to the biblical narrative. It pervades apparently nonideological narratives written by men (for men) about women. As feminist studies of androcentric fiction demonstrate, male-authored female characters reveal more about the wishful thinking, fears, aspirations, and prejudices of their male creators than about women's lives/experiences/perceptions. The pragmatic or ideological aspect of the literary work characterizes all literary works (Uspensky). The objective or neutral "reflection" of reality in literature is an illusion (Booth).

The fact is that the ideological aspect prevails in all literary characterization. The ascription of motivation, thought, action, and word to a certain character constitutes an indirect means of authorial judgment which exists even in what appears to be the most neutral and objective tale. This is especially the case in the best ideological literature, like the Bible. Yet, even the scholars who acknowledged the didactic aspect of the biblical narrative have focused almost exclusively on its monotheistic ideology, ignoring completely its patriarchal ideology. Thus, for example, it has been suggested that the motif of the miraculous conception of a barren woman in the Bible implies that YHWH is the sole proprietor and master of human life (Alter, 1981:47–52). This fits well the biblical monotheistic framework. As we shall see, however, this recurrent motif is also motivated by the Bible's patriarchal ideology, which seeks to naturalize and legitimate man's political dominance.

The biblical annunciation type-scene consists of three major thematic components: the initial barrenness of the wife, a divine promise of future conception, and the birth of a son (Alter, 1981:49). While these components function largely as constants, the actual scenes vary in narrative span and complexity. As has already been pointed out, the deflections from the standard structure are not coincidental; they function often as foreshadowing techniques alluding to future events in the life of the future son. For our purpose, the most significant variations pertain to the role of the potential mother in the annunciation type-scene (Alter, 1983); these variations, as we shall see next, constitute a consistently increasing emphasis on the potential mother as the true heroine of the annunciation type-scene.

The first biblical annunciation type-scene is preceded by YHWH's direct address to the potential father, Abraham, regarding the future conception of his barren wife, Sarai, "And God said to Abraham, 'As for Sarai your wife, you shall not call her name Sarai, but Sarah shall be her name. I will bless her, and moreover I will give you a son by her; I will bless her, and she shall be the mother of nations; kings of people shall come from her'" (Gen 17:15-16).[2] Although Sarai's status and thereby her fate are discussed in this dialogue, she is referred to in the third person.

YHWH blesses Sarai in her absence and changes her name through her husband. The act of naming signifies a recognition of identity, an endowment of new essence and being, and it suggests the namer's authority. YHWH changes Abram's name to Abraham (17:5) in his direct dialogue with him, yet the names of his wife and his son, which are also determined by YHWH, are to be given by Abraham who represents God's authority as husband and father. More importantly, the blessings of Sarai and the change in her name are preceded by a restatement of YHWH's covenant with Abraham. The transformation of the barren Sarai into a fertile Sarah is a logical and necessary procedure required by YHWH's commitment to Abraham: "And I will make my covenant between me and you, and you shall be the father of a multitude of nations" (vv 2, 4).

In the annunciation type-scene itself Abraham continues to occupy center stage. The scene opens with an introductory verse which leaves no doubt as to the actual addressee of YHWH: "And the Lord appeared to him by the oaks of Mamre, as he sat in the tent door in the heat of the day" (18:1). When the three messengers arrive at the tent, Abraham the generous and hospitable host invites the guests to rest up and refresh themselves, while instructing Sarah, who is inside the tent, to prepare cakes for the men. Sarah's function in this context is no different from that of Abraham's servant who is enjoined to prepare a calf for the meal. Unlike Abraham, who is implicitly praised for this generosity and eagerness to please his guests, Sarah, who is not privy to what is happening outside the tent, receives no credit for her work, since she functions as her husband's adjunct. Throughout the meal, Sarah shows no interest in the guests. The text repeats the fact that Sarah remains inside the tent in Abraham's response to the messengers' query concerning her whereabouts (v 9). This repetition is not coincidental; it emphasizes Sarah's absence from this fateful scene and by contrast, Abraham's central role in it. Instead of becoming actively involved in the conversation Sarah eavesdrops on her husband and guests "at the tent door behind him" [Abraham] (v 10). Once again, although Sarah is the subject of YHWH's address, she is referred to in the third person while her husband functions as the actual addressee: "YHWH said, 'I shall surely return to you when the season comes round and Sarah your wife shall have a son'" (v 10). Even when Sarah is reprimanded for laughing to herself in disbelief, she is addressed through her husband. Only when she denies having laughed, does YHWH speak directly to her, "saying, 'No, but you did laugh'" (v 15).

YHWH's only direct reference to Sarah takes the form of an implicit accusation.

The juxtaposition of the husband and wife in this scene enhances the attributes of the first and the drawbacks of the latter. Abraham's activity outside the tent is contrasted by Sarah's passivity. Seventeen verbs predicate Abraham's dedication to his guests. The verbs "run" and "hasten" are repeated twice. Sarah, on the other hand, is the subject of four verbs, none of which demonstrates a high level of exertion: to hear, laugh, deny, and fear. Although there is reason to believe that Sarah obeyed her husband's instructions and, like a good housewife, baked cakes for the guests, the text does not mention this fact explicitly. Sarah emerges from the scene as confined, passive, cowardly, deceptive, and unfaithful. Sarah's participation in the annunciation type-scene amounts to a troublesome interference. If the text is trying to establish a correlation between YHWH's benevolence and the uprightness of his subjects, it is clear that the manifestation of this benevolence, namely, the annunciation type-scene, is related causally to the man's demeanor and concessively to the woman's. The implication is that YHWH violates nature's rules and gives the barren woman a child because of her husband's magnanimity and despite her pettiness. But the fulfillment of the divine promise does not follow the annunciation in the narrative sequence; instead, it is postponed to chapter 21, which opens with a characteristic formula: "And the Lord remembered Sarah" (21:1). The interpolated narrative material refers to Abraham's intercession on behalf of the citizens of Sodom and Gomorrah, the destruction of the iniquitous cities by YHWH (chap. 19) and the episode in Gerar in which Abraham presents his wife as his sister (chap. 20). Sarah is absent from chapter 19 which dramatizes Abraham's compassion and altruism. In chapter 20, she appears as a passive object of sexual possession, taken by Abimelech, King of Gerar, and narrowly saved from committing adultery by the direct intervention of YHWH.

Although Sarah is given full credit for giving birth to Isaac, in chapter 21, the text continues to stress that she is mostly instrumental, and that the miracle is performed for Abraham. Verse 2 does not simply state the fact that Sarah bore a son but that "she bore Abraham a son." Verse 3 repeats this idea twice: "Abraham called the name of his son who was born to him, whom Sarah bore him, Isaac." Abraham proceeds to establish his paternal authority over his newborn son by naming and circumcising him (v 4), while Sarah comments again on the risibility of her belated conception (v 6).

As we noted, the first annunciation type-scene starts with YHWH's address to Abraham, without being previously solicited by either Abraham or Sarah. In the second annunciation type-scene, Isaac initiates the first move; he pleads with YHWH on behalf of his barren wife, and YHWH grants his prayer (Gen 25:21). Once again, the wife's conception is attributed to the good relationship of her husband with YHWH; it is not contingent upon the qualities or actions of the wife. Nevertheless, it is YHWH's response to

Rebekah that the text reports and not his response to Isaac. In response to Rebekah's complaint about her painful pregnancy, YHWH explains that she is bearing twins, and that the younger of the two will prevail over the older. Whereas in the first annunciation type-scene, YHWH discusses the future son with the father; here He shares his prescience with the mother. Another indication of Rebekah's greater involvement in the future of her children occurs in their naming. Whereas in the case of Isaac, YHWH endows Abraham with the exclusive right to name his son, here the children are named by both parents: "The first came forth red, all his body like a hairy mantle; so they called his name Esau. Afterward, his brother came forth ... so his name was called Jacob" (vv 25–26). Unlike Sarah, Rebekah appears at center stage, alongside Isaac. She receives greater recognition from YHWH as potential mother, and there is not so much as an allusion to a moral discrepancy between the man and his wife at this point.

The third annunciation type-scene is preceded by a description of the plight and despair of the barren wife. The text presents Rachel as a jealous co-wife, exasperated by the fertility of her rival, Leah. In her despair, Rachel turns to Jacob with what appears to be an impetuous and immature demand: "Give me children, or I shall die" (Gen 30:1). The reader is expected to sympathize with Jacob's angry response: "Am I in the place of God who has withheld from you the fruit of the womb?" (v 2). Indeed, the previous type-scenes bear Jacob's statement out, for was it not YHWH who gave Sarah and Rebekah children? Jacob chastises Rachel angrily and self-righteously. His response implies that his wife's barrenness is outside his sphere of control; he disclaims all responsibility for his wife's condition. The ensuing list of the sons born to Jacob by other concubines and by Leah intimates that Jacob may not be concerned because his progeny was ensured by other means. Finally, the conventional formula announcing divine intervention appears: "Then God remembered Rachel, and God hearkened to her and opened her womb" (v 22). The formula differs from both previous formulas of divine intervention. The first formula presents YHWH's intervention as a fulfillment of a promise: "The Lord visited Sarah as he had said, and the Lord did to Sarah as he had promised" (21:1). The second formula presents divine intervention as a direct response to the husband's plea: the Lord granted his prayer"(25:21). The third formula, however, stresses the fact that YHWH intervenes in response to Rachel's plight, by repeating that He "remembered her" (*zkr*) "and hearkened to her" (*šm'*). In addition, Rachel, like Leah, reserves the right of naming her sons. Jacob accepts the names given to his sons by his wives with the exception of Benjamin. Jacob changes the name Rachel gives to her second son from *ben-'ônî* ("the son of sorrow"), to *binyāmîn* ("the son of my right hand") (35:18).

The fourth annunciation type-scene, on the other hand, presents the potential father, Manoah, as somewhat of a schlemiel, whereas his unnamed wife emerges as the clear protagonist of the scene. Manoah is absent when the angel of the Lord appears to his wife and informs her that she is to conceive a son who will be a Nazirite and a national redeemer (Judg 13:3–5). Not only is the woman apprised of the future of her son, but she is given a set of instructions to follow during her pregnancy, implying a close interdependence between the mother's actions and the future son's life. When Manoah hears the news, he entreats the Lord to send his messenger once again. When the angel reappears, it is once again the women who sees him first, while sitting alone in the field. The open field points up metonymically the woman's independence, just as the tent underscored Sarah's confinement. Similarly, the words "and Manoah arose and went after his wife" (v 11) signify the husband's dependence on his wife. This constitutes a reverse analogy to the posture of Sarah inside the tent behind Abraham (Gen 18:10).

In response to Manoah's requests, the angel repeats his instructions to the woman, adding nothing at all to what he had previously said to Manoah's wife and to what she had already reported to her husband. Whereas the woman perceives immediately that the messenger is "a man of God," and compares his appearance to the "countenance of an angel of God, very terrible " (Judg 13:6), Manoah treats the divine messenger as a human being, inviting him for a meal. When the angel declines Manoah's invitation, hinting at his divine identity by suggesting that Manoah should use the meal as a burnt offering for the Lord, Manoah misses the hint and proceeds to inquire about the stranger's name, so that "when your words come true, we may honor you" (v 17). This request contrasts with the woman's conscientious and respectful silence (v 6). Even when the stranger answers enigmatically, pointing out that his name is "wondrous" (or "mysterious"), Manoah remains unaware of the stranger's true identity. only when he witnesses the miraculous ascent to heaven in the flame of the burnt offering, "*then* Manoah knew that he was the angel of the Lord" (v 21). The emphasis on the temporal adverb at the beginning of the sentence adds an additional dash of irony to the satirical presentation of the obtuse husband. But now, Manoah panics: "We shall surely die, for we have seen God" (v 22). Once again, Manoah's wife demonstrates her superior intelligence by pointing out the futility of showing miracles to people who had been singled out for death. The text vindicates her point of view by following this interchange with the final component of the annunciation type-scene, the fulfillment of the divine promise: "And the woman bore a son and called his name Samson" (v 24). The woman does not bear a son "to" her husband; neither does she consult her husband about their son's name.

The thematic and structural parallels between Judges 13 and Genesis 18 highlight the radical shift in the characterization and respective status of the potential mother and father figures. Whereas the hospitality of Abraham is graciously accepted by the three messengers, Manoah's hospitality is rejected. The first scene uses Araham's hospitality to enhance his uprightness, the latter exposes Manoah's hospitality as maladroitness. In the first scene,

YHWH addresses Sarah indirectly and peripherally; in the fourth scene God turns to the woman first, and only repeats for her husband things already known to her. Sarah emerges from the first scene as skeptical and parochial housewife, vastly overshadowed by Abraham's magnanimity. Manoah's wife, on the other hand, is perspicacious, sensitive, and devout, outshining her inept husband. Sarah's unnecessary interference in the course of the first annunciation type-scene parallels to a great extent the dispensable contributions of Manoah.

In the next scene, the potential father is pushed even further away from the focus of the story. Hannah, like Rachel, suffers not only from her barrenness, but also from the provocations of Peninnah, her fertile rival. But unlike Rachel, Hannah does not turn to her husband, Elkanah, for help. She decides to address her plea directly to YHWH. She does not even call on Eli, the priest, who is visibly stationed by the doorposts of the temple, but instead pours out her bitter heart in prayer and directly enlists God's help, by offering to dedicate her future son to His service. This is the first time the barren woman is shown to turn directly to YHWH; Rebekah, it will be remembered, turns to YHWH to complain of her difficult pregnancy, not to ask for children. This is also the first time the type-scene reports in direct speech the barren woman's prayer for children.

Hannah circumvents the authority of both Elkanah and Eli by making a vow to YHWH on her own initiative. The text implies support for her initiative by pointing out that Elkanah fails to understand his wife's misery (1 Sam 1:8) and by satirizing Eli as an obtuse old man, who misinterprets Hannah's chagrin for drunkenness. Sure of his perception, he rebukes the embittered woman with harsh words: "How long will you be drunken? Put away your wine from you" (v 14). But confronted with Hannah's eloquent response, Eli retracts his rash accusation and bids the woman to go in peace, adding: "and the God of Israel grant your petition which you have made to him" (v 17). It is not clear whether Eli is promising YHWH's help, or merely expressing his wishful blessings. Either way, Eli remains unaware of Hannah's specific request, which does not add much to his already suspect stature as divine oracle and representative of YHWH.

Unlike the divine messengers earlier, Eli fails to anticipate the miraculous conception. Whereas the previous messengers anticipate and initiate the annunciation, Eli reacts to Hannah's initiative. Furthermore, Eli fails to understand Hannah's plight and, although reacting favorably to her plea, the text implies that he remains unaware of its specific nature.

Neither does Elkanah, the potential father, understand Hannah's anguish. "And Elkanah, her husband, said to her, 'Hannah, why do you weep? And why do you not eat? And why is your heart sad? Am I not better to you than ten sons?'" (v 8). Elkanah's repeated questions indicate his concern for his wife, but at the same time they imply helplessness and a basic lack of understanding for the childless woman. Elkanah's speech functions as ironic self-betrayal; it dramatizes the husband's exaggerated sense of self-importance and his inability to realize that his love cannot compensate for his wife's barrenness. Elkanah's lack of insight into what the Bible presents as woman's greatest tragedy places him in a marginal role within the framework of this drama. Unlike the previous husbands who came in direct contact with divine emissaries (or, in Jacob's case, spoke on behalf of YHWH), Elkanah is absent from the scene dramatizing the divine element.

In his capacity as YHWH's representative, Eli promises Hannah God's help. Fulfilling his role as husband, Elkanah has intercourse with his wife, but none of these male characters are shown to have any awareness of the special significance of their actions. Both are excluded form the privileged point of view of Hannah, the omniscient narrator and the implied reader. Juxtaposed with these male foils, Hannah emerges as the incontestable heroine of the scene. Whereas in the case of Sarah, the text emphasizes that she bore a son "to Abraham," here the text presents the husband as an auxiliary character: "And Elkanah knew Hannah his wife, and the Lord remembered her, and in due time Hannah conceived and bore a son, and she called his name Samuel, for she said, 'I have asked him of the Lord' " (vv 19–20).

If Elkanah is a secondary character, the potential father in the final annunciation type-scene is barely a peripheral figure (Harvey). Gehazi, Elisha's servant, describes him as an old man (2 Kgs 4:14). The text dramatizes him as uninsightful and passive. His contribution to the annunciation scene proper is marginal. Prior to the son's birth, the potential father is referred to only in the third person. He is practically excluded from the interaction between the man of God, Elisha, and his wife, "the great woman of Shunem" (gĕdôlâ, v 8). The Shunammite is the one who goes out of her way to "seize" (wattaḥăzeq, v 8) Elisha, offering him meals whenever he passes through town. Discontent with her sporadic hospitality, she convinces her husband to dedicate a room in their house for Elisha. The text records the woman's suggestion in great detail and omits the husband's reply, thereby underscoring the woman's initiative and, by contrast, the husband's passivity and possible indifference.

This annunciation type-scene is the first to present the female protagonist as character before focusing on her as a maternal role model. The actions and speeches of the preceding female characters were mostly motivated by the desire for children or by the prospect of giving birth. These characters were described only in conjunction with the binary theme of barrenness-fertility, or with the fate and identity of their prospective sons. In the case of the great woman of Shunem, her character and her relationship with Elisha seem to deserve attention independently of the theme of childlessness. The text insists that the Shunammite's hospitality and generosity stem from her benevolence, not from an ulterior motive. When urged by Elisha to express her needs, in return for her favors, the Shunammite demurs: "I dwell among my own people" is her proud answer (v 13). Only when

Gehazi, Elisha's servant, informs him that the woman "has no son, and her husband is old" (v 14) does the reader realize that the Shunammite is childless. This is the first time in which the annunciation type-scene does not attribute childlessness exclusively to woman. The text does not define the woman as "barren" (*'ăqārâ*) or closed-wombed; on the contrary, by specifying that her husband is old, the text suggests that the man's age may explain the absence of children this time. When Elisha informs her that "at this season, when the time comes round, you shall embrace a son" (v 16), she is incredulous: "no, my lord, oh man of God; do not lie to your maidservant" (v 16). By introducing the woman's qualities prior to the actual annunciation, the narrative establishes a relationship of cause and effect between the episodes. This type-scene is the first to present YHWH's intervention as reward for woman's upright conduct. Hannah conceives, thanks to her ardent prayer to YHWH; the Shunammite conceives, thanks to her selflessness, benevolence, humility, and loyalty to YHWH's emissary.

The first type-scene establishes a causal link between the husband's uprightness and the wife's miraculous conception. The text makes it clear that the postmenopausal and barren Sarah conceives not because of her own conduct but thanks to YHWH's interest in Abraham. The hospitality, generosity, and humility initially ascribed to the potential father are now ascribed to the potential mother. On the other hand, the reticence, passivity, and indifference displayed by the potential mother towards the divine messengers in the first type-scene are transposed to the potential father in the last. Significantly, the text does not stress that the Shunammite bore a son "to" or even by her husband; omitting the husband from the final phase of the scene, it states: "But the woman conceived and bore a son about that time the following spring, as Elisha said to her" (v 17).

The passivity of the Shunammite's husband is further dramatized in his reaction to his son's disease and subsequent death. When the boy complains of a severe headache, his father orders a servant to "carry him to his mother" (v 19). When the Shunammite hurries to see Elisha, her husband, unaware of the disaster, argues "Why will you go to him today? It is neither new moon nor Sabbath" (v 23). The husband's protestations expose his limited understanding of the events. His criticism of his wife backfires. The husband's unanswered questions function here as irony of self-betrayal. As in Elkanah's case, these questions are potential obstructions rather than accelerating factors in the plot progression towards the happy denouement. Whereas Hannah leaves Elkanah's questions unanswered, the Shunammite responds to her old man's irrelevant arguments with a short "*šālôm*" ("It shall be well" [v 23]).

Yet, the husband is not the only character ridiculed by the narrative. I tend to agree with Robert Alter that the narrator of 2 Kings is rather ambivalent towards the figure of Elisha in general (1981:126). In our particular scene, Elisha is not aware that his benefactor is childless and acts on her behalf only after Gehazi apprises him of the situation. Furthermore, when the Shunammite comes to see him concerning her dead son, he is unaware of the disaster and instructs his servant to greet her and ask her if it is well with her, her husband, and her son (v 26). Realizing that the woman is in great distress he admits that the "Lord has hidden it from me, and has not told me" (v 27). Elisha remains in the dark until the Shunammite speaks; but instead of hurrying to the dead boy, he dispatches his servant Gehazi, instructing him to put his staff on the boy's face (similar to the husband who sends the sick boy to his mother with a servant), a solution which proves later to be ineffective. Only when the woman insists on his personal involvement does Elisha consent to follow her (v 30). The detailed description of Elisha's technical attempts to revive the dead son presents the process of resuscitation as a medical rather than miraculous ordeal. Despite the woman's impeccable conduct and profound piety, Elisha continues to refer to her as "the Shunammite" and sometimes with the more derisive "that Shunammite" (*haššûnammît hallāz* [v 25]), as if he never condescended to learn her name. But clearly Elish'a attitude is not representative of the narrator's point of view.

The growing recognition of the potential mother figure suggests an ever-increasing emphasis within the biblical framework on the institution of motherhood. As Adrienne Rich points out, the social and legal *institution* of motherhood is distinctly different from the personal and psychological aspect of motherhood; the latter refers to "the *potential relationship* of any woman to her powers of reproduction and to children," whereas the former refers to the mechanism aimed at "ensuring that that potential—and all women—shall remain under male control" (xv). The institution of motherhood is a powerful patriarchal mechanism. Male control of female reproductive powers in conjunction with patrilocal and monogamous marriage (for the wife), secures the wife as her husband's exclusive property and insures the continuity of his name and family possessions via patrinomial customs and patrilineal inheritance patterns. The institution of motherhood as defined by the patriarchal system guarantees that both the wife and her children will increase his property during his lifetime and perpetuate his achievements and memory after his death.

The annunciation type-scenes surveyed in this study clearly define motherhood as patriarchal institution, *not* as personal tendency of woman. All the mother figures in these scenes are married wives. There is no instance in the biblical narrative in which an unmarried barren woman is visited by God or divine emissary and miraculously released from her barrenness. This would be unthinkable, since the child born out of wedlock would not be able to carry on his father's lineage, and would be ostracized from the community as a *mamzēr* (Deut 23:3), while his mother would at best be branded as *zônâ* ("whore"). YHWH, in the biblical narrative, restricts his interest in barren women to married women and to situations which leave no doubt as to the identity of the potential father. What seems to be a sentimental narrative about the happy transition from emptiness to fullness and from failure to victory is a carefully constructed story intended among other things to promote the institution of motherhood. All the narrative details are designed and orchestrated in accordance with this ideological perspective, from the selection of thematic materials to the organization of motifs, dialogue, plot structure, and characterization. The growing emphasis on the figure of the potential mother may be misinterpreted as a growing recognition of the importance of woman's reproductive powers. The fact is that the annunciation type-scene, in its many variations, drives home the opposite message: that woman has no control at all over her reproductive potential. YHWH has control, and he is often andromorphized in the biblical narrative. Furthermore, all the divine messengers, dispatched to proclaim the imminent miraculous conception, are male figures. The literary constellation of male characters surrounding and determining the fate of the potential mother dramatizes the idea that woman's reproductive potential should be and can be controlled only by men. It is true that the presence of the potential husband progressively decreases in the annunciation type-scene, but his presence is, nevertheless, essential.

Tamar, Judah's daughter-in-law, would be burnt at the stake and condemned as a harlot had she tried to procure children outside of her deceased husband's family (Gen 38:24). The only thing which saves her life and turns her into a biblical heroine is the fact that the man she sleeps with, Judah, is directly related to Er, her deceased husband, who left her with no children. Ruth, too, is extolled as a heroine, thanks to her faithfulness to her deceased husband's patrilineage. What turns her into a biblical heroine is not the fact that she prefers to follow Naomi to the land of Judah rather than to stay in Moab, but the fact that Naomi is her mother-in-law, the mother of Mahlon, her deceased husband who left her childless. She is not merely extolled for her ability to survive physically in adverse circumstances or for her initiative and energy in general as Phyllis Trible suggests (195–96). For Ruth succeeds in finding and marrying *a direct relative of Elimelech,* her father-in-law, and giving birth to children who would carry on the patrilineage of her deceased husband.

Tamar and Ruth achieve the high status of biblical heroines, thanks to their voluntary and active support of the patriarchal institution of the levirate, which insures the patrilineage of a deceased husband (Fuchs). But the biblical narrative is careful *not* to establish too close a link between the interests of patriarchy and woman's sacrifice. On the contrary, the heroine's motivation is normally shown to be self-seeking. Both Ruth and Tamar are shown to fight for their *own* benefit and security. By projecting onto woman what man desires most, the biblical narrative creates womanhood in its own image.

The motif of motherhood in the biblical narrative seems to be closely associated with the motif of female rivalry. The mother-harlot who steals her roommate's son away and encourages the king to kill him acts on the same motivation that drove Sarah to drive out Hagar and her son Ishmael (Gen 21:9–10). Rachel too seems to be driven to despair by her jealousy of her fertile sister. The motif of female rivalry is intertwined with the motif of motherhood in the story of Hannah and Peninnah. The fertile Peninnah taunts and humiliates Hannah for her barrenness (1 Sam 1:16). It is rare to find a biblical narrative presenting mutually supportive mothers. This may be explained as a clever literary strategy in the service of biblical sexual politics. By perpetuating the theme of women's mutual rivalry, especially in a reproductive context, the narrative implies that sisterhood is a precarious alternative to the patriarchal system.

Both the positive and the negative mother-figures are shown to prefer their sons' well-being to their own. The best consolation offered to Hagar, who has been driven out by Sarah, refers not to herself but to her son: ". . . and the angel of God called to Hagar from heaven and said to her, 'What troubles you Hagar? Fear not; for God has heard the voice of the lad where he is. Arise, lift up the lad, and hold him fast with your hand; for I will make him a great nation' " (Gen 21:17–18). This consolation which focuses exclusively on the future son, Ishmael, is presented as the only and the most effective divine response to woman's predicament. Her own physical and emotional anguish is not taken into account. The only problem biblical mothers face concerns their sons' well-being, and the only solution to their problems is the assurance that their sons will survive. Thus the biblical narrative presents as the best palliative for a difficult pregnancy a message concerning the future sons. YHWH's promise to the pregnant Rebekah that she will bear twin sons seems to put an end to her intolerable pangs (Gen 25:22–24). Rachel's fatal delivery is presented as peripheral to the birth of Benjamin (Gen 35:17).

Woman's reluctance to give birth or to assume maternal responsibility for her child are options which are completely excluded from the represented reality of the Bible. These possibilities do not even appear as subjects for criticism as they do in the case of men. Onan, for example, refuses to "raise seed unto 'his brother Er' " and consequently is severely punished by YHWH (Gen 38:10). But woman is not even shown to be capable of *not* desiring sons. The biblical narrative is careful to ascribe the desire for sons to its female figures. Rachel is described as most desperate to give birth: "Give me sons, or I shall die" (Gen 30:1). Ironically, Rachel dies not through barrenness but through fertility.

Mother-figures are portrayed not only as desirous of children, but also as protective of their children and relentlessly devoted to them. Whereas conflicts between fathers and children appear as prevalent motifs in the biblical narrative (e.g., Laban versus Rachel and Leah; Jacob versus his sons, especially Simeon and Levi; Saul versus Jonathan and Michal; and David versus Absalom), they almost never appear in the context of mother-child relationship. The closest a mother-figure comes to being portrayed at cross-purposes with her child is Rebekah scheming against Esau, her elder son. But, we are told, Rebekah does it out of love for Jacob.

On the other hand, the "maternal instinct" is portrayed as highly selfish and confined inclination, mostly focused on one's own child. Sarah's concern for her son, Isaac, is presented as her primary motivation for driving Hagar and Ishmael out (Gen 21:9-10). The harlot who lost her son shows no pity for the son of her friend, and prefers to see him dead rather than alive in the arms of her rival (1 Kgs 3:26).

Woman's parenthood in the biblical narrative is largely restricted to reproductive and protective functions. Hagar, Zipporah, the Shunammite, and Rizpah all represent the maternal role at its most rudimentary—and reductive. When a mother appears to interfere on behalf of her son in a more sophisticated way, for example, to promote his rights over his siblings, she must circumvent her husband's authority. Thus, when Rebekah interferes on behalf of Jacob, she does not do so openly, for example, by attempting to convince Isaac that his preference for Esau is not in keeping with YHWH"s will. Rather, she resorts to deception, which indicates that only in this circuitous manner will she be able to prevail over her husband. But while Rebekah takes initiative independently, Bathsheba does not dare intercede with David on behalf of Solomon before Nathan encourages her to do so. Here, too, mother is forced to resort to a bit of histrionics in order to win over the father, the final authority over the fate of her child. The mother may be the decisive factor in giving birth to and preserving the life of her children, but she remains subservient to her husband's authority over her and her children.

It is interesting to note that whereas mothers are shown to interfere actively on behalf of their sons, they never interfere on behalf of their daughters. The story of Dinah's rape makes no reference to Leah. The only responsible parties are Dinah's father, Jacob (somewhat lamely), and her brothers. The story of Jephthah's daughter does not mention her mother either. The story of the concubine exploited to death by the Benjaminites refers to her father and her master only. Maacah, the mother of Tamar, is absent from the story about her daughter's rape. Aside from the victim, the story mentions only the aggressor, Amnon, the negligent father, David, and the avenger, Absalom, Tamar's brother. By expatiating on mothers who protect or interfere on behalf of their sons, the biblical narrative creates maternal role models which promote the interests of the male rather than the female child. Thus, all the annunciation type-scenes precede the birth of sons. The biblical mothers are usually desirous of sons. This is blatant in the case of Rachel, who demands from Jacob sons. The children born to previously barren mothers are all male. Similarly, Tamar and Ruth are rewarded with the birth of sons. When the biblical narrative mentions birth it almost exclusively refers to a male baby. The only exception is Dinah, Leah's daughter. But even here the daughter seems to be short-changed, since hers is the only case in which the Bible omits the etymology of the name (Gen 30:21). The motif of mother-daughter relationship is practically non-existent in the biblical narrative. Not only is motherhood defined in relation to a lawful husband-father, but it is also determined by the male gender of the child. Furthermore, it can be asserted that the presence of mother-figures in the biblical narrative is often contingent upon the identity and importance of their sons. In other words, the narrative frequently deals with the mother-figure due to its interest in her immediate or future offspring rather than in her own character. Some narratives involving a mother figure focus mainly on the circumstances leading to her son's birth. Soon after the birth of the son, the mother-figure is quickly whisked off the stage (Leah, Tamar, Samson's mother, Ruth). Other mothers survive in a few details concerning their protection of their sons, e.g., Sarah, Rebekah, the Shunammite, and Bathsheba. Sarah manages to drive Hagar and Ishmael away (Genesis 21) shortly before she expires (Gen 23:2). Rebekah disappears from the scene as soon as her protective role is completed, allowing the literary focus to shift from Isaac to Jacob. The Shunammite disappears as soon as her son is resuscitated by Elisha, allowing the focus to shift back to Elisha. And Bathsheba disappears from the text as soon as Solomon's rule is insured, allowing the focus to shift from David to Solomon.

The literary frame is particularly significant in the case of the annunciation type-scene, because of its unusual emphasis on the mother-figure. Even in these scenes the dramatic climax involves the birth of a son. Additionally, they all start with reference to the father. Even in the later scenes, featuring especially dominant mother-figures, the beginning deals with the father, and the ending with the son. The annunciation scene of Samson opens with an exposition relating first to Manoah and later to his wife: "And there was a certain man of Zorah, of the tribe of the Danites, whose name was Manoah; and his wife was barren and had no children" (Judg 13:2). Although Hannah clearly outshines her husband Elkanah, the annunciation type-scene opens first with reference to the man, presenting the potential mother as his barren co-wife (1 Sam 1:1–2). The Shunammite's story extols the woman's virtues, but still it constitutes only a part of a narrative series revolving around Elisha. Although she prevails over her husband in the annunciation type-scene, the narrative as a whole is presented as an additional enterprise of the man of God, another aspect of his divine power. This can be seen in the opening verses of the scene: "One day Elisha went on to Shunem, and there lived a great woman who urged (lit. seized) him to eat bread, and so whenever he passed there he would stop (lit. turn) there to eat bread" (2 Kgs 4:8). The Shunammite is introduced in a combined sentence which functions syntactically as a relative clause that refers to Shunem, the place where Elisha used to visit. This strategy is not restricted to the annunciation type-scene; it appears in the story of Tamar and Judah (Gen 38:1–5) and in the story of Ruth and Boaz (Ruth 1:1–5). Despite the unquestionably central role played by mother-figures in annunciation type-scenes and in narratives about significant births, the literary frame of the unit, opening and concluding with information regarding male characters, attests to the patriarchal ideology underlying them.

These constraints on the biblical mother-figures explain their literary flatness. None of the biblical mother-figures matches the depth and complexity of father-figures like Abraham, Jacob, Jephthah, and David. Only father-figures are shown to experience conflict between, for example, parental love and the exigencies of divine authority (Abraham and Jephthah). Only they demonstrate the complexity of a situation in which a parent is called upon to scold his most beloved son, or to hide his love for fear of sibling revenge (Jacob). Only they exemplify the human conflict between love for and fear of one's own child (David). The parental role played by the father-figure constitutes only one aspect in the character, one that contributes to the depth and many-sidedness of this character. It does not eclipse his other qualities. This is the difference between a multifaceted, well-developed literary character and a type, or a role model. We must conclude that although the procreative context is the only one which allows for a direct communication between woman and YHWH (or his messenger), and although motherhood is the most exalted female role in the biblical narrative, the biblical mother-figures attain neither the human nor the literary complexity of their male counterparts. The patriarchal framework of the biblical story prevents the mother figure from becoming a full-fledged *human* role model, while its androcentric perspective confines her to a limited literary role, largely subordinated to the biblical male protagonists.

NOTES

[1] "Sexual Politics" refers to the power-structured relations between men and women and more specifically to the economic, social, and ideological arrangements whereby males have traditionally controlled females. See Millet (31–81). "Biblical Sexual Politics" refers to the ways in which the Bible promotes the idea of woman's subordination to man. "Patriarchy" refers to a value system which legislates women's political subordination as divinely ordained or natural.

[2] This and all the following quotations are based on the *Revised Standard Version* with occasional revisions, unless otherwise stated.

WORKS CONSULTED

Alter, Robert
    1981   *The Art of Biblical Narrative*. New York: Basic Books.
    1983   "How Convention Helps Us Read: The Case of the Bible's Annunciation Type-Scene." *Prooftexts* 3:115–30.

Arpali, Boaz
    1970   "Attention: a Biblical Story." *Hasifrut* 2:580–97 (in Hebrew).
Beauvoir, Simone de
    1952   *The Second Sex*. Trans. ed. H. M. Parshley, New York: Vintage.
Bird, Phyllis
    1974   "Images of Women in the Old Testament." Pp. 41–88 in *Religion and Sexism*. Ed. Rosemary Ruether. New York: Simon and Schuster.
Booth, Wayne C.
    1961   *The Rhetoric of Fiction*. Chicago: University of Chicago.
Briffault, Robert
    1927   *The Mothers*. Vol. I. New York: Johnson.
Daly, Mary
    1973   *Beyond God the Father*. Boston: Beacon.
Fuchs, Esther
    1982   "Status and Role of Female Heroines in the Biblical Narrative." *The Mankind Quarterly* 23:149–60.
Harvey, W. J.
    1965   *Character and the Novel*. Ithaca: Cornell University.
Millet, Kate
    1969   *Sexual Politics*. New York: Ballantine.
Perry, Menahem and Meir Sternberg
    1968   "The King Viewed Ironically: On the Narrator's Devices in the Story of David and Bathsheba." *Hasifrut* 1:263–92 (in Hebrew).
Rich, Adrienne
    1976   *Of Woman Born*. New York: Norton.
Sternberg, Meir
    1977   "The Structure of Repetition in the Biblical Story." *Hasifrut* 25:110–50 (in Hebrew).
Trible, Phyllis
    1978   *God and the Rhetoric of Sexuality*. Philadelphia: Fortress.
Uspensky, Boris
    1973   *A Poetics of Composition*. Berkeley and Los Angeles: University of California.

Response

BETWEEN READER AND TEXT: A GENERAL RESPONSE

James G. Williams

The studies in this volume represent so many different methodologies and take up such a varied assortment of narrative texts that it is difficult to respond to them all appropriately. I have therefore decided to comment primarily on certain theoretical and methodological aspects of the research that, in my opinion, either represent signs of progress in the study of biblical narrative or are particularly problematic.

Mary Gerhart's essay is the only contribution that seeks to lay out a theoretical basis for analyzing narrative texts, and she goes on to apply this theory to the work of some representative biblical critics. All of the other contributions are instances of working criticism. Some of them draw on particular theories or critical sources that are applied or assessed in a new way: *Thomas B. Dozeman* on spatial form in the Sinai narrative, drawing on Smitten and Daghistany; *George W. Coats* on form-critical themes of the Hexateuch, discussing Noth, von Rad, and his own previous work; *Everett Fox* on reading Genesis as a book, evidently influenced by recent trends in literary criticism and the "canonical criticism" of Childs; *Naomi Steinberg* on the priority of genealogy in the narrative structure of Genesis 12–50, using Todorov's analysis of narrative equilibrium; and *Nelly Furman* on the meaning and function of garments in the Jacob cycle, applying Barthes' notion of textuality to arrive at a new feminist reading. Others do not foreground their theoretical debts so sharply, but are interesting and valuable discussions arising out of the interstices of contemporary forms of social, historical, and literary criticism; *Antony F. Campbell* on the reported story; *Phyllis A. Bird* on the harlot as a central figure in certain stories; *Anne M. Solomon* on the structure of Chronicles and the organization of the Pentateuch; *Joel Rosenberg* on the relation of political and literary history as exemplified in 2 Samuel 11; and *Esther Fuchs* on the dominance of patriarchal ideology in type-scenes concerning the barren mother.

Of these essays in working criticism, Campbell's article is the one that could break new ground for specific literary and social critical applications if it is followed up appropriately. He proposes that "reported stories" often function as condensations or aide-mémoire for other storytellers, a thesis supported by Burke Long's essay on field studies in oral literature. I myself have encountered a similar thesis only once before, in a meeting of the Jesus Seminar at Redlands, California (March 6-9, 1986), where Dominic Crossan argued that most of the parables of Jesus as we have them are "plot summaries" which may have been greatly lengthened in some oral settings. It would make a tremendous difference in our reading of texts to establish whether or not this scribal summarizing or epitomizing was a common practice among the writers and redactors responsible for the biblical narratives. A book or monograph on the subject could be a boon for critics concerned with narratology.

I. Narrative: A Generic Approach

Gerhart holds that although much has been accomplished in literary critical analysis, a comprehensive theory of narrative is needed in order to expose unexamined assumptions. She proposes that a view of narrative as generically cognitive, historical, and theological is the key to biblical interpretation. She calls her understanding of narrative "postcritical," which I gather is practically synonymous with "postmodern." I understand her to mean a theory (1) that takes into account the interpreter's own assumptions; (2) that is not based on a "naive realist epistemology" (language and texts do not *simply* refer to objects apart from them, whether persons, events, or writers of the texts); and (3) that does not appeal to an absolute (God or Reason) which is external to the interpreter.

Gerhart's point about narrative as generically cognitive is that it is simultaneously a mode of knowing and a comprehensive genre. Following Ricoeur, she stresses that the reader/hearer is induced by narrative to think and arrive at judgments in multiple ways: by qualities juxtaposed, images reinforced, assumptions questioned through metaphor and various stylistic patterns. In other words, narrative as a mode of knowing, in this postcritical sense, must involve a notion of "reader of competence" (see also Gerhart). Reader competence is an essential concept because "the narrative 'whole' is located *between the text and the reader's reconstruction of its parts*" (emphasis mine). In this view, to read or follow a narrative "... is not to master, but to find events cognitively acceptable *after all*."

These considerations of narrative as cognitive raise a question about Rosenberg's otherwise very solid treatment of the role of story in political history. I do not doubt there is an interrelationship of story, history, and institutions, and he certainly shows this in clear fashion. The question that goes begging is his stance *vis-à-vis* the supposedly "real history" (his term) that the Samuel text weighs and assesses. He states that "the art of storytelling ... is the currency of thought itself," but he seems to assume a close relationship of story to history apart from the storyteller's construction of certain events. This construction is one in which the woman, Bathsheba, is a pawn in a world of male rights and values. There is even a possible implication that Bathsheba herself may be at fault in the death of Uriah, if Joab's oblique reference to Abimelech's death at the hand of a woman (2 Sam 11:21) is intended as an allusion to Bathsheba (see Bal). *If* there is a core of "real history" in the biblical narrative (i.e., David made Bathsheba do his sexual bidding and this affected the course of events), the narrative is nonetheless shaped by an androcentric ideology.

As for narrative as generically historical, Gerhart draws upon Habermas in stressing the historical horizon of the interpreter and the condition of all genres as historically bound. She also refers extensively to Jameson, who characterizes dialectical thinking as "historical reflexivity," which involves not only the study of something, but also the study of the concepts and categories the interpreter necessarily brings to the study. In other words, there is no "untainted" representation of an object studied.

What Gerhart leaves opaque, in my estimation, is how this historical reflexivity is related to narrative as such. I surmise that she is getting at the narrative character of consciousness that is both affected by and affects its own remembering and historical circumstances. Both of these — remembering (and forgetting) and being part of a larger, social narrative frame — belong to narrative as a mode of history. It is for this reason that I think Nelly Furman's thought provoking essay is lacking in one important respect: in following Barthes' notion of textuality she does not attend to the sociohistorical dimension of reading. That is to say, the textual fabric of a narrative is *more* than "the product of the interaction of the narrator's and the reader's subjectivities." Critics like Jameson have taught us to be sensitive to the ways in which these subjectivities are informed by a larger history, which inevitably means ideology. Furman acknowledges this point, in effect, by making reference to her own "feminist and critical concerns" and in asserting that the narrator of Genesis 39 "embraces the ideological structure which Joseph serves, namely, the male desire for an exclusive bond between men." Contemporary feminist criticism and ancient Israelite patriarchal storytelling both belong to a complex of assumptions about reality that far transcend the narrator's or the critic's predilections. In this sense narrators and critics seldom "embrace" an ideological structure as much as they *represent* it.

In treating narrative as generically theological, I gather Gerhart has in mind the context of research in biblical narrative. I think, however, it would be better to say that narrative is generically *interpretive*. In any case, Gerhart suggests that in becoming engaged with a narrative, we explicitly or implicitly pose questions and answer them: "*Which* texts? *Which* interpretations? and By *what* criteria [are they to be evaluated]?" These questions and responses arising out of our narrative activity "become foundational to an understanding of self and world."

At the point of Gerhart's claim for narrative as foundational I find myself diverging from a theory that is otherwise very appealing. Although I agree that for the broader framework of their existence human beings cannot articulate meaning without narrative, particularly mythic narrative, there are nonetheless non-narrative forms that are as important as narratives in specific settings; these often stand in tension with narrative or even call it into question. Crossan has referred to the world-subverting function of parable: "It is possible to live in myth and without parable. But it is not possible to live in parable alone. To live in parable means to dwell in the tension of myth *and* parable" (60). By "parable" Crossan means, of course, a certain kind of brief, metaphorical narrative, but I would substitute "aphorism" for "parable" in his statement. As I have elsewhere stated, aphoristic modes of discourse offer a needed alternative to story for engaging in theology (Williams, 1981:89–90). Narrative, particularly as it moves toward the broader functions of myth in establishing world (continuity and coherence), is naturally of basic significance to theological reflection in its constructive aspects. For theology's critical role, however, aphorism should be given more attention, for as Pascal pointed out, the true subject of theology cannot be subjected to order; therefore he wrote aphoristically:

> J'ecrirai ici mes pensées sans ordre et non pas peut-etre dans une confusion sans dessein. C'est le véritable ordre et qui marquera tourjours mon objet par le désordre meme. (I will write here my thoughts without order and not, perhaps, in a confusion without design. This is the true order, one that will always indicate my goal by disorder itself) (Pensée 532).

II. Recreating the Past

The contributions of Fox, Solomon, and Steinberg all touch on a narratological issue that should be explored: the recreation of the past. Frank Kermode has recently commented on this issue in terms of anteriority and authority (1988). Drawing on Bakhtin and Todorov, he discusses the ways in which the sort of discourse Todorov calls polyvalent demands recourse to anterior texts. Whether or not the anterior text previously existed, or existed in the form cited, it functions in the narrative both as a source to be explicated and as a touchstone of authority. For example, in the Gospel of Mark the parable of the sower (Mark 4:3–8), which was presumably already present in the Jesus sayings tradition, becomes an oracle to be deciphered (Mark 4:10–13), and its interpretation is rendered as a dominical control of the tradition of interpretation (Mark 4:14–20). This interpretive control is dependent, in turn, on another anterior source, "the Scriptures" or Hebrew Bible as a kind of "seminar" or seedbed of the gospel narrative (Williams, 1985:179–88; cf. Kermode, 1979:85).

So now, what questions arise if we read Genesis as a "book" with Fox? If it "has been painstakingly knit together with artistic tools of a high caliber," what are we to make of the layers and seams? David Gunn has made the point that "reading biblical narrative in terms of its final form is a more radical proposition than perhaps is realized by those who most enthusiastically have embraced the program. . . ." (71). He goes on to ask some questions that we can reword and adapt to this context: Is Genesis really a book? Does this mean "unified narrative"? Can Genesis be viewed as a book in relation to canon in any fashion analogous to the way a modern book would be viewed in relation to some list of classics, or even other books by the same author? Is there *one* narrator, let alone a reliable one?

However any of us may deal with these questions, it is clear that viewing Genesis as a book in Fox's sense of thematic unity is to create a new source. Fox acknowledges this in part in saying that the title of his paper "reflects the era in which it has been written." Genesis as thematic unity that is artistically composed is not the same as the source studied in the earlier tradition or in modern scholarship prior to the emergence of literary criticism. The new text created by Fox has a basic structure he deduces from a fourfold scheme. He sums up this structure as "selection and survival amidst struggle and disaster." If one were to read Genesis as simply a *sēper* of Torah, and if Torah were understood as a book, one would presumably find a basic structure much more expansive than that. But what if one were to go back into the layers and seams of Genesis? The layer that has been called J seems to place as much emphasis on struggle and disaster as survival and selection. On the other hand, has not P created a new anterior source by rooting selection in the covenant of circumcision (Genesis 17) and beginning the whole story with the creation of the cosmos? There is now a *bĕrē'šît* or a Torah—depending on how one wishes to focus the subject—that gives concrete assurance of selection from the beginnings. With the establishment of the Sabbath as the crown of creation, the picture of Adam as a kind of king among creatures whose divine image is transmitted without effacement (Gen 5:1–3), and the promise of an unconditional everlasting covenant to Abraham (Gen 17:13), the assurance of God's presence and choosing of Abraham's posterity is not in question. The mystery that emerges is why it is necessary to experience history as the narration of struggle and disaster if creation and covenant are on Israel's side as literarily represented in the final form of the Torah.

In other words, one can read Genesis as a book, but it is still polyvalent. The sources and redactions identified in earlier criticism are shifted into a new mode, but in some sense they are still there and may be just as troubling or disruptive. There are voices from past contexts, words and worlds already inhabited which are placed in new words and worlds. Recreated, in other words. That process of recreation is what must be addressed, even if we read narrative in terms of its "final" form.

I will be briefer in commenting in the same vein on the essays of Solomon and Steinberg. Steinberg says, "Todorov's design for narrative plot leads us to conclude that the family stories of the book of Genesis must be read in the context of the genealogies of Israel's ancestors." I do not doubt that Genesis in its final form gives numerous signals to read the text in this way. What I would stress is that reading Genesis in the context of the genealogies is to create a new anterior source and to recognize the validity of another authority. Whenever the genealogies may have been inserted, to make them the points of reference means that those who are responsible for interpreting creation and history as genealogy, as well as the works this group produced (Genesis, Torah in its final form), have determined the reading process. Likewise, if Solomon is on the right track in her argument about the structure of the Chronicler's history—and I find myself in accord with her analysis for the most part—then there was a determination of the reading process on a grand scale. In the postexilic period the priestly revision of Israel's story achieved a new sense of anteriority and a new source of authority that still affects our approach to the texts.

Of course, a new past, a new reading, a new work that is read—all these make up a "narrative," a "whole" of some sort that occurs between the text and the reader's reconstruction thereof.

III. Gender and Narrative

Narrative is a tricky thing, as is language in general (See Bal, 1988: 136–37). That is, one can argue that ambiguity and a tendency toward deception is inherent in the very structure of signs. I will return to this proposition shortly, after I give my comments on Bird's essay.

Bird's study is a rich probing of literary art and its relation to historical reality. What I would comment on is the "location" of the harlot as protagonist in the literary, social, and semantic senses. Bird summarizes in the last sentence of her abstract:

> The study argues that each of the texts [Gen 38:1–26; Josh 2:1–24; 1 Kgs 3:16–27] requires as its presupposition a view of the harlot as a marginal figure in the society, tolerated but despised, and that fundamental ambivalence toward the harlot's role is not resolved by any action of the harlot, either in literature or in life.

The key word in my view is *marginal:* the harlot is like the female figures in many biblical tales and ancient Near Eastern myths, but at the same time her standing is even more ambiguous and tenuous (see essays in Exum and Bos). She is on the margin of socially acceptable persons and roles. On the other hand, as marginal she is different to the point of being *too* different. If one distinguishes between the signs of the potential victim within the social order and the potential victim outside the social order, then the harlot has all the marks of the potential victim within the social order (see Girard, 1986).

It is interesting that two of the tales discussed by Bird occur in relation to a border or some marginal situation fraught with confusion. In the story of Tamar the setting is Canaanite or non-Israelite. It is not clear whether

Tamar herself is Canaanite, but the chain of events is set in motion when Judah "went down from his brothers" (Gen 39:1), i.e., departed from the realm of Israelite community. In the account of Rahab and the Israelite spies, Rahab's house is located in the wall of the city. Like the arche-mothers and other important women in biblical narratives, Rahab functions as mediator between the male protagonist and a threatening world (see Williams, 1982: 114–23).

It would be interesting to determine how many of the significant women in biblical stories appear in marginal situations or even at borders according to the geography of the narrative, and to compare these results with a study of men in marginal situations and at borders. One would, of course, expect man male figures to be at boundaries, for one of the essential features of ancient Israelite narrative, as of myth generally, is that founding figures cross boundaries into zones of testing or into regions where a boon may be obtained. Nonetheless, if a higher percentage of women were localized or particularized in such settings, that would be a significant fact. As I reflect immediately on the question, I think of these women who act at a border or in foreign territory or are associated with a foreign land: Delilah (in Philistine territory?); Esther (taken into the Persian court); Hagar (Egyptian, she is cast into the wilderness); Ruth (Moabite, crosses into Judah with Naomi); Sarah (as the wife-sister in Egypt and Gerar); Zipporah (on the way from the Sinai Peninsula into Egypt). Then there are many others who appear in a situation of confusion or crisis. Is there a pattern here?

What I am getting at is the possibility that the very form of narrative itself, particularly as it stems from patriarchal culture, carries with it a bundle of assumptions about women in the world—about the relation of woman and world. The relations of woman/world, woman/man, woman/God, etc. are actualized in boundary situations where the woman, by virtue of her very tenuous, sometimes marginal status, can lead the male protagonist over the threshold into a safer or better zone for his survival and success.

I propose that René Girard's theory of language and culture helps to explain this marginal situation of the woman in biblical narrative. Esther Fuchs, to whose essay I will return, has put it well, even if her statement will not hold without remainder for *all* biblical narrative: "the biblical narrative creates women in the image of patriarchal desire." "The image of patriarchal desire" is precisely the point. Let me explain by summarizing Girard's thesis.

Girard argues that violence has its roots in "mimetic desire," a concept by which he challenges Freud's theory of the Oedipus complex. Mimetic desire is the drive to imitate the respected and feared model that always puts the subject in a double bind. The mandate of the model is: Imitate me! Yet if one were to imitate the model completely one would be and have what the model is and has; therefore, any actual model is an implicit rival. The extreme form of rivalry would be to displace the model absolutely, that is, eliminate — kill — the other. On the other hand, if this rivalry is rejected and repressed, the subject is then bent into slavish submission to the model.

The predicament of mimetic desire, which involved this unconscious process of rivalry, would result in complete social chaos without some means of breaking out of it or regulating it. The universal tendency of human groups has been to engage in an unconscious process of regulation by finding a victim, a "scapegoat" in the broad sense, in order to impute the community's ills to the victim. Human communities maintain their order—and order means language, status, possessions, gods, etc.—through a system of differences. These differences are threatened by violence within the group. Here is where *sacrifice* enters the picture.

Sacrifice is a momentary reversion to the chaos of violence in order to maintain the system of differences. Myths and theologies are typically rationalizations of an original and initial act of violence which the group must camouflage and conceal from itself. Thus it is quite common for the sacrificial victim to be apotheosized as a god.

Everything I have said about Girard's thesis so far can be found in *Violence and the Sacred*. In addition, I would mention two other aspects of his theory, one found in *Things Hidden Since the Foundation of the World* and the other in *The Scapegoat*. In the *Things Hidden* Girard identifies the basic structure of the sign in language generally as the victim and the meaning of the victim.

> The signifier is the victim. The signified is all actual and potential meaning the community confers on to the victim and, through its intermediary, on to all things (103).

The sign in its totality "is the reconciling victim." The fact that a sign can be identified as what "can be used in order to lie" (Bal's statement of Eco's definition of a sign; 1988:136) is a manifestation of the huge cover-up operation taking place in culture—the denial of the victim standing behind the sign.

The other aspect I wish to touch on is Girard's analysis of stereotypes of persecution, which is found in *The Scapegoat*. These are (1) accusation of crimes eliminating distinctions, (2) person already bearing signs of the victim (an outsider, disabled in some manner, or otherwise different in some unacceptable way), and (3) victim's difference either within or outside the social system. Girard's favorite example is the Oedipus myth. If one retold this story in terms of victim stereotypes which are activated in a time of crisis, then it may be reread or retold precisely as a text of persecution; a crippled outsider appearing at a time when harvests are bad, animals are dying, and social unrest is rampant, is accused of parricide and incest. In the myth as we have it in Sophocles' play this order of events is reversed and the crimes become the cause of the community's misfortunes.

Whoever exists primarily as an image of someone's desire leads a precarious and potentially victimized existence. If she is sought after because her suitor is imitating the desire of his model-rival, or if she conducts herself in a certain way because she accepts the image represented in this imitated desire, then she will be blamed if she steps outside of the "home territory" of this image into "alien territory." Therefore Fuchs is right—up to a point. In those tales where the woman acts only for the sake of the hero or the man's world, she is a persona on the boundary, a mediator who may quickly become a victim.

At the same time, women in biblical narrative are not *completely* enclosed "in the image of patriarchal desire." Fuchs herself, at least in the abstract of her contribution, speaks of "the subversire power of motherhood in the genealogical economy of patriarchy." If feminist criticism amounts to nothing more than reducing the biblical texts to their rootage in patriarchal ideology with the male figures as the bad guys and the female figures as the good gals, then criticism and hermeneutics will amount to no more than an obvious reductio ad absurdum.

In another essay Fuchs has faulted me for not pursuing, in *Women Recounted*, the association of the feminine with language and mediation, stating that "the failure to bring out the political aspect of the troublesome relationship of language and women in the Hebrew Bible risks mystifying and validating this relationship" (69). She correctly stated that I did not deal with the politics—or regulation of power—of the relation of the feminine to language and mediation. I agree with her that this should be done. But she goes to the opposite extreme of unwillingness to see anything more than political ideology wherever she turns in the stories of men and women. How is it possible then to find the subversive power of motherhood within patriarchally conceptualized narratives? Or how is it possible to find, as Furman does, that "by pluralizing the meaning of a piece of attire, Rebekah, Potiphar's wife, and Tamar explode and thereby subvert the closure of the patriarchal representational system and symbolic code"? How does this feminine, if not feminist, perspective slip through?

A Girardian hermeneutic will help sort out some of these questions, even if the interpreter does not accept every aspect of Girard's theory. It offers illumination on the relation of sign and victim and on why the female figures in certain stories function in a manner similar to language. And it also proposes another insight: that there is a biblical tradition of God and the narrator siding with the victim, beginning with Cain and Abel and reaching an apex in the Hebrew Bible with the Suffering Servant of Second Isaiah and Job, and in the New Testament with the crucifixion of Jesus as a disclosure and demythicizing of the victimary mechanism. Where there is siding with the victim, are the narratives taking the part of only the *male* victims? If one replies that Tamar gains her rights, Rahab gains her life and livelihood, Hannah gains her fertility, Ruth gets her man and child for Naomi, et al.—all without breaking free from a patriarchal, androcentric world, then I would ask: What other world does one expect them to inhabit? If we reduce meaning to the world of any text or subject, we have come back again to a reductio ad absurdum. If the interpreter pits an image of the text's world against her own and holds, in effect, that one of the two must be eliminated, then that is a good example of one kind of radical actualization of mimetic desire—the desire to imitate the model completely by obtaining the power that the model (supposedly) has. (The other radical form is to submit completely to the model/rival.) But as Gerhart says, "Reader competence is an essential concept because 'the narrative "whole" is located between the text and the reader's reconstruction of its parts.'" To read or follow a narrative ". . . is not to master, but to find events cognitively acceptable *after all."*

The interpreter's task is not to master, but to find, after all, a cognitively acceptable story that lies somewhere between her and the text.

WORKS CONSULTED

Bal, Mieke
    1987   *Lethal Love: Feminist Literary Readings of Biblical Love Stories.* Bloomington and Indianapolis: Indiana University.
    1988   "Tricky Thematics." *Semeia* 42:133–55.

Crossan, J. Dominic
    1975   *The Dark Interval: Towards a Theology of Story.* Niles, IL: Argus Communications.

Exum, J. Cheryl and Johanna W. H. Bos
    1988   Eds. *Reasoning with the Foxes: Female Wit in a World of Male Power. Semeia* 42. Atlanta: Scholars.

Fuchs, Esther
    1988   "For I Have the Way of Women: Deception, Gender, and Ideology in Biblical Narrative." *Semeia* 42:68–83.

Gerhart, Mary
    1988   "Genric Competence in Biblical Hermeneutics." *Semeia* 44:29–43.

Girard, René
    1977   *Violence and the Sacred.* Baltimore: Johns Hopkins.
    1986   *The Scapegoat.* Baltimore: Johns Hopkins.
    1987   *Things Hidden Since the Foundation of the World.* Stanford: Stanford University.

Gunn, David M.
    1987   "New Directions in the Study of Biblical Hebrew Narrative." *JSOT* 39:65–75.

Kermode, Frank
    1979   *The Genesis of Secrecy: On the Interpretation of Narrative.* Cambridge: Harvard University.
    1988   "Anteriority, Authority, and Secrecy: A General Comment." *Semeia* 44:155–67.

Pascal, Blaise
    1963   *Pensées,* in *Pascal: Oeuvres Complètes.* Ed. L. Lafuma. Paris: Editions de Seuil.

Williams, James G.
- 1981 *Those Who Ponder Proverbs: Aphoristic Thinking and Biblical Literature.* Sheffield: Almond.
- 1982 *Women Recounted: Narrative Thinking and the God of Israel.* Sheffield: Almond.
- 1985 *Gospel Against Parable: Mark's Language of Mystery.* Sheffield and Decatur: Almond.

www.ingramcontent.com/pod-product-compliance
Lightning Source LLC
Chambersburg PA
CBHW031314150426
43191CB00005B/222